Y0-BDG-435

CRIT[illegible]
INSI[illegible]
Benjamin

CRITICAL INSIGHTS

Benjamin Franklin

Editor
Jack Lynch
Rutgers University

Salem Press
Pasadena, California   Hackensack, New Jersey

Cover photo: Hulton Archive/Getty Images

Published by Salem Press

∞ The paper used in these volumes conforms to the American National Standard for Permanence of Paper for Printed Library Materials, Z39.48-1992 (R1997).

Library of Congress Cataloging-in-Publication Data

Benjamin Franklin / editor, Jack Lynch.
p. cm. -- (Critical insights)
Includes bibliographical references and index.
ISBN 978-1-58765-640-8 (alk. paper)
1. Franklin, Benjamin, 1706-1790--Criticism and interpretation. I. Lynch, Jack (John T.)
PS752.B46 2009
818'.109--dc22

2009026435

PRINTED IN CANADA

Contents

Career, Life, and Influence

Critical Contexts

Critical Readings

Resources

About This Volume

Jack Lynch

Where does one begin discussing a figure as various, and as complicated, as Benjamin Franklin? Statesman, memoirist, philosopher, politician, inventor, wit, scientist, bon vivant—there are so many sides to Franklin that it is difficult to know where to start. Plenty of people have tried to sum him up; countless biographies, historical essays, and critical studies have striven to make us understand this most engaging of personalities. And yet he remains frustratingly sphinxlike, even as he remains perpetually familiar.

The intention of this collection is to bring together representative essays from a variety of critical perspectives, partly to give some sense of Franklin's achievement but also to draw attention to some of the inconsistencies, contradictions, and even failings that made him who he was. The book tries to examine Franklin from many points of view, in the hope of offering a composite portrait—though with no expectations that even the composite portrait will be complete or comprehensive.

The collection opens with several short introductory essays before moving on to a section on Franklin's critical contexts, which contains a series of wide-ranging overviews of his life, his works, and his legacy. A longer and more focused section, "Critical Readings," follows, with samples of critical close readings from a number of schools of thought. The volume is rounded out by a chronology of the important events in Franklin's life, a list of his works, and a bibliography with suggestions for further reading.

CAREER, LIFE, AND INFLUENCE

On Benjamin Franklin

Jack Lynch

The word *iconic* has become our age's all-purpose adjective to describe anything famous or important. Benjamin Franklin is certainly that: he was among the most famous people in the world in his own day, and his fame and importance have only grown in the two centuries since his death. But he is also iconic in the original etymological sense, "like a portrait immediately recognizable, an image suited to adoration." Franklin has one of the most familiar faces in history—he grins at us from our hundred-dollar bills, and he makes appearances in Disney cartoons and sitcoms. Whenever we see the bald pate, the round glasses, and the wise and tolerant smile, we know we are in the presence of one of the most influential people in American history.

It is a position Franklin earned over the course of a remarkable lifetime. A phrase like "came from humble beginnings" is now a tired cliché, but it was not when Franklin was born. He made his way through a world in which social mobility was almost unheard of—and yet, somehow, this child of a poor candle maker managed to turn himself into the most famous American in the world. "Having emerged from the poverty and obscurity in which I was born and bred," he writes in the *Autobiography*, "to a state of affluence and some degree of reputation in the world"—it is one of the great understatements in American literature, about both the obscurity of his beginnings and the reputation he found in his maturity. That "degree of reputation" is clear in the fact that his is the only name that appears on the four most important documents in the establishment of the United States: the Declaration of Independence, the Treaty of Paris, the Treaty of Alliance with France, and the United States Constitution. He also achieved fame with an astonishing series of inventions and innovations. When confronted with a trivia question in the form of "Who gave us the first [blank] in America?" one can rarely go wrong by answering "Benjamin Franklin," who gave us things as diverse as the first bifocals, the first circulating library, the first fire department, the first post office, the first insurance company, and the first zoo.

All these things could have come only from one of the most wide-ranging minds in history, and that breadth of knowledge and experience is evident in the way Franklin is studied today. In high schools and colleges, his name appears not only in history and literature classes but also in sociology, economics, political science, anthropology, psychology, physics, and even math classes—in all of these fields he was not merely a dabbler but a genuine presence responsible for lasting contributions. But that very diversity of interests makes it hard for us to get a handle on Franklin. How should we put all these different perspectives together and see him as a whole? Thus the range of essays collected here, all of which provide new angles from which to look on this most enduring, and endearing, of sages.

Perhaps it is inevitable that the author of one of the most famous autobiographies in history is remembered above all for his life story; interpretations of Franklin's works can never escape the gravitational pull exerted by his biography. The *Autobiography* therefore has pride of place here, appearing prominently in most of the essays, though we should remember that it was not a famous book in Franklin's day. The work was left unpublished, appearing in an unreliable edition in French translation a year after he died. It was read by very few during Franklin's own century, and not published in a good English edition until 1868. Even the title is not his own; the word *autobiography* was not coined until seven years after his death. And yet, though the word was not his, he made the form his own, especially in his tone, one that manages to be wise and wicked, sage and witty, ironic and profoundly serious all at once, as is clear in the opening paragraphs:

> I shall indulge the inclination so natural in old men, to be talking of themselves and their own past actions; and I shall indulge it without being tiresome to others, who, through respect to age, might conceive themselves obliged to give me a hearing, since this may be read or not as any one

> pleases. And, lastly (I may as well confess it, since my denial of it will be believed by nobody), perhaps I shall a good deal gratify my own vanity. Indeed, I scarce ever heard or saw the introductory words, "Without vanity I may say," &c., but some vain thing immediately followed. Most people dislike vanity in others, whatever share they have of it themselves; but I give it fair quarter wherever I meet with it.

There follows a wealth of information about his life, from his birth to the early days of his involvement in national politics. For all the *Autobiography*'s appeal, however, it is dangerous to rely on this work for an objective account of a life, since Franklin's story has been largely mythologized. And that mythology was created in large part by Franklin himself, a talented literary artist who was consciously shaping his image for his audience. The best interpreters of the *Autobiography*, therefore, know when to use the factual information he offers there and also know that the work must be approached as a literary text.

Yet Franklin was no one-hit wonder. His reputation depends not on a single book but on the elaborate web of published and unpublished writings that interconnect across his life and works. Those works fill many library shelves, even without any of the copious commentary. The standard scholarly edition of his writings, under way since 1959, fills thirty-nine volumes, and it is not yet complete. Even the most useful selection of his essential writings, published by the Library of America, occupies two stout volumes running to 2,400 pages. Many of these other writings make appearances here—*Poor Richard's Almanack*, the political writings, the scientific treatises—and all help to illuminate Franklin the man.

Still, Franklin cannot be understood in isolation from his historical and cultural context; we cannot separate our readings of Franklin from our understanding of early America. The man and the nation come together. In writing, and in living, one of the archetypal success stories, Franklin provided the paradigm of the poor boy who makes good. We now think of it as the definitive American story, and to understand it well we have to see how it connects to contemporary movements in economics, science, religious thought, politics, and so on. All these subjects and many more appear in the contributions to this collection.

* * *

Franklin's kite-and-key experiment is one of the most famous moments in the history of science, comparable to Archimedes' "Eureka!" and Sir Isaac Newton's falling apple. It also has, unlike Newton's apple, the merit of being a true story. Franklin informed his European correspondents about "the *Philadelphia* experiment for drawing the electrical fire from clouds," advising them how to construct a kite. "To the end of the twine, next the hand" he writes, "is to be ty'd a silk ribbon, and where the silk and twine join, a key may be fastened. This kite is to be raised when a thunder gust appears to be coming on." And his scientific contributions were not limited to electricity. He did important work on optics, medicine, fluid dynamics, and meteorology. It is fitting, therefore, that at least one essay in this volume considers the scientific Franklin.

Franklin's most famous scientific work, of course, has to do with the "electrical fire" or "electrical fluid," a subject much in the news during Franklin's lifetime. As Samuel Johnson, who would later meet Franklin in London, wrote in his famous *Dictionary* of 1755, "the industry of the present age . . . has discovered in electricity a multitude of philosophical wonders." And some of those philosophical wonders had to do with health, both bodily and mental, which is why Sherry Ann Beaudreau and Stanley Finger look at Franklin's early experiments in "medical electricity." The conjunction of physical and mental health is important. The last few centuries have worked to separate those two spheres, body and mind, treating one of them as gross and material, the other as abstract and spiritual—two utterly different and irreconcilable things. When we talk about some physical conditions being "only in your head" or attribute a mental condition to a "chemical imbalance," we are taking it for granted that body and mind are different things, even different kinds of things. Only recently have physicians and psychologists begun to try to put them back together, to recognize that any separation between them is artificial. In Franklin's day, that separation had not yet taken place. Following the lead of the German professor Johann Gottlob Krüger, Franklin conducted experiments in which electrical shocks—from power stored in the newly created Leyden jars, an early kind of power cell—might be used to cure both physical maladies (palsy, blindness) and what we would classify as mental disorders (hysteria, melancholy).

Betsy Erkkila takes a very different approach to the separation of mind and body. Franklin's century is often supposed to be a product of the Enlightenment, an Age of Reason—terms that suggest a kind of abstraction incompatible with the messiness of physical existence. Erkkila insists, though, that Franklin was still very much a material body, subject to stresses and strains, capable of feeling pleasure and pain, and demanding much attention just to continue running.

Some of those fleshly needs inform A. Owen Aldridge's essay here, a careful examination of one of Franklin's less familiar short pieces in which he makes an erotic proposal to one of his closest friends in Paris, Anne Catherine Helvétius, the widow of one of the most famous philosophers and social theorists of eighteenth-century Europe, Claude-Adrien Helvétius. Mme Helvétius was a distinguished intellectual in her own right, and this is no doubt part of what attracted Franklin to her. But was the attraction purely intellectual? And what kinds of evidence should we use to answer a question like that? Was Franklin's "unmistakably frank entreaty for her to become either his wife or his mistress" sincere?—just a humorous flirtation?—something else altogether? There is no question that the piece is playful, with the kind of clever inside jokes and sexual wordplay that the ironist always used. But was the elderly Franklin seriously proposing a physical relationship? This has been a long-standing critical and biographical mystery, and Aldridge uses it as an opportunity to think about the value of different varieties of evidence.

The private Franklin remains a source of perpetual interest, but he would never have come to our attention if Franklin had not lived a very public life, above all as one of the Founders, and therefore one of the forces behind the American Revolution. Franklin was always a practical man, and he recognized some of the practical problems in separation from Britain. Wars are expensive, but where were the Revolutionaries to get the money to carry out their struggle with Britain? Virtually all contemporary economic theorists were convinced that hard currency of silver or gold was the only reliable basis for wealth, because coins had *intrinsic* worth. But hard currency was in short supply in the New World, and the young nation was forced to depend on the purely *symbolic* worth of paper money. Paper money was the source of much anxiety in the eighteenth century. A silver dollar held its value the world over, but a Continental dollar would become worthless if the government fell. This lack of confidence in the worth of American paper money was a national obsession in the 1770s, as the Continental Congress watched the value of its money plummet. The answer lay in *credit*, a word that derives from the Latin word for *believe*: to offer credit was to testify to one's belief in an institution or a person. Here Jennifer Jordan Baker, an authority on the intersection of economics and literature in early America, offers a fascinating account of Franklin's use of credit, both personal and institutional, to prop up the economy of Revolutionary America and to fashion his own identity.

Economic policy gives us taxes, one of the two things in this world that Franklin famously believed "can be said to be certain." The other, of course, was death, one of Franklin's recurring concerns. Jennifer T. Kennedy is one of several contributors to this volume who dwell on Franklin's early career as a printer—a fact that was central to his self-conception. He repeatedly referred to the mistakes he had made over the course of his life as "errata," the errors in a printed book. This playful metaphor allows Franklin to figure life itself as a book, which in turn makes the afterlife a kind of "second edition." And this metaphor is not the product of modern critical ingenuity, not Kennedy's imposition on the text; Franklin himself had it in mind, even as a young man, when he penned this proposed epitaph for himself:

> The body of
> B. Franklin, Printer
> (Like the Cover of an Old Book
> Its Contents torn Out
> And Stript of its Lettering and Gilding)
> Lies Here, Food for Worms.
> But the Work shall not be Lost;
> For it will (as he Believ'd) Appear once More
> In a New and More Elegant Edition
> Revised and Corrected
> By the Author.

And yet, despite his concerns about death, Franklin usually handled the subject with a light touch, as when, in 1733, he twitted a rival almanac writer, Titan Leeds, by predicting his death and then refusing to believe Leeds's own protestation that he was still drawing breath. *Who are you going to believe?* Franklin playfully asked—"I shall convince him from his own words that he is dead." That playfulness characterized his own life and has even stayed with him in the afterlife. As Kennedy writes, "Even from the grave, Franklin always has the last laugh."

Laughter was one of Franklin's defining characteristics, a trait he shared with one of the great laughing figures of his day, Laurence Sterne. Christina Lupton looks at the two men together and pays particular attention to how they put their own early works to new uses later in their careers. In Sterne's famously eccentric novel *Tristram Shandy*, the characters discover a handwritten draft of a sermon, "The Abuses of Conscience," which becomes the center of one of the novel's more memorable comic episodes. The sermon, however, was originally written by Sterne himself, not in his persona of a novelist but in his day job as a priest. In other words, the sermon was originally intended seriously—not as "literature" (to use a notoriously troublesome term) but as a genuine piece of devotion to be read aloud in church. Franklin, too, recycled some of his own writing, and Lupton's examination of it in two contexts—that of its original appearance and that of its later reincarnation—gives us new insights into both texts.

It may come as a surprise to some readers to hear that Franklin, one of America's Founders, had a profound distrust of unfettered press freedoms. "If by the *liberty of the press* were understood merely the Liberty of discussing the Propriety of Public Measures and political opinions, let us have as much of it as you please," he wrote, but he knew not everyone was similarly high-minded. "If it means the Liberty of affronting, calumniating, and defaming one another," therefore, he says, he would "cheerfully consent to exchange my *Liberty* of Abusing others for the *Privilege* of not being abus'd myself." Freedom of expression is a good thing, but only when it is in the service of a higher good. When newspaper writers are no better than "malevolent Criticks and Bug Writers, who will abuse you while you are serving them, and wound your Character in nameless Pamphlets," when they are no better than "those little dirty stinking Insects, that attack us only in the dark, disturb our Repose, molesting & wounding us while our Sweat & Blood is contributing to their Subsistence"—in such cases, Franklin felt, it is better to restrict the freedoms. Ralph Frasca's essay, the last in this volume, explores the ways Franklin's abstract principles concerning liberty of the press were tested and shaped by his actual involvement in newspaper publishing.

* * *

Taken together, these essays offer us many perspectives on Franklin—some familiar, some unexpected. Despite their diversity, however, they could never pretend to approach him from every possible angle, and this collection cannot hope to give the final word on him.

Franklin is too complicated, too various, for any simple summing up. He will continue to exercise critical minds for centuries to come.

Perhaps the reason for this continued fascination is the way he embodies paradoxes. In Franklin we have the stern moralist who fathered an illegitimate child, the prudent peacemaker who led America to war, the proponent of moderation who enjoyed all the good things in life, the brilliant entrepreneur who gave his ideas away for free, the slaveholder who campaigned for abolition, the fatherly figure who fought against his own son in the Revolutionary War, the supporter of Christianity who challenged the divinity of Jesus, the polymathic sage of his country who was celebrated abroad as a rustic backwoodsman in a beaver hat. These contradictions, inconsistencies, and paradoxes make him a frustrating subject for study—but also an endlessly rewarding one.

Biography of Benjamin Franklin

Clark Davis

Benjamin Franklin was the son of Abiah Folger and Josiah Franklin, a poor soap boiler and tallow chandler. His formal education between 1714 and 1716 consisted of tutoring and a year's study at the Boston Grammar School. He eventually acquired prodigious learning from his own experience and study, which included vast readings in American, British, and West European books and newspapers.

After working almost two years for his father, Benjamin was apprenticed to his half brother, James Franklin, editor of the *New England Courant*, from 1721 to 1723. James encouraged his brother's first known literary efforts, the "Silence Dogood Essays," satirical imitations of Cotton Mather's *Bonifacius: An Essay upon the Good* (1706). Theocratic officialdom was outraged by these and other articles, and the editor was warned to desist. Shortly before the *New England Courant* was suppressed, Franklin broke the terms of his indenture in 1723 to emigrate to Philadelphia with little besides the clothes on his back. He worked for a year in a printing house there. Encouraged by Pennsylvania's eccentric governor, William Keith, to begin his own printing business, Franklin sailed to England, but he soon discovered that Keith's letters of credit were worthless. After saving enough from London printing jobs to return to Philadelphia in 1726, he clerked for a merchant before establishing himself as a printer.

In 1727 Franklin founded the Junto discussion group, the first American adult education class. In 1730 he became the owner of the *Pennsylvania Gazette*. In 1731 he started the Library Company of Philadelphia, the first American circulating library. He promoted Philadelphia's advanced street paving, cleaning, and lighting. In 1749 he helped found the Academy of Philadelphia, which opened in 1751 and is now the University of Pennsylvania. He soon gravitated into colonial politics and patronage, serving as postmaster of Philadelphia (1737), state printer, clerk (1736-1750) and member (1751-1754) of the Pennsylvania Assembly, member of several Indian commissions, delegate to the intercolonial Albany Congress (1754), deputy and joint postmaster general (1753-1774) for British North America, and Pennsylvania's agent in London (1757-1762, 1764-1775).

During these years, the most sustained of Franklin's literary productions was *Poor Richard's Almanack*, the proverbs of which illustrated his belief that Puritan virtues have immense utilitarian value. A Deist and natural rights philosopher believing in the perfectibility of man, Franklin felt obligated to show others how they, too, could rise from rags to riches by consciously leading a frugal, industrious life. He considered experiential tests superior to a system's logical consistency in evaluating the worth of concepts, but he carefully distinguished between end and means. Franklin's *Poor Richard's Almanack* sold about ten thousand copies per issue and enabled him to retire in 1748 from active conduct of his printing and newspaper business, from which he thereafter derived an income of one thousand pounds yearly.

To devote himself to moral and natural philosophy and to further their study by others, Franklin helped establish the American Philosophical Society at Philadelphia in 1743. The popular conception of him as a mere inventor of practical devices, such as his stove and lightning rod, does great injustice to Franklin the abstract scientist. He discovered the first law of electricity, gave to electrical charges their positive and negative designations, and deduced that the electrical properties of bodies depend on their shapes, a discovery that today controls condenser design. His compendious *Papers, Experiments and Observations on Electricity* won for him at home and abroad memberships in the major cultural and scientific societies and many honorary degrees. In a different field, Franklin's discovery that Atlantic "nor'easter" storms move against the wind was a fundamental advance in the science of weather. In *Observations on the Increase of Mankind, People of Countries, &c.* he anticipated theories later elaborated by Thomas Malthus.

At the Albany Congress of 1754, Franklin advanced his prophetic plan of union, which embodied the federal principle. (He asserted, throughout his life, that adoption of his plan, rejected by the colonies and by Parliament, would have averted the American Revolution.) In 1766, while representing Pennsylvania in London in disputes with the Penn proprietors, he helped persuade Parliament to repeal the Stamp Act as an impractical measure. His humility and reasonableness won new friends for America and increased his prestige so that other colonies designated him their agent. Although he feared that the disputes between Parliament and the Colonies had become irreconcilable, he labored for conciliation until the Coercive Acts of 1775.

Returning home, Franklin represented Pennsylvania in the Second Continental Congress. On the committee to draw up a declaration of independence, he made a few changes in Thomas Jefferson's draft. As chairman of the foreign affairs committee, he drafted the Treaty Plan of 1776. Although he was not on the constitutional committee, his was the strongest single influence on the Articles of Confederation because he submitted a revised plan of union and because his 1776 constitution for Pennsylvania afforded practical examples of the operation of the unicameral legislature, an executive of weak powers, and a denial of compulsive force by central authority—all soon to be salient features of the new federal government under the Articles of Confederation.

Appointed by Congress in 1776 as one of three treaty commissioners, Franklin went to France, where his *oeuvres* had been published in translation in 1773 and where his prestige was so great that he completely overshadowed his cocommissioners. The canny Franklin's intimacy with Foreign Minister Charles Gravier, comte de Vergennes, helped win, in 1778, recognition of the United States' independence and a treaty of alliance with France. A few months later, in 1779, Franklin became sole plenipotentiary to France. Though the treaty with France forbade either country to arrange a separate peace, Franklin had already begun in 1781 separate negotiations with Great Britain.

In 1782 he, John Adams, and John Jay formed a Peace Commission that effected a separate armistice, to the ostensible surprise and indignation of Vergennes. This preliminary, however, made possible the signature of a general peace treaty at Paris in 1783. Upon Franklin's long-standing request, he was recalled to the United States in 1785.

Pennsylvania honored the now ailing Franklin with the presidency of its Executive Council (1785-1787). As one of its delegates to the Federal Convention in 1787, Franklin made few specific proposals, but his affable spirit, shunning the doctrinaire, promoted compromises based on practical experience. His federal principle was greatly strengthened, but his other notions of governmental machinery found little or no place in the new constitution.

Franklin married Deborah Read in 1730; she died in 1774. She was illiterate, but she was devoted to him. They had two daughters, one of whom survived infancy and married Richard Bache. Tolerant of her husband's infidelities, Deborah even raised his illegitimate son William Franklin, later royal governor of New Jersey and a Loyalist.

It was to guide William that Franklin began his *Autobiography* in 1771 at Twyford, England. By far his most widely read work, it has continued to influence readers for more than two hundred years, both as a guide to personal success and as an archetypal American story of the self-made individual. Franklin continued writing his memoirs up to the year 1757. He died in Philadelphia on April 17, 1790, and European countries joined the United States in mourning the passing of the man whom David Hume had hailed as the first philosopher and great man of letters in the New World.

From *Cyclopedia of World Authors, Fourth Revised Edition*. Pasadena, CA: Salem Press, 2004.

Bibliography

Aldridge, A. Owen. *Benjamin Franklin and Nature's God.* Durham, N.C.: Duke University Press, 1967. Study of Franklin's theology treats his religious beliefs in relation to both his practice and his literary works, including "Speech of Polly Baker," "Extract from an Account of the Captivity of William Henry," and "Letter from a Gentleman in Portugal." Intended for the serious student.

Anderson, Douglas. *The Radical Enlightenments of Benjamin Franklin.* Baltimore: The Johns Hopkins University Press, 1997. Focuses on the literary and intellectual career of Franklin in his early years; provides close readings of a number of Franklin texts.

Brands, H. W. *The First American: The Life and Times of Benjamin Franklin.* New York: Doubleday, 2000. Thorough biography provides comprehensive information on the multifaceted Franklin.

Campbell, James. *Recovering Benjamin Franklin: An Exploration of a Life of Science and Service.* Chicago: Open Court, 1999. Presents a thoughtful look at Franklin's life.

Durham, Jennifer L. *Benjamin Franklin: A Biographical Companion.* Santa Barbara, Calif.: ABC-CLIO, 1997. Encyclopedic format offers brief essays on Franklin's life and achievements in an A-to-Z format. Supplemented with selections from his writings, chronology, bibliography, and index.

Franklin, Benjamin. *Benjamin Franklin's Autobiography.* Edited by J. A. Leo Lemay and P. M. Zall. New York: W. W. Norton, 1986. Critical edition presents the authoritative text of Franklin's *Memoirs of the Life*, superseding all multivolume editions of Franklin's writings. Particularly useful are thirty pages of biographical notes concerning the contemporary and historical figures mentioned in the autobiography. Other valuable sections contain relevant extracts from Franklin's letters and selected commentaries by outstanding critics from Franklin's times to the mid-1980s.

____________. *Benjamin Franklin's Writings.* Edited by J. A. Leo Lemay. New York: Library of America, 1987. Outstanding collection contains not only the quintessence of Franklin's literary production but also valuable annotations and a thorough index.

____________. *Franklin on Franklin.* Edited by P. M. Zall. Lexington: University Press of Kentucky, 2001. Newly edited early draft of Franklin's autobiography, with expunged passages restored and the last decades, unrecorded by Franklin, filled out with correspondence and diary entries.

Granger, Bruce Ingham. *Benjamin Franklin: An American Man of Letters.* 1964. Reprint. Westport, Conn.: Greenwood Press, 1988. Subjects Franklin's periodical essays, almanacs, letters, bagatelles, and autobiography to close stylistic analysis, developing the "persona" of his sketches and the tropes of his essays and conversely dissecting "such rhetorical figures as analogy, repetition, proverb and pun." Successful as far as it goes, but fails to consider the intensely human message of Franklin's best writing.

Locker, Roy N., ed. *Meet Dr. Franklin.* Philadelphia: Franklin Institute, 1981. Sixteen prominent historians contribute to this compilation of essays analyzing various aspects of Franklin's career, including the literary. Intended for the nonspecialist, the essays cover the essentials of Franklin's life and thought.

Middlekauff, Robert. *Benjamin Franklin and His Enemies*. Berkeley: University of California Press, 1996. Focuses on Franklin's acrimonious relations with Thomas Penn and John Adams.

Morgan, Edmund S. *Benjamin Franklin*. New Haven, Conn.: Yale University Press, 2002. An admiring portrait written by the chair of the administrative board overseeing the publication of the multivolume *Papers of Benjamin Franklin*.

Van Doren, Carl. *Benjamin Franklin*. 1938. Reprint. Birmingham, Ala.: Palladium Press, 2001. One of the most readily obtainable and most comprehensive biographies of Franklin accessible to the general reader. Extensive quotations from Franklin's works provide a "speaking voice" for both the historical figure and the human personality.

The *Paris Review* Perspective

Bradley Bazzle for *The Paris Review*

Instead of a royal dynasty or a national deity, we Americans have the Founding Fathers. It's a peculiar pantheon. Many of the founders have left us extensive writings and, because of early America's economic flexibility, a surprising number of them rose to prominence from humble origins. The combined effect is that our national creation myth is unusually accessible. Nowhere is the myth told more dramatically than in Benjamin Franklin's *Autobiography*, which reads, in part, as a "how to" manual on becoming the founding father of a nascent country.

Born in Boston in 1706, Franklin was pulled out of school at the age of ten and at twelve was apprenticed to his brother as a printer. His brother published his first articles, *The Dogood Papers*, before Franklin was seventeen, but Franklin chafed under the stricture of apprenticeship and soon bolted for Philadelphia. By 1730 he had been appointed Pennsylvania's public printer. There he created the first circulation library in the United States, founded the American Philosophical Society, wrote *Poor Richard's Almanack*, conducted groundbreaking electrical experiments, and transformed himself into an all-purpose diplomat, politician, and man of letters. So the questions that pull us into the *Autobiography*, since most of us know a little about Franklin already, are how a person with so little education could rise to prominence so quickly, and how he could achieve so many monumental and diverse accomplishments in a single lifetime.

The simple answer is industriousness, which quickly emerges as Franklin's most singular quality. It is also the one most easily appreciated today, because hard work remains a central ideal of American society. What is startling is the degree of Franklin's industriousness. In the *Autobiography*, anecdotes of work ethic, frugality, and commitment to his trade pile up until they culminate, halfway through the book, in Franklin's description of what he calls the "bold and arduous project of arriving at moral perfection." As we examine this project—a rigorous procedure for eliminating vices from one's character, complete with helpful charts and a list of thirteen virtues—we realize, just in case there was any doubt, that we have followed Franklin into uncharted territory. What sort of autobiographer interrupts the narrative to give his readers a self-help lesson? An autobiographer for whom projects of self-improvement were as formative as childhood: without them, we would not understand his subject. Franklin's unceasing effort to perfect himself—an ambition at once fascinating and disturbing—is the centerpiece of his *Autobiography* because it is the centerpiece of his life, from which flow all of his experiences and accomplishments.

It is worth noting that the *Autobiography* is split into two halves and that the moral perfection business comes at the beginning of the second. Franklin wrote the second half for a wide audience at the urging of friends who had read the first half and were eager to read more. As a result, the second section suffers from a showy style, and it is crammed with opinions on everything from patents to the education of women. In contrast, the first half, which Franklin addresses to his son, is surprisingly candid. Franklin himself explains the discrepancy: "One does not dress for private company as for a public ball." There are moments in the first half when we do feel like "private company."

It is conventional to take the *Autobiography* as a performance, but to do so is to miss the humanity of it. The Franklin that emerges in the first half, though terrifyingly industrious, struggles, starves, is duped, and dwells on his mistakes. Those mistakes—"errata," as he calls them—are so few that Franklin seems to think he can call attention to them all and still come off untarnished. He is wrong. Tellingly, many of the errata involve his treatment of other people. For all of the "acquired friends" he impresses and charms, Franklin cannot maintain substantive friendships. Everyone disappoints him. In one of the more difficult passages to stomach, Franklin makes a pass at his friend Ralph's mistress, and then uses the rift this creates between them to distance himself from Ralph, who has become a besotted embarrassment. There is a surprising lack of commentary on the episode, the only explanation for which is that Franklin, after all these years, is still sore; that part of him misses the few friends he has had in his otherwise illustrious life. Despite the author's controlling hand, characters like Ralph and the hapless printer Keimer, Franklin's employer and rival, transcend the *Autobiography* like Shakespearean sidemen.

There is a museum-like quality to Franklin's *Autobiography*. It charmingly exposes some of the lies with which we romanticize the colonial period. Franklin reserves harsh words for few things, but tallow chandling and soap boiling are among them; in our current era of boutique candle stores and designer soaps, it is easy to forget that these were once the products of industries so filthy that they nearly drove the adolescent Franklin out to sea. The *Autobiography* also gives us glimpses into cultures that shaped early American society but have since dwindled in their influence, from the Native Americans of the northeast to Pennsylvania's once thriving Moravian community. Historical figures come alive within Franklin's pages and, more often than not, are given unsolicited advice. Franklin befriends the Methodist evangelist George Whitefield and devises an experiment to test Whitefield's claim that he can preach to thirty thousand people at once. Franklin gathers supplies for General Edward Braddock, the commander in chief for North America in the French and Indian War, and uses the opportunity to counsel him on wartime strategy.

Art is given special distinction within the *Autobiography*. Practical artists who value sense, like the writers Alexander Pope and John Bunyan, earn particular attention, and even reverence, from Franklin. It may be difficult for modern readers to react to *The Pilgrim's Progress* with excitement, but Franklin is deeply impressed by the way it "mixes narration and dialogue, a method of writing very engaging to the reader"—giving us a fascinating window into the mind of an eighteenth-century reader. Franklin seems to consider art to be one of the few areas of human achievement beyond his considerable capacity. He disparages his own attempts at verse and is careful never to liken himself, even in metaphor, to an artist; he is careful always to portray himself as a craftsman.

One cannot help but wonder if the reason Franklin chose to write nonfiction can be traced to a word of advice from his father, who told him early on that "verse makers were generally beggars." But perhaps it could not have been any other way. The hero of Franklin's story is Franklin himself, after all, a figure deliciously human and frighteningly inhuman at once. There are moments, reading the *Autobiography*, when we ask ourselves, When will it end? When will he stop achieving so much, making us feel worthless by comparison? It never does stop, but we don't put down the book; we read on, shaking our heads in mirth and dismay.

CRITICAL CONTEXTS

Benjamin Franklin:
A Cultural Context

Neil Heims

For Neil Heims, Franklin was, first and foremost, a "public man," and his *Autobiography* was concerned above all with crafting a "public self." Even as Franklin seems to speak to us in that book as the private man, we are never allowed to forget that he was always in the public eye, and so he wanted to be, for his public position was what enabled him to try to influence the world for good. So involved was he with so many aspects of eighteenth-century life that he can be understood only in a public context. In this essay Heims explores some of those intellectual, social, and cultural contexts, including the invention of printing with movable type, Lockean philosophy and psychology, the slave trade, and questions of empire in early American politics. — J.L.

1

Benjamin Franklin has come to be regarded as a model of a self-made man, an exemplar of a characteristic American type and a preeminent American virtue. "Having emerged from the poverty and obscurity in which I was born and bred," he writes in the opening paragraph of his *Autobiography*,

> to a state of affluence and some degree of reputation in the world, and having gone so far through life with a considerable share of felicity, the conducing means I made use of, which with the blessing of God so well succeeded, my posterity may like to know, as they may find some of them suitable to their own situations, and therefore fit to be imitated.

Even more fitting a designation than "self-made," however, may be to describe Franklin as a public man. The self that he constructed and then set about to preserve in his *Autobiography* was a public self. Writing an autobiography—rather than a confession, as Saint Augustine or Jean-Jacques Rousseau did, for example—is to perform a public, civic, act. It is designed to influence the public good and the manner of civic association rather than, as is the end of writing a confession, to effect the good of the soul, whether to cleanse one's own or to guide the souls of others. Franklin's aim in the *Autobiography* is to guide his readers to seek and to sustain the capacity to live life in the state of liberty, free of crippling dependencies through the attainment of competence. Provoking his readers' interest in his life and creating a desire in them to emulate it was his way of securing his investment in the new American nation he had been instrumental in creating and of ensuring that its future follow the course he had prepared.

Competence, the mastery of a set of skills and the ability to undertake and accomplish projects by using those skills, permits the achievement of self-sufficiency and the consequent ability to do good and useful acts, good because useful. It is only when an aggregate of individuals are self-sufficient and competent that they can form a society that is itself self-sufficient, and through the interplay of their several competencies it can be therefore a free and independent society. Franklin's self-made model is the model for realizing democracy and cooperation.

Franklin's religious credo did not invoke religion as its own end but established the utility of religious precepts in shaping social consciousness. "I had been religiously educated as a Presbyterian," he explained in the *Autobiography*,

> and tho' some of the dogmas of that persuasion . . . appeared to me unintelligible, others doubtful, and I early absented myself from the public assemblies of the sect, Sunday being my studying day, I never was without some religious principles. I never doubted, for instance, the existence of the Deity; that he made the world, and govern'd it by his Providence; *that the most acceptable service of God was the doing good to man*. (80; emphasis added)

Although he did attend services at the behest of his friend the Presbyterian minister George Whitefield, Franklin soon stopped attending because "their aim seem[ed] to be rather to make us Presbyterians than good citizens" (81).

2

Although Franklin was of Puritan stock—his father, Josiah Franklin, having left England for the colonies in 1683 with the double hope of securing his salvation and his livelihood—the doctrines of faith and belief were of little value to Franklin; nevertheless, the injunction to practice virtue, shun vice, and do good had been bred into his bones—and it was reinforced and given direction by his reading of Cotton Mather's *Essays to Do Good* or *Bonifacius*, published in 1710. In these essays, Mather asserted that a person's primary duty is to perform such acts and undertake such projects as contribute to the betterment of society.

Josiah Franklin's Puritan influence had made the need for a light to follow a strong constituent of his son's character. But by the end of the seventeenth century, that light was no longer the single beam of sectarian dogma it had been for his godly ancestors. It had become the illumination cast variously throughout the Creation. It was discoverable not through Divine revelation but through the efforts of the intellect and by the method of experimentation. It was not a light that shone upon the path to otherworld salvation but a light that made clear the way to negotiate the byways of this one. That light was cast, paradoxically, as an emanation from the black print set against the white pages of books.

The invention of movable type by the German goldsmith and printer Johannes Gutenberg in the 1440s changed the course of European history as much as the ecclesiastical and political events of the succeeding centuries. In fact, it is easy to argue that those events were clearly related to, if not actual and even inevitable results of, the revolution Gutenberg began. The invention of movable type allowed for the wholesale printing and distribution of books, pamphlets, journals, and broadsides; of ideas, opinions, and exhortations. It democratized speech and thought even when speech and thought were still officially constrained, and it gave men (men) the ability to broadcast their ideas and extend their influence.[1]

The seventeenth century was the time in England when the revolution in printing exploded and written matter became pervasive and relevant. Much of the writing of the seventeenth century in England was done for the sake of expressing the arguments, opinions, and beliefs upon which people staked their sacred honor and for which they would fight and die. One indication of the importance of writing and of the power and influence of printing is that the defense of publishing was the subject of John Milton's great argument in the *Aereopagitica*.

"From a child I was fond of reading," Franklin wrote near the beginning of his *Autobiography*, making it clear that reading was not the diversion of idle hours but a serious activity that he credited as essential to the formation of his intellect, character, values, and the very habits of his life and the way he lived and engaged the surrounding world. Among the authors he studied, John Locke and Daniel Defoe were essential influences. It was Franklin's genius and his good fortune that they were not only essential influences upon him but also upon the age in which he lived.

In his *Essay Concerning Human Understanding* (1690) Locke set out "to consider the discerning faculties of a man, as they are employed about the objects which they have to do with." Locke wanted to know how we know the things that we think we know, to determine the validity of that knowledge, and to discover the way to achieve knowledge. He hoped to "give any account of the ways whereby our understandings come to attain those notions of things we have" and to "set down any measures of the certainty of our knowledge." He wanted to be able to reject faulty methods that lead to false knowledge and to verify procedures that lead to authentic knowledge. The certainty of knowledge can be measured, he suspected, and he sought to determine how. But he was hardly sure he would be able to. He predicted, as he began his inquiry, that he "may perhaps have reason to suspect, that either there is no such thing as truth at all, or that mankind hath no sufficient means to attain a certain knowledge of it" (Introduction, 2, "Design"). This is not as blasphemous as it sounds, for Locke is not talking about Divine truth, which had been taken to be the fruit of indisputable revelation, but about phenomenological truth, about observable facts and events. To the extent that Locke was removing the focus of thought from the Divinity and revelation and centering it on humanity and perception, there is an element of possible impiety in his pursuit. But his skepticism also leads to a search for methods of discovery that will stand in the face of skepticism.

Given the instability of knowledge and the tendency to take opinion for knowledge, Locke sought to "examine by what measures, in things whereof we have no certain knowledge, we ought to regulate our assent and moderate our persuasion" (Introduction, 3, "Method"). The word *measures* suggests measuring, methods, calibrations, means of determining the properties of something and gaining, thereby, knowledge of it. Pursuing this course of action brought Franklin his fame whether he was dealing with lightning; designing a stove; fashioning bifocal eyeglasses; ordering the postal system; establishing a library, a militia, a hospital, or a university; or making a revolution and establishing a government. He undertook practical engagement with phenomena and events. He intruded into the order of things and experimented. He endeavored to understand what phenomena were and how they worked by submitting them to the intervention of his reason and through mechanical means that he devised, such as the iron pipe that he made into a lightning rod. Becoming an inventor was the result of being an experimenter.

Franklin often made himself the object of his observation and the field of his experimentation. Going from New York to Philadelphia in his youth, having endured a wet and cold sleepless night aboard ship, "in the evening I found myself very feverish," but "having read somewhere that cold water drank plentifully was good for a fever," he "follow'd the prescription" before he "went in to bed." He "sweat plentiful most of the night." His "fever left [him] and in the morning, [after] crossing the ferry," he "proceeded on [his] journey on foot" (24). He undertook character building in a similarly scientific way. When Franklin "conceiv'd the bold and arduous project of arriving at moral perfection," he "contrived" a "method" (82) for accomplishing it:

> I made a little book, in which I allotted a page for each of the virtues. I rul'd each page with red ink, so as to have seven columns, one for each day of the week, marking each column with a letter for the day. I cross'd these columns with thirteen red lines, marking the beginning of each line with the first letter of one of the virtues, on which line, and in its proper column, I might mark, by a little black spot, every fault I found upon examination to have been committed respecting that virtue upon that day. (85)

He kept careful entries and afterward, as a scientific observer does, reviewed the notes he made throughout the course of the experiment and "was surpris'd to find myself so much fuller of faults than I had imagined; but I had the satisfaction of seeing them diminish" (88). But he is not concerned only with the results of his investigation but also, in the manner of a responsible scientist, with the quality of its apparatus:

> To avoid the trouble of renewing now and then my little book, which, by scraping out the marks on the paper of old faults to make room for new ones in a new course, became full of holes, I transferr'd my tables and precepts to the ivory leaves of a memorandum book, on which the lines were drawn with red ink, that made a durable stain, and on those lines I mark'd my faults with a black-lead pencil, which marks I could easily wipe out with a wet sponge. (84)

Locke's challenge was to determine "how far the understanding can extend its view, how far it has faculties to attain certainty; and in what cases it can only judge and guess" (Introduction, 4, "Useful"). Arguing for the value of the scientific method and the pursuit of learning, Locke provided the intellectual impetus that directed Franklin in everything he undertook.

Locke did not despair of our ability to achieve knowledge with certainty. The Deity "has put within the reach of their discovery, the comfortable provision for this life, and the way that leads to a better." By "discovery" Locke implies inquiry and experimentation. By "better," Locke is referring to the quality of life in this world, not the next one. "We shall not have much reason to complain of the narrowness of our minds," he asserts, "if we will but employ them about what may be of use to us; for of that they are very capable." As a measure of their capacity, he argues that "we shall then use our understandings right, when we entertain all objects in that way and proportion that they are suited to our faculties, and upon those grounds they are capable of being proposed to us; and not peremptorily or intemperately require demonstration, and demand certainty, where probability only is to be had" (Introduction, 5, "Our capacity").

To assert that we must not "require demonstration, and demand certainty, where probability only is to be had," Locke must distinguish between Divine and earthly knowledge, suggesting there is a method for knowing the things that fall below theological disputation: experimentation and "demonstration." We have the power of "observation," which can be "employed either about external sensible objects, or about the internal operations of our minds." What we observe can be "perceived and reflected on by ourselves, [and observation] is that which supplies our understandings with all the materials of thinking. These two [perception and reflection] are the fountains of knowledge, from whence all the ideas we have, or can naturally have, do spring" (bk. II, ch. 1, 2, "All ideas"). Reliable knowledge is possible when one "will suffer himself to be informed by observation and experience, and not make his own hypothesis the rule of nature" (bk. II, ch. 1, 21, "State of a child"), when one follows the scientific method of observation and experimentation, as Franklin did. Locke taught Franklin that to live means to experiment with life, to reflect upon one's perceptions and to experiment with one's circumstances, always paying attention to making one's knowledge as complete as possible so that one's actions can be as informed and consequently as useful or beneficial as possible.

The other important influence on the young Franklin was Daniel Defoe, the author best known for *Robinson Crusoe*, his novel of industriousness and self-sufficiency. In his *Essay upon Projects* (1697), Defoe is practical to the point of being cynical when he considers the capabilities as well as the disposition of humankind. Defoe begins his meditation on human industriousness, social responsibility, worthwhile social undertakings, and valuable social and economic institutions, what he calls "projects," by reflecting:

> Man is the worst of all God's creatures to shift for himself; no other animal is ever starved to death; nature without has provided them both food and clothes, and nature within has placed an instinct that never fails to direct them to proper means for a supply; but man must either work or starve, slave or die. ("Of Projectors," para. 1)

This is a grim realism that focuses on "man" only as a physical, earthly creature. Defoe mitigates his original bleakness by conceding that man

> has indeed reason given him to direct him, and few who follow the dictates of that reason come to such unhappy exigencies; but when by the errors of a man's youth he has reduced himself to such a degree of distress as to be absolutely without three things—money, friends, and health—he dies in a ditch, or in some worse place, a hospital. ("Of Projectors," para. 1)

The ironic repositioning that makes a hospital a worse place to die than a ditch is the spur that provokes the entire work. *An Essay upon Projects*, although written from the point of view of a cynic, is really quite a socially conscious exercise concerned precisely with building rational social institutions to provide "money, friends, and health" for an often crippled and needy humankind. Franklin drew from Defoe the spirit of projecting. He was a prime mover in establishing and maintaining social institutions devised for the common good, institutions such as insurance societies, schools, hospitals, banks, and militias.

As well as following Defoe, Franklin was carrying on a tradition laid down by William Penn, the Quaker founder of Pennsylvania. In *No Cross, No Crown*, written in 1668 while he was confined in the Tower of London on charges of blasphemy, having published a pamphlet decrying both the Catholic Church and the Puritans and challenging the concept of the Trinity, Penn wrote, "True Godliness don't [*sic*] turn Men out into the World, but enables them to live better in it and excites their Endeavors to mend it" (quoted in Wright 26). It was in a commonwealth founded on this philosophy of brotherhood and responsibility that Franklin lived, worked, and thrived.

As the basis for his theory of human knowledge, John Locke formulated the idea of a tabula rasa, asserting that people are born without innate ideas and that knowledge is accumulated through learning, by observation, experience of, and reflection upon the surrounding world. The world into which Benjamin Franklin was born and in which he grew up was itself the nearest thing to a "blank slate" that the world might be. It was a New World, informed by the history of Europe and attached to European culture, yet no longer really of that Old World nor willing to conform to it. It was a world in the process of being built, in the early stages of physical development, in which all the social institutions, supportive or oppressive, that had governed human behavior and human commerce in Europe had to be re-created and, consequently, reviewed and revised, and not necessarily re-created as they had existed in Europe. It was a world that encouraged, that demanded, observation, speculation, and invention.

It was a world that offered not just an overwhelming sense of newness and the possibility of a new beginning. It was challenged by the tension of old ways and institutions struggling to co-opt that newness, to usurp it and reinstitute the forms, manners, and institutions that continued to prevail in the Old World. In a world like that, for a man like Franklin, there was an identity in the act of creating himself and of creating his environment. Franklin realized himself as he employed his talents constructing and transforming the surrounding world. He devoted the first half of his eighty-four years to building that world, shaping and defining it, installing in it institutions, according to the lights of his reason and the wisdom of his mentors, in service to individual advancement and the common good. During the second half of his life, he worked to secure the concrete fruits of his vision and actions in the revolutionary struggle against England.

3

In 1731, Franklin founded a circulating library; in 1736, a fire brigade; in 1737, he was appointed postmaster of Philadelphia and elected to the Pennsylvania Assembly. Between 1742 and 1744, he invented the Franklin stove (and declined to patent it and profit financially from it), inaugurated the establishment of the University of Pennsylvania, and established the American Philosophical Society. In 1747, he published his experiments with electricity and organized the Pennsylvania militia. He did these things "hands on," as a tradesman, an inventor, and a citizen.

Until he retired from his trade as printer in 1748, a wealthy man,[2] and while the relationship between England and the American colonies was essentially cordial, Franklin's concerns had been personal and civic, pursuing his own designs and designing the surrounding world. Once he had established himself as a gentleman rather than a journeyman, once he had garnered civic authority and administrative power, and once relations between England and the American colonies had become contentious, Franklin's social engagement became a matter of political conflict rather than civic activity. Chief among his concerns was preserving the idea and the ideal of himself and of his society that his industry, frugality, and social activity had established despite his elevation in social position.

Ever industrious, Franklin taught himself Latin, French, Italian, Spanish, and German, at least well enough to read in those languages. He moved his place of residence from his shop and rented a house in a better part of town. He had a portrait of himself painted, the first of a great many that were done in the succeeding years, and designed a Franklin coat of arms with which he sealed his letters. He had always paid attention to the kind of image he cast. In his *Autobiography*, he noted that he paid attention not only to being frugal and industrious but also to seeming so. "To show that I was not above my business," he explained,

> I sometimes brought home the paper I purchas'd at the stores thro' the streets on a wheelbarrow. Thus being esteem'd an industrious, thriving young man, and paying duly for what I bought, the merchants who imported stationery solicited my custom; others proposed supplying me with books, and I went on swimmingly. (66)

Franklin also bought several slaves. It is perplexing that he did. He had begun, around 1740, to print pamphlets by his friend the reverend George Whitefield attacking slavery. Whitefield condemned slaveholders as "monsters of barbarity" who treated their slaves worse than their dogs, who "cut [them] with knives," and "by their unrelenting scourges, have ploughed upon their backs, and made long furrows, and at length brought them even to death itself." Whitefield judged that were slaves to "get the upper hand . . . all good men must acknowledge the judgment would be just." Franklin himself wrote in the *Pennsylvania Gazette* in 1751 that "whites who have Slaves . . . are enfeebled. . . . The white children become proud, disgusted with Labor, and being educated in Idleness, are rendered unfit to get a Living by Industry." Franklin's argument appears callous, directed as it is, in the main, to showing how slavery impairs the virtues of self-reliance and industry in the slaveholders. It seems almost an afterthought when he says, "The Slaves being worked too hard, and ill fed, their Constitutions are broken, and Deaths among them are more than the Births." He seems to challenge the way the institution of slavery is carried on rather than condemn the institution itself. His response to the existence of slavery in the American colonies, in 1751, was provincial, and it did not address the slave trade. "Why increase the Sons of *Africa*," he wrote, "by Planting them in *America*, where we have so fair an Opportunity, by excluding all Blacks and Tawneys, of increasing the lovely White and Red?" (quoted in Fruchtman 29-31; emphasis in original).

Franklin was a man of his time. Even Whitefield, despite his dawning awareness and humane concern, did not advocate the abolition of slavery or the slave trade. For Franklin to come to these positions, which he did by the 1770s, he had to encounter several thinkers more radical than Whitefield. Anthony Benezet was born a Huguenot in France, fled to England to escape Catholic persecution, and became a Quaker in England and then, in Philadelphia, an abolitionist. There, Benezet opened two schools, one for white children and one for free black children. Thanks to his friendship with Benezet, Franklin got to observe black children in his school. On the strength of this observation, practitioner of scientific method that he was, Franklin began to dislodge the prejudice that had disabled his reason. In 1673, writing about his tour of Benezet's schools, Franklin said of the black youngsters, "Their Apprehension [was] as quick, their Memory as Strong and their Docility [i.e., their ability to learn] in every Respect equal to that of White Children" (quoted in Fruchtman 32).

Franklin's response to slavery was changing, as were the responses of many in the northern American colonies, spurred by the work of Benezet and Thomas Bray, an English missionary in Baltimore with whom Franklin had become acquainted in London. Bray founded a society in Baltimore to support libraries and schools for black people. In 1769, Franklin read *A Representation of the Injustice and Dangerous Tendency of Tolerating Slavery*, by Granville Sharp, an English abolitionist. In 1770, Franklin himself wrote *A Conversation on Slavery*, an imaginary exchange among an Englishman, a Scot, and an American.

In it Franklin makes the Englishman accuse Americans of hypocrisy: they claim that they wish to further liberty, but, as slaveholders, they deny others freedom. They can hardly expect to be taken seriously. Two years later Franklin wrote to Benezet, "I have commenc'd an Acquaintance with Mr. Granville Sharp, and we shall act in Concert in the Affair of Slavery" (quoted in Fruchtman 40). Franklin had become, and remained, an abolitionist.

4

Unlike most of the other American colonies, with the exception of Maryland, Rhode Island, and Connecticut, Pennsylvania was not a British Crown Colony. In 1681, in order to pay off a debt of £20,000 (roughly the equivalent of $20,000,000 today) owed the Penn family, King Charles II granted a charter to William Penn that gave him the land in North America that became Pennsylvania. Penn's heirs refused to pay taxes on the lands they owned in Pennsylvania. In order to compel them to pay, Franklin determined to wrest governance of Pennsylvania from the Penns and make it a royal colony, subject to the Crown.

During the 1750s, while France and England were at war for possession of the North American continent, Pennsylvania, ill equipped for self-defense, being neglected by the Penn family, and guided largely by a culture of Quaker pacifism, was particularly vulnerable to attack from the French and their Indian allies. Franklin took part in organizing a militia in the colony and, in 1754, sought to forge a defense alliance of all the colonies under the Albany Plan of Union. The plan failed. Yet even as it began as a pro-British move, it had, as a movement to unite the colonies, the seeds within it of a movement against the authority of England.

In 1757, the Pennsylvania Assembly dispatched Franklin to London to negotiate with the Penn family to pay taxes on their properties. While there, Franklin published a series of articles in the English press condemning the Penns and supporting the authority of the monarchy and the value of the empire. Franklin succeeded in getting the Penns to agree to be taxed on land that had been surveyed, but he was forced to allow that all of their land that had not been surveyed would not be taxed.

London was a more exciting city than Philadelphia, and Franklin became a vital part of its intellectual life. In addition to his official business, he attended meetings of the Royal Society, studied electricity, traveled to Scotland, Belgium, and Holland, improved the design of chimneys and simplified the mechanisms used in clocks, studied weather phenomena, and invented the glass harmonica, an instrument for which both Mozart and Beethoven subsequently wrote. He returned to Pennsylvania in 1762. After two years in Philadelphia, where he headed the colonial post office, served on a number of legislative committees, and helped to negotiate peace treaties with the Pontiac Indians, Franklin returned to London, in 1764, as the agent for Pennsylvania. One of his commissions was to reduce further the authority not of England over the colonies but of the Penns over Pennsylvania. In a 1764 pamphlet regarding the English presence in the New World, *Cool Thoughts on the Present Situation of Our Public Affairs*, Franklin wrote:

> That we shall have a standing army to maintain, is another bugbear raised to terrify us from endeavoring to obtain a King's government. It is very possible that the Crown may think it necessary to keep Troops in America henceforward, to maintain its Conquests, and defend the Colonies; and that the Parliament may establish some Revenue arising out of the American Trade to be apply'd towards supporting those Troops. It is possible too, that we may, after a few Years Experience, be generally very well satisfy'd with that Measure, from the steady Protection it will afford us against Foreign Enemies, and the Security of internal Peace among ourselves without the Expence or Trouble of a Militia. (quoted in Wright 142)

This is hardly the position of a colonial revolutionary.

Franklin's appreciation of British imperial authority diminished as his disapproval of the way Parliament handled its imperial responsibilities increased. With the Molasses Act of 1733, Parliament taxed the sale of molasses in the colonies in order to give an advantage to the English makers and vendors of molasses over the French. Poor enforcement and widespread corruption rendered the law ineffective. In 1764, in order to strengthen the Molasses Act, Parliament passed the Sugar Act. Lord Grenville, Chancellor of the Exchequer, sent the British navy to Boston Harbor to enforce it. Franklin, like most of the colonists, objected, but he hoped that, once back in London, he could broker a compromise between the Crown and the colonies and preserve the empire. He failed to do so. Parliament levied the Stamp Act of 1765 on the colonies. Designed to pay off British war debts, fund the English military presence, and pay for the exploration of territories England had wrested from France, the act placed taxes on a variety of paper products, from legal documents to newspapers and pamphlets to playing cards.

Outraged at being taxed by a body in which they had no representation, the colonists considered the Stamp Act a presumption aimed at their very autonomy. Franklin did not, at first, regard the Stamp Act as profoundly preemptive, as did his fellow colonists, but since he wanted, in the interest of imperial unity, to see the colonies represented in Parliament, he did agree that the Stamp Act represented one more instance of the exclusion of the colonies from Parliament. He saw the Stamp Act not as an attack on independence from England but as an attack on confederation with England. The act was, as Franklin had warned, a disaster. It infuriated the Americans and failed, because of their boycotts, to bring England the intended revenues. Franklin testified against it before Parliament in 1766, insisting that the colonists would not pay *any* taxes imposed by Parliament; rather, taxes had to be levied by "the several assemblies" of the individual colonies (Wright 196). Parliament grudgingly rescinded the tax. The colonists saw the repeal as Franklin's victory, and Franklin was moved closer to the colonial, anti-imperial cause. In 1767, no longer the man who had written

Cool Thoughts, he wrote "On the Propriety of Taxing America," in which he staunchly opposed parliamentary taxation.

From 1766 through 1775, Franklin remained in England as the representative of the colonies. Always hoping to mediate between their interests and the interests of England, he was regarded by the colonists as too English and by the English as too American. The increasing tension between the colonies and England, as it moved the Americans further away from identification with England, made the idea of colonial representation in Parliament, which also had no support in Parliament, less appealing to Franklin. In 1771, Franklin wrote to Sam Adams and Otis Cushing that it appeared to him that Parliament, "in the system of customs to be exacted in America" had "sown the seeds of a total disunion of the two countries" (quoted in Wright 220). Note that he refers to the colonies as a country.

In 1772, eight boatloads of colonists boarded the *Gaspee* off Pawtucket, overpowered the crew and burned the ship. The men who launched the attack were not found, but in response, Governor Hutchinson of Massachusetts resolved that he and the judges of the Superior Court would take their salaries from the king and not from the colonial assemblies, distancing themselves, thereby, from colonial authority. Additionally, Hutchinson wrote a series of letters to Thomas Whatley, who had been Lord Grenville's secretary, calling for "an abridgement [in the colonies] of what are called English liberties" (quoted in Wright 224). This kind of response strengthened the resolve of the colonists, expressed by Franklin in a letter to Thomas Cushing, to resist English authority and to establish a congress for the colonies along with a military capability "which will make us more respectable, our Friendship more valued and Enmity feared" (quoted in Wright 221). The degree of Franklin's alienation from England and resentment of its colonial presumptions can be seen in a hoax "edict" he wrote alleging that the King of Prussia claimed the right to tax England because of the number of Germans who had settled there (Wright 222-23).

In 1772, Franklin was shown Hutchinson's letters by a friend in Parliament whose name he never revealed. Franklin sent them to Cushing with instructions that they be shown around to colonial leaders and not published. They nevertheless were published, and their appearance served to heighten colonial anger. On Christmas Day in 1773, soon after the Boston Tea Party, Franklin admitted to sending the letters to Boston. In November 1774, Josiah Quincy, Jr., writing from England to Massachusetts, reported that Franklin's "ideas are not contracted within the narrow limits of exemption from taxes, but are extended upon the broad scale of total emancipation" (quoted in Wright 236). Franklin's continuing presence in London became dangerous. He was nearly arrested, and he returned to Philadelphia on May 5, 1775.

In Philadelphia, Franklin showed the same skills and the same capacity to respond to his era that had propelled him to world prominence as a younger man. He was active in organizing militias for the defense of Philadelphia and in organizing the printing of money and the manufacture of saltpeter, the basic component of gunpowder. He was also involved in the establishment of a continental post office and military hospitals. He improved the design of the musket and designed marine obstacles to hinder the movement of British ships. He contributed, in gold, to the support of General Washington's army. And he contributed wording to the Declaration of Independence. He also broke with his son William and never reconciled to him afterward, because William remained loyal to the British.

In October 1776, Franklin left on a mission to France. He spent the Revolutionary War years there, lobbying the court of France for aid in the war. Because of Franklin's diplomatic skill and his reputation as a scientist and a philosopher, he was uniquely able to enlist French support, financially and militarily, in the Continental cause. He was greatly admired by the French. His works had been translated into French, he had dined with the king on a previous visit, his likeness was cast on medals that were in wide circulation, and his portrait was painted a number of times. He lived luxuriously on the largesse of admirers, and he hobnobbed with intellectuals, writers, and aristocrats at a time when many in France were attracted to republican ideas. He was thoroughly at home in France.[3]

Franklin returned to Philadelphia on September 14, 1785, and remained there until his death, on April 17, 1790, engaged as always in the politics of forming a free and civil society. He continued, too, to work on his *Autobiography*, hoping to extend the reach of his formative influences and his numerous accomplishments, and to make them count in shaping the character of the nation he had helped to establish, sensing the fundamental reciprocity at work in the movement of history: that the cultural context of an era creates its people and its politics, and the people and the politics of an era create its culture.

Notes

1. Luther's 1522 translation of the Bible, for example, could have the historic importance it did in his rebellion against Rome, bring the unmediated gospel to the people, and have its authority supplant the authority of the Church fathers only because it could be printed in quantity and widely distributed.

2. Franklin retired as a journeyman, but he maintained his partnership in the business. He "owned three printing firms in three different colonies," had "established at least eighteen paper mills," and "may have been the largest paper dealer in the English-speaking world." In addition, "he owned a good deal of rental property in Philadelphia and many coastal towns," and he "was a substantial creditor, practically a banker, with a great amount of money out on loan." Franklin's income once he had established himself is estimated to have been around two thousand pounds per year, twice the amount earned by the governor of Pennsylvania and ten times the amount earned by lawyers practicing in England (Wood 54).

3. After a visit to Paris in 1767, Franklin wrote to his friend Mary Stevenson, "I had not been here Six Days before my Taylor and Peruquier had transform'd me into a Frenchman. Only think what a Figure I make in a little Bag Wig and naked Ears! They told me I was become 20 Years younger, and look'd very galante; so being in Paris where the Mode is to be sacredly follow'd, I was once very near making Love to my Friend's Wife" (quoted in Wood 172).

Works Consulted and Cited

Clark, Ronald W. *Benjamin Franklin: A Biography*. 1983. New York: Barnes & Noble, 2004.

Crane, Verner W. *Benjamin Franklin and a Rising People*. New York: HarperCollins, 1954.

Defoe, Daniel. *An Essay upon Projects*. 1697. http://ebooks.adelaide.edu.au/d/defoe/daniel/d31es/index.html

Franklin, Benjamin. *The Autobiography of Benjamin Franklin*. 1791. New York: P. F. Collier & Son, 1909. http://etext.lib.virginia.edu/etcbin/toccer-new2?id=Fra2Aut.sgm&images=images/modeng&data=/texts/english/modeng/parsed&tag=public&part=all

Fruchtman, Jack, Jr. *Atlantic Cousins: Benjamin Franklin and His Visionary Friends*. New York: Thunder's Mouth Press, 2005.

Lemay, J. A. Leo. *The Life of Benjamin Franklin: Journalist, 1706-1730*. Philadelphia: U of Pennsylvania P, 2006.

Locke, John. *An Essay Concerning Human Understanding*. 1690. http://oregonstate.edu/instruct/phl302/texts/locke/locke1/Essay_contents.html

Lucas, F. L. *The Art of Living: Four Eighteenth-Century Minds: Hume, Horace Walpole, Burke, Benjamin Franklin*. New York: Macmillan, 1959.

Seavey, Ormond. *Becoming Benjamin Franklin: The Autobiography and the Life*. University Park: Pennsylvania State UP, 1988.

Van Doren, Carl. *Benjamin Franklin*. 1938. New York: Viking Press, 1956.

Wood, Gordon S. *The Americanization of Benjamin Franklin*. New York: Penguin Press, 2004.

Wright, Esmond. *Franklin of Philadelphia*. Cambridge, MA: Belknap Press of Harvard UP, 1986.

Benjamin Franklin:
The Critical Reception

Gurdip Panesar

Franklin was one of the most famous people in the world during his lifetime, and he has remained so—but the reason for his fame has shifted over the centuries. In this essay Gurdip Panesar looks at the ways critics have read Franklin's works and suggests that one of the reasons we have trouble making sense of Franklin is the multiplicity of his interests and talents. Which discipline does he "belong" to? Was he a literary author who happened to be involved in politics and science? Was he a historic figure who happened to write and do scientific experiments? Was he a scientist who happened to publish and shape the course of a nation?

Of course Franklin was all of these things and more, but most critics, and most ages, have been able to see only part of the picture at a time. Thus the Franklin who appears in the pages of both learned journals and popular biographies has changed his character: sometimes he is the practical man of business, sometimes the protagonist of the archetypal poor-boy-makes-good story, sometimes the infallible sage, sometimes the deeply flawed and conflicted human being. As Panesar points out, the people of each age see in Franklin what they want to see, or perhaps what they need to see. — J.L.

Benjamin Franklin is known as a great man who wrote much but not necessarily as one of America's greatest literary figures. We can identify several reasons for this. First of all, he is such a multifaceted individual that it often appears something of a daunting task to try to approach him from any critical angle. The phrase "many-sided Franklin," the title of Paul Leicester Ford's 1899 biography, has often justly been invoked in relation to him. He remains one of the relatively few figures in world history who could genuinely be called a Renaissance man or polymath, given that he was a politician, a journalist, a writer, a printer, a diplomat, a scientist, and an inventor. Furthermore, he had, of course, a fundamental role in shaping the independent United States as one of the Founding Fathers, a role that has embedded him in the national consciousness. Indeed, Franklin is a public figure of such standing that he has become enshrined in myth as well as history, a "massively symbolic folk hero" (Wood ix) as much as, if not more so, than his illustrious political contemporaries Jefferson, Madison, and Washington.

Biographies of Franklin have abounded over the past two hundred-odd years. His achievements in so many fields have naturally resulted in a multiplicity of approaches in Franklin scholarship—political, philosophical, sociological, and scientific. Trying to extract him from the realm of legend and from his variety of public roles in order to concentrate on him purely as a man of letters can be an arduous task. Even here, literary criticism remains generally mixed with the subject of "life writing" in his case, owing to his famous *Autobiography* and other writings on various aspects of his public roles. In a purely literary sense, it is not easy to know just what approach to take in examining his writings. It is therefore not too surprising that a purely literary approach has historically not been much in evidence among Franklin scholars.

Another reason for the paucity of "pure" literary criticism on Franklin is the relative lack of critical appraisal of the colonial/eighteenth-century period of North American literature as a whole. Studies and introductions to that era of literature of course have been produced—a very recent and notable work of reference being *The Oxford Handbook of Early American Literature*, edited by Kevin J. Hayes—but it remains overshadowed by the great flowering of American literature in the following two centuries. Literary criticism of this period has often tended to break down into discussion of the era's most important writers, such as Jonathan Edwards and Cotton Mather, with whom Franklin is often usefully compared. As a literary period the eighteenth century in America remains a fairly tenuous area of scholarship (in stark contrast to the British literature of that time).

Finally, we can point to the nature of the bulk of Franklin's own writings to account for why he has not received quite as much attention solely as a literary figure as many other writers. He wrote voluminously, but not in the forms that are most familiar in literature today—novels, drama, or poetry. Of course, he did write in the forms common to his time—satirical essays and sketches, and the like—but he did not concern himself with the kind of subjects that are generally seen, from the Romantic age until today, as being the province of the best literature. As Esmond Wright notes in *Franklin of Philadelphia*, Franklin lacked an "aesthetic response" (3)—he never wrote about nature, or about relationships between men and women, or really of the mind or spirit, as many great writers before and after him were seen to do. Instead, Franklin's writings are very much focused on matters of business, politics, civic affairs, duty, and wealth.

In his two most famous works, his *Autobiography* and *Poor Richard's Almanack*, this essentially hardheaded, pragmatic attitude is generally seen to prevail. The *Autobiography* is the story of a successful businessman, the exemplar of the self-made man, and *Poor Richard* is a collection of homely sayings and maxims encouraging practical wisdom and the accumulation of wealth. These writings have often attracted charges of dull rationalism, practicality, and even vulgarity, and as such have often been deemed unworthy of examination as "great" literature. Albert Henry Smyth remarked in 1889 that "Franklin's mind was attentive to trifles; his philosophy never got beyond the homely maxims of worldly prudence" (20). Franklin's personal friend David Hume might have nominated him as the first great American man of letters, and great he undoubtedly was; he has also often been thought of as "the first American"—to quote the title of a 2000 biography by H. W. Brands—owing to his decisive role in shaping the American Constitution and arguing the cause of the new nation in the Old World as well as his role in improving civic and public life, not to mention his discoveries and inventions in the field of science. However, the value of Franklin's literary preoccupations has often been called into question from his day down to ours, leading sometimes to the suspicion that somehow he was not really a literary man, as exemplified in one of the early pieces of Franklin criticism by John Foster in the *Eclectic Review* in 1818: "his deficiency of literature, in the usual sense of the term, was excellently compensated by so wide an acquaintance with the world." This has been a common position adopted by many Franklin critics over the centuries: that he was first and foremost a product of eighteenth-century enlightenment and rationalism, which he applied to every sphere in life in the most practical manner and manifested in his writings at the expense of beauty, real feeling, and sublimity. For all that, however, his works have been studied continually, as much as his contributions to public and political life, amid changing times and fashions, while his actual place in literature continues to be much debated. It has been observed that two of his most noted biographers of the nineteenth century, Paul Leicester Ford and John Bach McMaster, could not finally decide just what role Franklin occupies in American literature (Huang 272), and more than a century later the evaluation of his writings is still very much an ongoing process.

Benjamin Franklin was born in Boston on January 17, 1706, into a devout Puritan household. His father, Josiah Franklin, an émigré from England, was a tallow chandler. The young Franklin had little formal schooling but read widely and was apprenticed to his older brother James, a printer, at age twelve. James started the publication of the first independent newspaper in the colonies, the *New England Courant*. Franklin's first published work was in this paper, a series of satirical letters written in the persona of a middle-aged widow named Silence Dogood. At age seventeen, at odds with his brother, Franklin ran away to Philadelphia and found work in a printing shop. Soon afterward he sailed to England with the intention of setting up his own business. He worked for a while in a printing house in London and then returned to Philadelphia in 1720, where he opened his own print shop in 1728 and established the *Pennsylvania Gazette*, to which he also contributed. In 1727 he also set up the Junto, a discussion group with a view to bringing about improvements to civic life; this organization's achievements over the years were to include the establishment of a library, a hospital, a fire company, and an academy that would eventually grow into the University of Pennsylvania. In 1732, Franklin established a common-law marriage with Deborah Read; they had two children, one of whom died in infancy (Franklin also had an illegitimate son named William).

In 1733 Franklin began publishing *Poor Richard's Almanack* under the pseudonym Richard Saunders; its wise and pithy sayings relating to everyday life became extremely popular. Franklin invented virtually none of them but rather reworked them from other sources into memorable form for ordinary Americans. He also embarked on scientific experimentation, his most famous contributions in this area being his demonstration of the electrical nature of lightning and the invention of the Franklin stove. He wrote copiously on his discoveries and inventions, with the first publication of his scientific observations appearing in 1751. In that year he was also elected to the Pennsylvania Assembly, and from that time onward his involvement in matters of political importance increased. In 1747, he had published his propaganda piece *Plain Truth*, which succeeded in persuading the largely peaceful assembly to organize a militia to fight the French and Indian Wars on behalf of the British Empire. In 1758 the preface to the final edition of *Poor Richard* was published as "Father Abraham's Sermon" (thereafter generally published as *The Way to Wealth*); this work cemented his reputation as a purveyor of wise and homely sayings.

The latter part of Franklin's life brought the most high-profile events of his career. Although at first loyal to the British, he became increasingly disenchanted with such controversies as the Stamp Act in the 1760s. In 1773 he published perhaps his two most famous political satires—*An Edict of the King of Prussia* (on the vexing question of colonial tax) and *Rules by Which a Great Empire May Be Reduced to a Small One*. In 1791, the year after Franklin's death, the first part of the work that was to be his most lasting legacy as a writer, the *Autobiography*, was published in French; the first English translation appeared in

1793. This account of his life ends abruptly in the year 1775, when he still had his most famous political exploits ahead of him. Returning to America from England in 1775, his disillusionment with the British Empire complete, he helped draft the Declaration of Independence.

After independence was achieved, he continued his work as diplomat, serving as commissioner to France from 1778 to 1785; it was there that he wrote some of his most delightful sketches, known as "The Bagatelles." Returning to America in 1785 in great honor, he became president of Philadelphia for three years. He continued to write on political matters: in 1789 he published "A Plan for Improving the Condition of the Free Blacks," and his final published work was a political satire, *Sidi Mehemet Ibrahim on the Slave Trade* (also known simply as *On the Slave Trade*). He died on April 17, 1790.

From the first, literary observers and critics were aware of the strengths of Franklin's writings. The chief merits of his prose, the graceful, balanced, elegant style consciously modeled on major English eighteenth-century writers, such as Addison and Steele—whose journal *The Spectator* he openly admired—were never in doubt. For instance, in 1806 Lord Jeffrey commented that "his style has all the vigour, and even conciseness, of Swift, without any of his harshness. It is no degree more flowery yet both elegant and witty" (quoted in Swinton 166). His lucid style was also seen to be of great service in other areas of his work, such as his scientific writings; the eminent English physicist Humphry Davy declared that it was "almost as worthy of admiration as the doctrine" (quoted in Mott and Jorgenson 49). In the 1903 edition of a biography first published in 1898, Sydney George Fisher decreed that "the test of literary genius is the ability to be fascinating about stoves" (158), thus praising the way in which Franklin was capable of elevating dull, ordinary material into fascinating reading. Franklin did not merely imitate the style of the English writers; he also imitated their subject matter in his satires and "hoaxes" such as *An Edict of the King of Prussia*.

Although Franklin's style was naturally seen as imitative of the eighteenth-century English masters, he was also credited by some with helping to foster a new "American" idiom. These critics detected a new vigor, a "native raciness" underneath the polite style (Trent and Erskine 8). I. Bernard Cohen in 1953 declared that "one of the outstanding needs in Franklin scholarship is a study of his humorous writings and satires. . . . I am certain that when such a job has been done, Franklin will emerge as America's first humorist, in the tradition of Will Rogers, of Mark Twain, Mr Dooley" (xi). Compare Esmond Wright in his 1986 study *Franklin of Philadelphia*: "His prose heralded Mark Twain, his ribaldry and anecdotage anticipated Lincoln" (357). Franklin's satire has also been usefully examined from the point of view of a distinct American tradition in *American Satire: An Anthology of Writings from Colonial Times to the Present*, edited by Nicholas Bakalar. There is the view, then, that Franklin did not merely copy the eighteenth-century English masters but actively contributed to the development of a kind of truly American literature, thus signaling a certain shift away from critics' viewing him as little more than a successful imitator of his eighteenth-century English neoclassical counterparts.

If Franklin's style has generally attracted favorable comment, however, the nature of his preoccupations in the bulk of his writings—matters of business, political affairs, material wealth—very often have not. With the dawning of the Romantic age in literature at the end of the eighteenth century, with its exalted themes of nature and transcendence and matters of the mind and spirit, Franklin's light sketches, political satires, and witty essays began to seem out of place. The poet John Keats, for example, remarked scornfully that there was nothing "sublime" about Franklin, or indeed about Americans as a whole (quoted in Wood 5).

It is even more illuminating, however, to compare Franklin's standing with American writers in the later nineteenth century, particularly canonical American writers, as he exerted a considerable influence on them, albeit in a generally negative sense. They created rather disparaging portrayals of him as a shrewd, worldly, and essentially small-minded type, for instance in Edgar Allan Poe's 1845 sketch "The Business Man" (which does not actually mention Franklin by name) and Herman Melville's *Israel Potter: His Fifty Years of Exile* (1855). Twain, meanwhile, in his 1870 essay "The Late Benjamin Franklin," scoffed that Franklin "prostituted his talents to the invention of maxims and aphorisms" (quoted in Wood 4).

Franklin remained the standard of worldly and material success well into the twentieth century for American writers, in F. Scott Fitzgerald's *The Great Gatsby*, for example. However, in the twentieth century criticism of Franklin became more unrelenting owing to new ideas pertaining to psychology and the depths of human nature that were embraced by many writers on both sides of the Atlantic. Also influential was sociologist Max Weber's magisterial work *The Protestant Ethic and the Spirit of Capitalism* (1904-1905), which famously crystallized the image of Franklin as the man who helped usher in the modern capitalist, entrepreneurial age. Thus the attack on Franklin became double-pronged. In a 1929 biography, Bernard Faÿ declared that "of all his titles to glory, the most outstanding one is that he was the first bourgeois in the world" (vii), but in the ferment of new social and political ideas in the early twentieth century, "bourgeois" was generally a derogatory label.

Along with the middle-class values and morality that Franklin was seen to espouse, the lack of psychological depth in his writings provided fresh ammunition for his detractors, most memorably the writer D. H. Lawrence, in a 1923 study of American literature:

> Middle size, sturdy snuff coloured Dr Franklin. . . . The soul of man is a dark vast forest, with wild life—think of Benjamin fencing it off. . . . He made himself a list of virtues, which he trotted inside like a grey nag in a paddock. . . . he tries to take away my wholeness and my dark forest, my freedom. (quoted in Wright, *Franklin* 2)

William Carlos Williams echoed this decades later in his essay "Franklin and the Rejection of the American Wilderness": "He was the dyke keeper, keeping out the wilderness with his wits" (86-87). Franklin was thus seen as a shallow figure, unaware of, or perhaps willfully repudiating, the deeper truths and emotions of the human condition that had come to be regarded as the proper subjects for any serious writer. Critic Charles Angoff summed up the mood in 1931. Referring to a remark by Thomas Carlyle a century before, that Franklin was the "Father of the Yankee people," he caustically observed that "this was a libel on the tribe, for the Yankees had produced Twain, Hawthorne, and Emily Dickinson" (2:310).

In the first decades of the twentieth century, therefore, the literary verdict being returned on Franklin was not particularly favorable; he was seen to be wholly at odds with illustrious writers of both Britain and America. Thereafter, however, such virulent attacks on Franklin's literary credibility faded. He was still seen by many as having fairly limited value as a writer, as illustrated by an entry in an American literary encyclopedia of 1956: "It was perhaps his failure to look much beyond his didactic aim that kept his work minor" (Cady 129). There was, however, an increasing willingness to regard him more on his own terms and once more in his original eighteenth-century context. In 1964 there was the welcome appearance of Bruce Ingham Granger's full-length and detailed literary study that carefully examined Franklin's different writings according to the terms and conventions of various literary genres. However, his work continued to be more commonly approached from biographical, sociological, and cultural angles. He continued to be seen, as he always had been in some measure, as very representative of his time, a product of the eighteenth-century Enlightenment, the embodiment of reason, and compared and contrasted with other "representative" colonial figures such as Cotton Mather and Jonathan Edwards—for instance, in Mitchell Robert Breitwieser's searching study *Cotton Mather and Benjamin Franklin: The Price of Representative Personality.*

Such works still tended to concentrate on Franklin's thought and outlook rather than purely on the literary qualities of his writings.

However, in the latter part of the twentieth century there was also increasing recognition of the fact that Franklin the man was a more complex case than had previously been assumed; he began to be seen not just as a straightforward exponent of middle-class materialistic values or representative of eighteenth-century "reason." Robert Sayre, in a 1964 study, remarked that Franklin's works reveal a sense of "change and discontinuity" and that he readily slipped into different poses in his writings, not, as earlier critics had held, because he was merely imitating the rhetorical devices common to eighteenth-century models such as Swift, but because "he lived in a fluid world" (23). Particularly from the 1960s onward, critics were more ready to admit that there was far more to Franklin than the enduring image of the self-complacent, successful businessman. Following the trend of postmodernist criticism, some challenged the notion that he stood for any definable set of values of philosophy at all; Michael Zuckerman remarked that there was no center to Franklin's thought: "he experimented playfully . . . with beliefs and values" (448-449).

All this had major implications for what has always remained Franklin's most celebrated work, the *Autobiography*, which in recent decades has come under ever closer scrutiny. For instance, Joseph Fichtelberg offers a structuralist reading in his article "The Complex Image: Text and Reader in the *Autobiography* of Benjamin Franklin," and Wright posits the question "The *Autobiography*: Fact or Fiction?" and concludes that it is a work of art, or "at least of artifice" (42). The *Autobiography* has in recent years come to be valued more for its secrets and intricacies, and its playful use of language and persona, than for its apparently straightforward account of the rise of a self-made man.

Recent decades in Franklin criticism have also seen a new focus on works that previously received very little or no attention, following J. A. Leo Lemay's 1986 publication of *The Canon of Benjamin Franklin, 1722-1776: New Attributions and Reconsiderations*, in which various journalistic articles by Franklin come under review. These appeared to reveal a new unsuspected side to the man in the light of his articles on crime and vice. Ronald A. Bosco talked up the sensationalist edge to Franklin's reporting in the late 1980s, and some other critics, such as Robert D. Arner, also chose to focus on this hitherto neglected aspect of Franklin's writings (articles by both Bosco and Arner appear in *Reappraising Benjamin Franklin: A Bicentennial Perspective*, edited by Lemay).

Another development in Franklin scholarship that might finally be noted here is analysis of his work in comparison not just with neoclassical English writers or American writers but also with English writers in the Romantic age such as William Blake. William C. Spengemann takes this approach in chapter 5 of his radical 1994 survey of American colonial literature, *A New World of Words*. This strategy allows for emphasis on Franklin's acute awareness of being on the cusp of a rapidly changing world and postulates that he adopted the principle of reason and enlightened self-interest not out of self-confidence but simply out of necessity, in order to cope with the threat of an uncertain future. This alignment lends a certain air of poignancy to Franklin's writings, a quality that previous critics had not really associated with his work.

New approaches to Franklin the writer have therefore been in evidence in recent decades, and new aspects and angles to his work have been uncovered, but in the main his literary reputation still appears solid rather than spectacular, as it generally has over the two hundred-odd years since his death. Similarly, the most common approach in Franklin scholarship remains that of biographical criticism and life writing. It may also be observed that the problem inherent in literary criticism, and in Franklin criticism in particular, also remains, as stated in a concise 1962 literary introduction to Franklin:

> The final judgement upon the question of whether or not Franklin was a great writer rests upon the evaluation of his purposes. If the advancement of science and the resolution of political differences are of major importance, he was. If the exploration of the depths of human psychology is the

primary purpose of literature, he was not. If the great thing for the writer is to present a thought-provoking or satisfying philosophy of life, the question is debatable. (Hornberger 46)

The debates continue; and while Franklin may still not be regarded as being among America's very greatest literary men, his writings—most of all his *Autobiography*—will assuredly still be read and studied for many years to come.

Bibliographical Notes

As is to be expected in the case of so famous a figure, biographies of Franklin have appeared in a continuous stream ever since his death. See Carl Van Doren's *Benjamin Franklin*, first published by the Viking Press in 1938, for a richly detailed picture. More recent biographies include H. W. Brands's *The First American: The Life and Times of Benjamin Franklin*, published by Doubleday in 2000, and Walter Isaacson's *Benjamin Franklin: An American Life*, published by Simon & Schuster in 2003.

Several collections of Franklin's own works have been compiled over the years. John Bigelow edited *The Complete Works* in ten volumes in 1887-88. The biggest collection of Franklin writings is *The Papers of Benjamin Franklin*, edited by Leonard W. Labaree and others and published by Yale University Press; thirty-nine volumes of this series have been published from 1959 through 2009.

Many editions of the *Autobiography* have appeared since the first authentic version was published in 1868 by John Bigelow. One of the most useful is the 1986 Norton Critical Edition, edited by J. A. Leo Lemay and Paul Zall. *Autobiography and Other Writings*, edited by Ormond Seavey—first published by Oxford University Press in 1993 and reissued in 2008—provides a handy single-volume collection of Franklin's major and lesser-known works.

Several Franklin bibliographies have been compiled. Earlier ones include that by Paul Leicester Ford (London, 1889); one of the latest is *Benjamin Franklin: Biographical Overview and Bibliography*, edited by Christopher J. Murrey and published by Nova Science in 2002. Also of interest is Melvin H. Buxbaum's *Benjamin Franklin: A Reference Guide*, published in 1983 by G. K. Hall.

Works Cited

Angoff, Charles. *A Literary History of the American People*. 2 vols. New York: Alfred A. Knopf, 1931.

Arner, Robert D. "Politics and Temperance in Boston and Philadelphia: Benjamin Franklin's Journalistic Writings on Drinking and Drunkenness." *Reappraising Benjamin Franklin: A Bicentennial Perspective*. Ed. J. A. Leo Lemay. Newark: U of Delaware P, 1993. 78-97.

Bakalar, Nicholas, ed. *American Satire: An Anthology of Writings from Colonial Times to the Present*. New York: Meridian, 1997.

Bosco, Ronald A. "Scandal, Like Other Virtues, Is Its Own Reward: Franklin Working the Crime Beat." *Reappraising Benjamin Franklin: A Bicentennial Perspective*. Ed. J. A. Leo Lemay. Newark: U of Delaware P, 1993. 52-77.

Brands, H. W. *The First American: The Life and Times of Benjamin Franklin*. New York: Doubleday, 2000.

Breitwieser, Mitchell Robert. *Cotton Mather and Benjamin Franklin: The Price of Representative Personality*. New York: Cambridge UP, 1984.

Buxbaum, Melvin H. *Benjamin Franklin: A Reference Guide*. Boston: G. K. Hall, 1983.

Cady, Edwin H., Frederick J. Hoffman, and Roy Harvey Pearce. *The Growth of American Literature: A Critical and Historical Survey*. New York: American Book Company, 1956.

Cohen, I. Bernard. *Benjamin Franklin: His Contribution to the American Tradition*. Indianapolis: Bobbs-Merrill, 1953.

Faÿ, Bernard. *Franklin: The Apostle of Modern Times*. London: Sampson Low, Marston, 1929.

Fichtelberg, Joseph. "The Complex Image: Text and Reader in the *Autobiography* of Benjamin Franklin." *Early American Literature* 23 (1988): 202-7.

Fisher, Sydney George. *The True Benjamin Franklin*. 1898. 5th ed. Philadelphia: J. B. Lippincott, 1903.

Franklin, Benjamin. *Autobiography: An Authoritative Text*. Ed. J. A. Leo Lemay and P. M. Zall. New York: W. W. Norton, 1986.

____________. *Autobiography and Other Writings*. Ed. Ormond Seavey. 1993. New York: Oxford UP, 2008.

____________. *The Complete Works of Benjamin Franklin*. 10 vols. Ed. John Bigelow. New York: G. P. Putnam's Sons, 1887-88.

___________. *The Papers of Benjamin Franklin*. 39 vols. Ed. Leonard W. Labaree et al. New Haven, CT: Yale UP, 1959-2009.

Granger, Bruce Ingham. *Benjamin Franklin: An American Man of Letters*. Ithaca, NY: Cornell UP, 1964.

Hayes, Kevin J., ed. *The Oxford Handbook of Early American Literature*. New York: Oxford UP, 2008.

Hornberger, Theodore. *Benjamin Franklin*. Minneapolis: U of Minnesota P, 1962.

Huang, Nian-Sheng. *Benjamin Franklin in American Thought and Culture*. Philadelphia: American Philosophical Society, 1994.

Isaacson, Walter. *Benjamin Franklin: An American Life*. New York: Simon & Schuster, 2003.

Lemay, J. A. Leo. *The Canon of Benjamin Franklin, 1722-1776: New Attributions and Reconsiderations*. Newark: U of Delaware P, 1986.

___________, ed. *Reappraising Benjamin Franklin: A Bicentennial Perspective*. Newark: U of Delaware P, 1993.

Mott, Frank Luther, and Chester E. Jorgenson. *Benjamin Franklin: Representative Selections*. New York: American Book Company, 1936.

Murrey, Christopher J., ed. *Benjamin Franklin: Biographical Overview and Bibliography*. New York: Nova Science, 2002.

Sayre, Robert. *The Examined Self: Benjamin Franklin, Henry Adams, Henry James*. Princeton, NJ: Princeton UP, 1964.

Smyth, Albert Henry. *American Literature*. Philadelphia: Eldridge, 1889.

Spengemann, William C. *A New World of Words: Redefining Early American Literature*. New Haven, CT: Yale UP, 1994.

Swinton, William. *Studies in English Literature*. New York: Harper, 1882.

Trent, W. P., and John Erskine. *Great Writers of America*. New York: Norgate & Holt, 1912.

Van Doren, Carl. *Benjamin Franklin*. 1938. Birmingham, AL: Palladium, 2001.

Williams, William Carlos. "Franklin and the Rejection of the American Wilderness." *Benjamin Franklin: Statesman-Philosopher or Materialist?* Ed. Wilbur R. Jacobs. New York: Holt, Rinehart and Winston, 1972.

Wood, Gordon S. *The Americanization of Benjamin Franklin*. New York: Penguin Press, 2004.

Wright, Esmond. "The *Autobiography*: Fact or Fiction?" *The Intellectual World of Benjamin Franklin*. Ed. Dilys Winegard. Philadelphia: U of Pennsylvania P, 1990. 29-42.

___________. *Franklin of Philadelphia*. Cambridge, MA: Belknap Press of Harvard UP, 1986.

Zuckerman, Michael. "Doing Good While Doing Well: Benevolence and Self-Interest in Franklin's *Autobiography*." *Reappraising Benjamin Franklin: A Bicentennial Perspective*. Ed. J. A. Leo Lemay. Newark: U of Delaware P, 1993.

Franklin as Father:
Didactic Discourse in the *Autobiography*

Maura Grace Harrington

Maura Grace Harrington investigates the place of fatherhood in Franklin's most famous book, with "fatherhood" understood as both a biological and a spiritual relation. "In order to set himself up as a credible and authoritative figure," she writes, "Franklin is careful to trace two important lineages: his genetic extraction and his spiritual inheritance."

We do not get to choose our biological parents, but other kinds of filiation are sometimes under our control. Harrington reminds us that Franklin is classed among the Founding Fathers, making him a kind of parent to the entire nation, and in enacting the part of the self-made man, Franklin became "the product of his own creation." But Franklin also knew that, for all his self-mythologization, he was not sui generis; he had his own connections to his ancestors—to the past. And while he could not escape that fact, he could reinterpret it. "Franklin," explains Harrington in a provocative close reading of his writings about fatherhood, "claims a moral lineage through his father to God." —J.L.

In his thought-provoking and insightful article "'Now, Gods, Stand Up for Bastards': Reinterpreting Benjamin Franklin's *Autobiography*," William H. Shurr traces the impression of Franklin as "the reverend figure of legend" (435) by many critics who have studied his memoir. At the conclusion of his exploration of Franklin's "seriously duplicitous" (446) character and motivations for penning the *Autobiography*, Shurr inveighs that so that readers can realistically understand the complexities of the *Autobiography*, "the actual Franklin needs to be decanonized" (447). Shurr makes a strong case for this necessity, debunking the myth of unity of purpose that enshrouds the composition of the *Autobiography*. The purpose of Shurr's article is to deconstruct Franklin's mythic status and authorial intentions; however, before such analysis can be appreciated fully, it is necessary to examine the techniques that Franklin uses in his *Autobiography* in order to build himself up to demigod status. Upon examining Franklin's use of language and his patrilineal emphasis, it becomes clear that he constructs himself as a member of a succession of fathers, stretching from God to himself, in order to assume a seminal role in the creation of the ideal American citizen.

Inaugurating himself as the very type of the American, Benjamin Franklin, in his *Autobiography*, asserts his individuality while simultaneously drawing on the authority of other figures. Franklin claims a moral lineage through his father to God. Franklin considers even his own mistakes exemplary, asserting that they serve to highlight values that should be important to Americans. In claiming a place of priority among Americans, Franklin reveals that he has been influenced by Puritan views of life and, more specifically, of the American project. While Franklin stops short of asserting that his existence as the model American has been prophesied in Scripture, he derives the authority that he claims from his independent decision to adhere to certain scriptural values with which his father had inculcated him. Ultimately relegating himself to the role of father, this author of what essentially becomes a manual for Americanization relies on distinguishing experience from inexperience, showing that being self-made paradoxically requires reliance on precedents.

In the *Autobiography*, Franklin ties together closely his idea of Father, as both his own biological father and God the Father, and the American Dream. The concept of attaining wealth and prestige, for Franklin, is related to his basis in biblical values and to his instruction from his father. Franklin explicitly points out these connections: "And my Father having among his Instructions to me when a Boy, frequently repeated a Proverb of Solomon, 'Seest thou a Man diligent in his Calling, he shall stand before Kings, he shall not stand before mean Men.' I from thence consider'd Industry as a Means of obtaining Wealth and Distinction, which encourag'd me" (75). In this passage, it is made apparent that Franklin has striven to acquire money and respect. He has been driven to do this by his father, and his father has gotten this idea from his ideological origins in the biblical God. While Franklin attributes much of his success to the constructive criticism of his father, he maintains that his success is also due to the presence of a higher power in his life: "And now I speak of thanking God, I desire with all Humility to acknowledge, that I owe the mention'd Happiness of my past Life to his kind Providence, which led me to the Means I us'd and gave them Success" (2). Deriving from his patrilineal values, Franklin's idea of the American Dream, which he attains and exhorts his readers to strive toward, hinges on both virtue and wealth. Franklin cites the description of Wisdom or Virtue in Solomon 3:16-17 as a particular inspiration to him in his pursuit of his goals: "'Length of Days is in her right hand, and in her Left Hand Riches and Honours; Her Ways are Ways of Pleasantness, and all her Paths are Peace'" (82). Although Franklin's various ideas about becoming a true American originate in his father's instruction, these concepts ultimately begin with biblically inspired concepts. At many points in his narrative, Franklin correlates his earthly father and God so closely that he minimizes the distinction between the two.

Franklin sees his life in terms of the journey he has undertaken in order to arrive at maturity and virtue, allowing him the privilege of serving as a model American, in his own estimation. His idea of virtue, or living a good life, is not necessarily tied to religion per se, but instead is based on his understanding of God and religion more as universal concepts than as specific and personal ideas. Franklin believes:

> That there is one God who made all things.
>
> That he governs the World by his Providence.—
>
> That he ought to be worshipped by Adoration, Prayer and Thanksgiving.
>
> But that the most acceptable Service of God is doing Good to Man.
>
> That the Soul is immortal.
>
> And that God will certainly reward virtue and punish Vice either here or hereafter. (92)

Franklin's life and his *Autobiography* are modeled on the principle of doing good for his fellow human beings. His goal is not particularly religious, and he records his shunning of various religious practices throughout the course of the *Autobiography*. For example, his first religious experience in Philadelphia, a visit to a Quaker meeting, proves to be less than stimulating and provides him with little benefit other than a much-needed nap (25). The process by which Franklin arrives at his state of moral maturity reflects the fact that he is inculcated with Puritan procedures for attaining superior virtue. Throughout this work, Franklin refers to his quest to attain a virtuous state, which state will inform his actions and betray to the world his secular sanctity. David L. Parker points out that Franklin's

> aim of "moral Perfection" is clearly not precisely analogous to the Puritan objective of sanctity. Nevertheless, the first paragraph he devotes to this subject suggests his probable familiarity with the standard Puritan conversion pattern through the attitudes it describes, through its methodical attention to the displacement of bad habits, and even, to a limited extent, through its terminology. (69)

Franklin will eradicate his faults, primarily because he intends for them to disappear; "His progress thus far roughly corresponds to that of the Puritan convert through the stages of conviction and compunction" (70). He at least somewhat consciously situates his eventual ascent to the status of self-made American in the context of the Puritan schema of the relationship between God and man.

Although Franklin seems to break totally from Puritanism by removing himself from organized religious practice, he does not completely remove himself from the framework of the Puritan mind-set. Perry Miller and Thomas H. Johnson assert the following about the Puritans' attitudes toward nature:

> The Puritan does not deny that truth can be discovered in nature, poetry, right reason, and the consent of nations. He does not deny that these things are emanations of God's wisdom and that from them men may gain all manner of valuable instruction. He does not doubt that there is a light in nature, which, he says, "consists in common principles imprinted upon the reasonable soul, by nature," and that man naturally inclines his assent to certain fundamental truths, not only such truths as that the whole is greater than the part, but that there is a God, that parents are to be honored, and that there is a difference between what is good and what is bad. (51)

For the Puritans, then, nature is anything but devoid of goodness. Nature is a medium through which divine truths can be more fully understood. Additionally, the Puritans give some credit to the "natural man" in that they believe that people are born with the propensity to follow certain general moral guidelines. Franklin, then, in his more secular views on virtue, is not totally separating himself from the sensibilities of his forebears but is instead taking up one train of their thought and developing it in an innovative way. Franklin molds the values that he has received so that they will be useful to him in the new landscape of America.

The steps by which Franklin attains his goal of being the exemplary American are not terribly clear. William C. Spengemann enumerates the factors to which Franklin grants responsibility for his arrival at his destination:

> At times he attributes his success to "foresight." . . . At other times, however, he ascribes this success to the quite different faculty of "hindsight." . . . Betraying a similar indecision about the value of experience, he assigns credit for his present reasonableness sometimes to "character"—an innate configuration of the soul, akin to innocence, which will eventually become manifest if he can preserve it from the taint of experience—and sometimes to experience itself, which molds character into an eventual shape that did not precede experience. (55)

Franklin, it seems, has been successful because of his own virtue, but he is not the only person who is responsible for his character; rather, Franklin's father has had an active role, both when near to and when far away from his son, in shaping the person Franklin has become.

Franklin attributes his success largely to the influence of his father, whom he characterizes as perspicacious and wise, whose judgment is omnipresent, and whose advice is a bulwark against evil. In portraying his father in this way, Franklin aligns his father with God. Franklin refers to his father as a judge of his worthiness and abilities. Regarding his father having saved him from embarking on a potentially dead-end career as a poet, Franklin remarks, "My father discourag'd me, by ridiculing my Performances, and telling me Verse-makers were generally Beggars; so I escap'd being a Poet, most probably a very bad one" (12). Franklin exposes his perception of his father's ability both to instruct his son in the ways of the world and to pick out his son's faults and, by exposing them, to prevent the young Franklin from doing harm to himself. Again ruminating of the guidance his father provided, Franklin explains that his forebear "observed that tho' I had the Advantage . . . in correct Spelling and pointing . . . I fell far short in elegance of Expression, in Method and in Perspicuity, of which he convinc'd me by several Instances. I saw the Justice of his Remarks, and thence grew more attentive to the *Manner* in Writing, and determin'd to endeavour at Improvement" (13). The judgment and advice rendered by his father not only allow Franklin to understand the error of his ways but also lead him to desire wholeheartedly to mend his errors. Franklin's father renders "Judgment" in the disputes between Franklin and his brother, to whom Franklin was apprenticed (18). Franklin aligns himself with his father by pointing out, "I fancy I was either generally in the right, or else a better Pleader, because the Judgment was generally in my favour" (18). Because the verdict favored him, Franklin had absorbed at least some of what his father had tried to teach him: either right judgment or self-presentation. In either case, Franklin, through writing that he has obtained his father's favor, indicates that he deserves to be victorious in his quarrels with his brother because he is on his way to becoming his father's successor.

By leaving Boston, Franklin hopes to free himself from the constraints under which he has lived while under apprenticeship to his elder brother. It is difficult to ignore, in this move, the analogous relationship between America and Britain; Franklin, like America (and like Americans who immigrate by choice), makes a purposeful, self-determining decision. Franklin, knowing that his father agrees with his elder son in the current dispute, is "sensible that if [he] attempted to go openly, Means would be used to prevent [him]" (20). By stealing away without giving notice to his family, Franklin is effectively severing ties with them, communicating that he no longer desires or requires any type of assistance from his parents. The influence of his father, however, follows Franklin into his self-imposed exile. Franklin reports to his "son," to whom the *Autobiography* is ostensibly written, that the governor of Pennsylvania encourages him to begin his own printing business but sends Franklin home to his father first for approval and for financial support. Franklin reports that when he approaches his father about this matter, he learns that "my Father, tho' he did not approve Sir William's Proposition was yet pleas'd that I had been able to obtain so advantageous a Character from a Person of such Note where I had resided, and that I had been so industrious and careful as to equip myself so handsomely in so short a time" (30-31). Although the governor is confident about the skills of the young Franklin, his father knows his son's character and is aware that his son is not yet ready to take on this challenge. Franklin's father, however, does allow Franklin to return to Philadelphia, and exhorts him

> to behave respectfully to the People there, endeavour to obtain the general Esteem, and avoid lampooning and libeling to which he thought I had too much Inclination; telling me, that by steady Industry and a prudent Parsimony, I might save enough by the time I was One and Twenty to set me up, and that if I came near the Matter he would help me out with the Rest. (31)

Franklin's father is portrayed as a God-like figure in that he is able to judge his son's character and to promise his assistance if Franklin is industrious. Although he expects his son to become an adult and to be able to support himself, Franklin's father retains his own authority over his soon-to-be mature son. Also, the control over the finances of his seemingly independent son parallels the authority that John Hull, a seventeenth-century Puritan colonist, ascribes to God. Hull attributes the financial hardships the colonists suffer to God: "trying, nurturing, lopping, and pruning his poor children, by his own fatherly hand, for their good" (quoted in Bercovitch 119-20). Franklin notes that when he embarks on his journey back to Philadelphia, he has obtained "some small Gifts as Tokens" (31) of the love of his parents, and, significantly, "their Approbation & their Blessing" (31), signifying that the power of Franklin's parents extends beyond their own immediate geographic area, into the life of their son.

Franklin is now on a mission to maintain his parents' favor and also to prove his own merit. His narrative persona, in retrospect, is keenly aware of the danger at this juncture, caused by the lack of paternal surveillance in his life during his young adult years. Franklin makes what he considers "one of [his] first great Errata" (33) on his journey back to Philadelphia, by using some of the money he is supposed to be holding in trust for a friend. Franklin observes, "This affair show'd that my Father was not much out in his Judgment when he suppos'd me too Young to manage Business of Importance" (33). His father's conclusions about his personal flaws have followed him into his new life and serve as a warning to Franklin about his future derelictions.

Franklin marvels that during his young adult years, his convictions about the role of virtues in leading a happy life

> with the kind hand of Providence, or some guardian Angel, or accidental favourable Circumstances and Situations, or all together, preserved me (thro' this dangerous Time of Youth and the hazardous Situations I was

> sometimes in among Strangers, remote from the Eye and Advice of my Father) without any *wilful* gross Immorality or Injustice that might have been expected from my Want of Religion. (56)

In so closely juxtaposing his spiritual distance from religion and his physical distance from his father, Franklin insinuates that the two are closely entwined. Being away from his father gives him the freedom to experiment spiritually, but this very distance also costs him the oversight that he knows will keep him safe. Because he is away from his father, Franklin is left to the care of "Providence," which care, luckily for Franklin, works out in his favor. Franklin, however, because of his belief that he must contribute to his own well-being, must not believe that his safety in his times of trial is due solely to God; instead, Franklin probably attributes his entrance into the realm of the "father" to his success in triumphing through trying experiences. He matures and achieves the status of being a judge of his own actions, retrospectively, and of the actions of others.

While Franklin realizes that not all of his contemporaries consider him to be perfect, he does not deem it necessary to address their criticism. Franklin justifies his decision to ignore his detractors by explaining, "I concluded to let my Papers shift for themselves; believing it was better to spend what time I could spare from public Business in making new Experiments, than in Disputing about those already made" (154-55). This drive to accomplish more while ignoring his critics paints Franklin as egotistical, but it also shows that he truly believes in his superiority to those who disagree with him. His assertions are irrefutable and need not be defended. Franklin believes himself to be a person who is worthy of being emulated. Spengemann asserts that

> the aim of the *Autobiography* . . . is not so much to explain how life is justified by some universal principle as to justify his life by persuading others to make its conclusions universal. . . . Franklin's *Autobiography* offers itself as a Scripture, the only one available to an audience that had over-

> thrown all forms of traditional authority and replaced them with the authority of personal conviction. By imitating his success, men can fulfill his prophecy and bring about the rule of human Reason, that earthly heaven in which Franklin will have his immortality. (54)

Franklin puts himself forth to his readers as a new model of what an American should be. Because he draws on Puritan ideas but interprets them in a secular way, he asserts himself as the first of a new generation of Americans to whom individualism is crucial. His "experiences create a truth that does not seem to precede them" (58). Franklin is entering new territory by becoming the prototype of the new, self-made American; he invites others to follow in his footsteps in order to achieve Americanization.

Although Franklin provides his example as one that can be universally emulated, imitating Franklin's actions will be just that: imitation. This is, once again, consistent with the Puritan roots of the American psyche. Implicit in Franklin's vision of Americanization is a certain degree of uniformity that proceeds from reasoned individuality. According to Miller and Johnson:

> Puritanism appears, from the social and economic point of view, to have been a philosophy of social stratification, placing the command in the hands of the properly qualified and demanding implicit obedience from the uneducated; from the religious point of view it was the dogged assertion of the unity of intellect and spirit in the face of a rising tide of democratic sentiment suspicious of the intellect and intoxicated with the spirit. It was autocratic, hierarchical, and authoritarian. It held that in the intellectual realm holy writ was to be expounded by right reason, that in the social realm the expounders of holy writ were to be the mentors of farmers and merchants. (19)

Putting himself forth as the standard by which all future generations of Americans could judge themselves allowed Franklin to create, in his mind, a new society that would not be under the threat of anarchy but instead would undergo a controlled revolution. Franklin treats "his own life as the source and model of a principle which could become universal if every man would only relinquish his own individuality and follow Franklin's example" (Spengemann 60). If all Americans follow Franklin's lead, there will be no chaos; instead, reasoned self-advancement will reign. By embodying universal virtues and showing them as the criteria for national leadership in his *Autobiography*, Franklin defines himself as what Sacvan Bercovitch refers to as a "prophetic exemplar of the country" (149).

Nominating himself as the exemplary American, Franklin puts himself forth as a man who is beyond the ordinary, and such a suggestion situates him, in the Puritan-influenced mind-set, in a position of potential greatness. To the Puritans, there was a distinction between men of genius and common men: "There must be the spark, the quickening insight, the subtle and inward genius, which makes all the difference between the men who see and understand and know, and ordinary men who live from hand to mouth, never pierce below surface meanings, and never achieve self-mastery and direction" (Miller and Johnson 53). Genius, or full understanding, cannot be achieved by just anyone; insight into matters of faith and morals are possible only for those "elect" few who have superior capabilities. Franklin, seeing himself as a man who has perspicacity enough to develop his own creed and to devise means by which any man who is so inclined may follow his example, thus allows for those of the lower ranks to advance in action, if not in comprehension.

Miller and Johnson assert that to the Puritan, "the will of God is exhibited in the world of nature and in the processes of right reason, but in order for man to perceive it, there must be something added to him" (52). Franklin purports to know exactly what needs to be added in order for the common American to understand his mission: Franklin's own example. Having little faith in the ability of the average American to follow his lead solely on the basis of knowing the outcomes of Franklin's actions, Franklin, by his *Autobiography*, allows the reader to travel through his life and to understand the influences on the decisions that he has made. By spelling out clearly how to be a self-made man, Franklin believes that he is enabling all Americans to live more fulfilling lives. This parallels the observation of Miller and Johnson that

> what the Puritan does insist on is that the natural man, if left to himself, will not read the lessons of nature and reason correctly. . . . Therefore God must draw up for man in black and white an exhaustive and authoritative code of laws, where he can find them in terms adapted to his imperfect and benighted state, in clear and unmistakable bold-faced type. (51-52)

Franklin believes that his task is to compose a handbook for Americans to follow; this manual takes the form of a narrative tale in which Franklin, by learning from his mistakes and by making wise decisions, becomes his own messianic hero. Franklin designs his *Autobiography* in such a way as to lead readers through his life experiences, producing a cathartic effect and inspiring them to become initiated into the American way of life by following his precepts.

In order to set himself up as a credible and authoritative figure, Franklin is careful to trace two important lineages: his genetic extraction and his spiritual inheritance. He is the "youngest Son of the youngest Son for 5 Generations back" (3) to a family whose lineage he traces in Ecton, England. Also, because his father, who instructed him in the wisdom of the Bible, has guided him, he is qualified to make statements about morality. However, in addition to his identifying himself as his father's son, readers are left with the distinct impression that Franklin is somehow the product of his own creation; perhaps he is a natural extension of his father, who has provided guidance and who surveyed his son's actions before Franklin had the capability to do so for himself. Spengemann writes:

> Franklin's evident feeling that this wayward boy was father to the successful man . . . makes the highly particularized boy a far more memorable, more completely realized figure than the rather bland and featureless adult he becomes as he sheds his distinctive, alienating traits. At the same time, the reader cannot help but feel that the supposedly peculiar boy, compelling though he is as a fictional character, is really a quite typical figure, a prodigal son, and that ostensibly representative adult is in fact a highly unusual and inimitable man. (56)

Despite the fact that Franklin claims to be self-generated, it is undeniable that he also owes much of his personality and success to those who guided him in his formative years. Mentioning this indebtedness prevents him from seeming as though he is a spider, spinning endlessly from himself a web of unqualified wisdom, but instead demonstrates that he is a member of a hierarchy, or a chain of command, into which he has been initiated. As Hugh J. Dawson observes, "In the medieval-Renaissance world picture inherited by the American colonists, men lived within a series of concentric spheres—family, church, state, and cosmos—each paternalistically governed" (279). By situating himself in this schema, Franklin appropriates for himself the power of the already established hierarchy. Through emphasizing this lineage, Franklin claims authority for himself and legitimates his own actions and those of his followers.

Franklin sees meaning in the many events of his life and believes that his recounting of his experiences can serve a meaningful purpose for his audience. Likewise, for the Puritans, every moment was packed with significance; every occurrence had meaning (Miller and Johnson 60). Miller and Johnson note: "There was nothing lukewarm, half-hearted, or flabby about the Puritan; whatever he did, he did with zest and gusto" (60). Related to this enthusiasm for life, and the recognition of the importance of its events, Puritan historiography is characterized by its specificity and its didacticism (84). Franklin's *Autobiography*, enumerating meaningful events in his life, does serve the function of instructing his readers in how to live the kind of life Franklin advocates. Included in the *Autobiography* is a letter from Franklin's friend Benjamin Vaughan in which Vaughan exhorts him: "Shew then, Sir, how much is to be done, both to sons and fathers; and invite all wise men to become like yourself; and other men to become wise" (71).[1] The inclusion of this letter shows that others see the authority that belongs to Franklin. As an experienced printer, Franklin mentions his shortcomings in his profession "as a Caution to young Printers, and that they may be encouraged not to pollute their Presses and disgrace their Profession by such infamous Practices, but refuse steadily; as they may see by my Example, that such Course of Conduct will not on the whole be injurious to their Interests" (95). Since the experienced Franklin is in a position to judge the actions that he undertook as a younger person, he can assess the ways in which knowing of even his dastardly deeds can be of help to burgeoning Americans.

It is quite clear that Franklin writes with a public agenda in mind. Dawson recognizes the "social dimension" of Franklin's project, asserting that Franklin's writing is "aimed at more than his individual improvement" (284). Franklin expresses his intention to instruct all lesser Americans when he discusses his *Almanack*: "I consider'd it as a proper Vehicle for conveying Instruction among the common People, who bought scarce any other Books. I therefore filled all the little Spaces that occurr'd between the Remarkable Days in the Calendar, with Proverbial Sentences, chiefly such as inculcated Industry and Frugality, as the Means of procuring Wealth and thereby securing Virtue" (93-94). Franklin intends to shape the minds of his readers, whom he sees as starved for intellectual stimulation, through reading. He uses the discourse of his father's values, and he instructs his readers in the ways of correct self-formation according to the values that he has found important in his own life. His instruction to others is not only through the example of his own actions but also, significantly to Franklin, through the system of language. Kaja Silverman, discussing Jacques Lacan's theory, writes: "Language mediates all other signifiers. . . . the subject participates in signification only after the acquisition of language" (165). Franklin's intent is to initiate his readers into the system of his rhetoric. By membership therein, Franklin's audience will be rendered able to participate in self-fashioning, which is essential to Americanization after Franklin's model.

While Franklin appears to be freeing his readers by opening up for them the possibility to participate in the new "Americanhood," he is actually confining them. As "language isolates the subject from the real, confining it forever to the realm of signification" (Silverman 166), Franklin, by encroaching on the freedom of his readers to develop into their own "American" selves, makes a concerted effort to mold them into the image of himself. Furthermore, through the discourse that Franklin attempts to impose on his readers, he aims both to subject them to his discourse and to deindividualize them. This parallels the Lacanian principle that "with the subject's entry into the symbolic order it is reduced to the status of a signifier in the field of the other" (Silverman 166). By encouraging his readers, through rhetoric, to exhibit certain thought patterns, Franklin hopes to induct them into following specified behaviors. Franklin writes an "auto-American-biography" by identifying his rhetoric about his own experience with an "assertion of the American self" (Bercovitch 184, 186). Franklin makes himself into a model for both fathers and sons, for both adults and children; his development into adulthood is to be imitated by Americans; he is to be for Americans what his father was for him.

Spengemann notes that in order to make his life appear to be imitable by all Americans, Franklin must generalize himself and avoid providing details about his own remarkable accomplishments (60). While this generalization is perhaps necessary for the aforementioned purpose, it is also beneficial for Franklin's other purpose: to add to his authority. By omitting specifics about his personality, especially late in the narrative, Franklin further deifies himself, rendering his observations and judgments universal. Franklin establishes himself as a member of the didactic, wise order, of which his father and God (as a symbol of authority) are members. He writes, of his moral journey, "I hope therefore that some of my Descendants may follow the Example and reap the Benefit" (88). He has followed his father's advice to work diligently, since he "did not think that . . . [he] should ever literally stand before Kings, which however has since happened" (75). By following his father's instruction, rooted in biblical wisdom, Franklin has effectively, by his assimilation of the secularized versions of the values of his father, become the updated version of his father, qualified to pass prejudgment on other Americans and to advise them on how to behave. Franklin's "virtuous" lifestyle, through which he displays the characteristics necessary to each American to maintain a harmonious society, is, to him, superior to strict religiosity. Although he breaks away from tradition by dissociating himself from organized religion, he legitimates himself by associating himself with his father, who is respectable because of his genealogy and his basis in the authoritative Scripture. Franklin sets himself up as an example; his story is a new salvation history of an unlikely hero who becomes self-actualized because of his adherence to the advice that is his father's and because of the sensibility that becomes his own set of values.

His father shapes Franklin's morals, observes him, surveys his actions, and approves. Franklin must, then, be reacting in appropriate ways to the traditional influences on his background. He associates his father with the entity to which Lacan refers as the "symbolic father" (Silverman 185). By doing this, Franklin draws a direct line from himself to the ultimate source of authority. Franklin has adopted what Jacques Lacan alludes to as the "master's discourse." The master must maintain a "dominant or commanding position," does not have justification for his power, and must show no weakness (Fink 131). The discourse of the Scripture that Franklin's father quotes is ostensibly of the master. Franklin's father's discourse is of this same type, since no justification is given for his judgments, and his advice and judgments are always sound. Franklin, as a boy, makes errors; however, once he arrives at adulthood, he is no longer fallible. Despite his self-deprecation, which mainly serves to endear him to his audience and to humanize the God-like figure that Franklin hopes to create, the reader is aware that Franklin's persona, in his own mind, is always in the right.

By the end of his narrative, Franklin has assumed a dominant position, and he intimates that there are two reasons that he achieved his status: diligence and the watchful eye of the father. His father, who incited him to it because this virtue is extolled in the Scriptures, inspires his diligence. Franklin also credits his father's and Providence's guidance and surveillance for his successes in life, allowing him to become a member of their order, having learned the proper methods of surveillance, and allowing him to become the example for all future Americans to follow. By following Franklin's directives, which are based on biblical and otherwise conventional wisdom, readers can devise plans for their own Americanization by actively choosing to conform to Franklin's precepts.

Note

1. The letter from Vaughan is not included in the Lemay and Zall edition of the text, although it is referenced. It is available in the 1990 Vintage Books edition of the *Autobiography.* This is the only citation in this article from the Vintage edition of the *Autobiography*; the rest are from the Lemay and Zall edition.

Works Cited

Bercovitch, Sacvan. *The Puritan Origins of the American Self.* New Haven, CT: Yale UP, 1975.

Dawson, Hugh J. "Father and Sons: Franklin's 'Memoirs' as Myth and Metaphor." *Early American Literature* 14.3 (Dec. 1979): 269-82.

Fink, Bruce. *The Lacanian Subject: Between Language and Jouissance*. Princeton, NJ: Princeton UP, 1995.

Franklin, Benjamin. *The Autobiography*. New York: Vintage Books, 1990.

____________. *The Autobiography of Benjamin Franklin: A Genetic Text*. Ed. J. A. Leo Lemay and P. M. Zall. Knoxville: U of Tennessee P, 1981.

Miller, Perry, and Thomas H. Johnson. *The Puritans*. New York: American Book Company, 1938.

Parker, David L. "From Sound Believer to Practical Preparationist: Some Puritan Harmonics in Franklin's *Autobiography*." *The Oldest Revolutionary: Essays on Benjamin Franklin*. Ed. J. A. Leo Lemay. Philadelphia: U of Pennsylvania P, 1976.

Shurr, William H. "'Now, Gods, Stand Up for Bastards': Reinterpreting Benjamin Franklin's *Autobiography*." *American Literature* 64.3 (1992): 435-51.

Silverman, Kaja. *The Subject of Semiotics*. New York: Oxford UP, 1983.

Spengemann, William C. *The Forms of Autobiography: Episodes in the History of a Literary Genre*. New Haven, CT: Yale UP, 1980.

Ben Franklin and the Lost Generation: The Self-Made Man in Fitzgerald, Hemingway, and Wright

Matthew J. Bolton

The phrase "American Dream" was apparently coined early in the twentieth century—the *Oxford English Dictionary* shows the first two examples of its use in 1911 and 1916. Surely it is no coincidence that the phrase entered the language at exactly the time one of America's great literary generations was making the transition from childhood to adulthood. Ernest Hemingway, F. Scott Fitzgerald, and Richard Wright were all adolescents when America began analyzing its national aspirations.

Since Franklin seemed, more than anyone else in history, to embody that dream, it is no surprise that he featured large in American consciousness at just that time. In this essay Matthew J. Bolton explores "the period's conflicted response to Ben Franklin's model of success." In examining the reactions of these three great writers, he offers an original interpretation of the so-called lost generation that began writing in the 1920s, because, as Bolton points out, "perhaps there is no decade in which the literary response to Benjamin Franklin's legacy is more complex and nuanced." — J.L.

Rising from humble origins to greatness through hard work, temperance, thrift, and ingenuity, Benjamin Franklin set the mold for the self-made man. He was the nascent country's first and best advocate of self-improvement, civic responsibility, and striving for worldly success. Franklin's annual publication *Poor Richard's Almanack* gave him a platform from which to espouse the simple virtues he saw as fundamental to a man's bettering himself. Twenty-first-century schoolchildren still learn Poor Richard's adages, such as "Early to bed, early to rise/ makes a man healthy, wealthy, and wise" and "A penny saved is a penny earned." Perhaps alone among the Founding Fathers, Franklin had an ability and desire to cast his personal philosophy into a series of maxims and principles that would become not part of official government documents but part of popular discourse and common sense.

Even in his own lifetime, Franklin's reputation began to assume mythic proportions. Statesman, inventor, scientist, author, and revolutionary, Franklin was a larger-than-life figure. He was aware of his own mythic stature when he sat down to write his *Autobiography*, a short, lively account of his life that would help to shape how future generations saw the great man. In the *Autobiography*, Franklin cultivates an image of himself as humble and hardworking, a man for whom success comes through steady application: he writes of forming a plan and then putting in the work to make that plan a reality. Franklin, through his life and his writing, might be considered the first architect of the American Dream.

Future generations would have to grapple with the legacy of Ben Franklin, embracing or rejecting his vision of self-determination and self-improvement. One does not have to read the *Autobiography* to be influenced by Franklin's story; the model of success that he represents is part of the larger fabric of American culture. There have been times and places where Franklin's life seemed to resonate as the quintessential American story. The success of various immigrant groups, for example—people who arrived at Ellis Island with nothing and built for themselves and their children productive and prosperous lives—seems to validate Franklin's vision of America as a land where one is surrounded by opportunity. Indeed, any rags-to-riches story is, to one extent or another, measured against the archetype of Franklin.

At other times and for other people, however, Franklin's principles and way of proceeding seem hollow. This reaction against Franklin is a strain that runs through nineteenth- and twentieth-century literature. Mark Twain, for example, was scornful of what he considered Franklin's Puritan platitudes, and Huck Finn's taking to the river might be read as a rejection of Poor Richard's value system. Herman Melville's Bartleby, the copyist who abruptly ceases all work, is another figure who stands opposed to Franklin's ideals. Melville himself acknowledged that Franklin was "the type and genius of his land," but lamented that he was "everything but a poet" (61). Many twentieth-century protagonists, from Salinger's Holden Caulfield to Updike's Rabbit Angstrom to Philip Roth's various avatars, likewise seem to struggle against the values Franklin espoused.

Perhaps there is no decade in which the literary response to Benjamin Franklin's legacy is more complex and nuanced than the 1920s. The "Roaring '20s" themselves seemed at once a rejection and a confirmation of Franklin's principles. The temperance and self-regulation that he espoused are made a mockery of by the failed public policy of Prohibition, in which alcohol was technically illegal but was consumed with abandon behind closed doors. Fortunes were made and lost with a speed that would have astonished the steady Franklin. The stock market crash of 1929 and the ensuing Great Depression might be seen as the end of a certain kind of American dream. In his epigraph to *The Sun Also Rises*, Ernest Hemingway recalled a comment Gertrude Stein had once made: "You are all a lost generation." Part of what the generation that came of age in the 1920s lost may have been its faith in the gospel of hard work. The literature of the 1920s reflects the period's conflicted response to Ben Franklin's model of success. In F. Scott Fitzgerald's *The Great Gatsby*, Jay Gatsby conceives of and puts into motion a Franklin-like plan for self-improvement. He gains the world but loses his soul, and the fate of Gatsby calls into question the validity of the American Dream itself. Jake Barnes, protagonist of *The Sun Also Rises*, seems at first glance to have rejected Franklin's model for living as surely as he has rejected America. Yet beneath the surface of his hard-drinking expatriate lifestyle, Barnes—like Hemingway himself—is driven by a set of principles that Poor Richard would have admired. Finally, Richard Wright's account of his own experiences as an African American youth in the 1920s shows a man exercising the principles of hard work and ambition that Franklin advocated but finding that the larger system does not recognize and reward them when they are practiced by a black man. Jay Gatsby, Hemingway and his protagonists, and Richard Wright might each be read as a version of Franklin's self-made man: characters who explore, in a less-optimistic age than Franklin's, the opportunities and liabilities that America offers them.

Jay Gatsby meets with a sordid, meaningless death on the grounds of his palatial Long Island estate. A victim less of fate than of mistaken identity, he is gunned down by a grieving husband who believes Gatsby, rather than Daisy Buchanan, was driving the sports car that struck and killed his wife. In one sense, however, it is fitting that mistaken identity should lead to Gatsby's undoing, for he has quite deliberately misidentified himself as "Jay Gatsby," a name born out of a poor boy's desire to be a rich man. To win back Daisy Buchanan, Jimmy Gatz systematically transforms himself into the wealthy and aristocratic Jay Gatsby. At Gatsby's funeral, his friend and chronicler Nick Carraway meets the dead man's father, a simple man who speaks to Gatsby's humble origins. Mr. Gatz shows Nick a schedule that Gatsby drew up for himself when he was a boy:

Rise from bed	6.00	A.M.
Dumbbell exercise and wall scaling.	6.15-6.30	"
Study electricity, etc.	7.15-8.15	"
Work	8.30-4.30	P.M.
Baseball and sports	4.30-5.00	"
Practice elocution, poise and how to attain it	5.00-6.00	"
Study needed inventions	7.00-9.00	"

GENERAL RESOLVES

No wasting time at Shafters or [a name, indecipherable]
No more smokeing or chewing
Bath every other day
Read one improving book or magazine per week
Save $5.00 [crossed out] $3.00 per week
Be better to parents

This schedule and list of resolutions is immediately recognizable to readers of Franklin's *Autobiography*. The Founding Father structured his day in just this manner, charting out what he would do by the hour. So important were his charts, tables, and lists of resolves to his success that Franklin includes them in the *Autobiography* as an integral part of his life story. Gatsby's choices of verbs echo Franklin's own: "rise . . . work . . . read . . ." appear on both lists. It is a regimen grounded in the Puritan work ethic and in the classical formulation of *mens sana in corpore sano*, a sound mind in a sound body.

Franklin's list of virtues is likewise the inspiration for Gatsby's "General Resolves." In a numbered and annotated list, Franklin resolves to exercise "temperance . . . silence . . . order . . . resolution . . . frugality . . . industry . . . moderation" and other qualities that he saw as essential to good conduct and long-term success (91-92). As if the chart itself did not telegraph his debt to Franklin, the boy who would become Gatsby includes two activities that ape Franklin's pursuits: "study electricity" and "study needed inventions." Growing up poor, Gatsby saw in Franklin a model for how one could rise in the world through self-discipline and the exercise of simple virtues. This Franklin-like regimen is a Rosetta stone that helps to explain how and why Jimmy Gatz became Jay Gatsby.

As a man, Gatsby retained many of the virtues that he resolved to cultivate in his youth. He is temperate in an age of intemperance, for example, and his sobriety sets him apart from the bacchanalian partygoers who flock to his mansion. The "elocution" and "poise" that he once studied have become integral to his personality; he is—at least until he meets Daisy again—sophisticated and unflappable. By most standards of his day, Gatsby is a wildly successful man: handsome, commanding, rich, and powerful. Yet Gatsby's rise in the world has come at a great cost. Despite the resolutions of his youth, Gatsby gained his wealth through vice rather than virtue. The figure of "Gatsby" may be Jimmy Gatz's own creation, but neither Gatz nor Gatsby can really be called a self-made man. Nick Carraway asks

Gatsby's gangster friend Meyer Wolfsheim whether he started Gatsby in business. Wolfsheim replies:

> Start him! I made him. . . . I raised him up out of nothing, right out of the gutter. I saw right away he was a fine-appearing, gentlemanly young man, and when he told me he was an Oggsford I knew I could use him good. (172)

This is a staggering revelation, one that flies in the face not only of Gatsby's presentation of himself as an aristocrat but of the reader's assumption that Gatsby remade himself through his own efforts. To use a formulation from Shakespeare's *Twelfth Night*, Gatsby neither was born great nor achieved greatness but had greatness thrust upon him. Moreover, that greatness came at the hands of a criminal. Wolfsheim is a gangster, and if he "made" Gatsby, then Gatsby is a gangster as well. Jay Gatsby's worldly success therefore stands in sharp contrast to that of Franklin; as a boy, Gatsby modeled himself on Franklin, but as a man he realized that to succeed in the world of men required something more than Franklin's simple work ethic and resolution.

Gatsby's illicit path to success suggests that postwar America operates according to rules that are different from those that held sway in Franklin's time. One of seventeen children of a candle maker, Franklin first rose from obscurity through steady application at another humble trade, that of printer. Yet Franklin never seems ashamed of his origins. Indeed, they are a source of pride for him, and rather than hide his background he often seems at pains to emphasize it. He writes that because of his father's encouragement, he "consider'd Industry as a Means of obtaining Wealth and Distinction" (88). Franklin's entire mythos involves rising out of obscurity, and to obscure his own origins would therefore be to diminish his accomplishments. Gatsby has a very different attitude toward his past. Ashamed of his humble background, he actually pretends to be someone else. He cultivates an aristocratic *sprezzatura*, as if those things that he worked hard for actually came to him easily. Something has changed in the notion of class between Franklin's time and Gatsby's. It is no longer enough to have achieved wealth and prominence; instead, Gatsby feels he must cover his tracks, achieving these markers of success only to pretend that he possessed them all along.

Ben Franklin and Jay Gatsby share a will to power, a capacity first to dream of a grand future and then to take the steps necessary to make that dream a reality. As a young man sailing from America to London, Franklin committed his dream to paper. Referring to the journal he kept during his voyage, he writes: "The most important Part of that Journal is the Plan to be found in it which I formed at Sea, for regulating my conduct in Life. It is the more remarkable, as being formed when I was so young, and yet being pretty faithfully adhered to quite thro' to old age" (56).

Franklin is both a dreamer and a doer, and his plan is the site where these two qualities of the abstract and the practical meet. Gatsby, too, conceives and executes a plan as a young man that will govern the course of his life. But Gatsby's plan, fixed as it is on re-creating himself as the kind of aristocrat for whom Daisy Buchanan left him, borders on monomania. In Jay Gatsby, Franklin's vision of the American as dreamer and doer has become a kind of madness. Gatsby will eventually meet his fate at the hands of a mechanic, a man who is part of the working class that he so desperately tried to escape. Gatsby's death suggests that it is not just one man but an age that has lost its way.

At first blush, Jake Barnes, the protagonist of Hemingway's 1926 novel *The Sun Also Rises*, seems to lead a life that stands at odds with that of Benjamin Franklin. Jake is an expatriate to Franklin's Founding Father and a hard drinker to Franklin's teetotaler. A denizen of Paris's floating world, Jake might chuckle at Poor Richard's injunction that "early to bed, early to rise, makes a man healthy, wealthy, and wise." Yet scratch Jake's cynical surface, and one finds a man who has a Franklin-like concern with his own conduct and industry. Jay Gatsby hid from the world both his humble origins and the resolve with which he achieved his greatness. Jake hides something else: not his identity or his origins, but the self-discipline and Puritan work ethic by which he still lives. In the midst of a dissolute, expatriate "lost generation," Jake privately hews to a distinctly American code of conduct that everyone around him seems to have forgotten.

Like Ben Franklin, Barnes is a newspaper man. The field has changed in the two hundred-odd years that separate these men, however, and the modern reporter cultivates an air of dissolution that might have frustrated and baffled the industrious Franklin. When Robert Cohn drops by Barnes's office, for example, Barnes does not simply say he is busy but instead uses a clever ploy to get rid of his visitor:

> "Come on down-stairs and have a drink."
>
> "Aren't you working?"
>
> "No," I said. We went down the stairs to the café on the ground floor. I had discovered that was the best way to get rid of friends. Once you had a drink, all you had to say was: "Well I've got to get back and get off some cables," and it was done. It is very important to discover graceful exits like that in the newspaper business, where it is such an important part of the ethics that you should never seem to be working. (11)

This is a fascinating dynamic, one that reverses the prototypical relationship between work and pleasure. Because a newspaperman "should never seem to be working," Barnes suggests that he and Cohn have a drink. In truth, however, Barnes would rather be working than relaxing in a café, and he goes downstairs with Cohn precisely because he wants to get back to his work. Whereas men of Franklin's age were openly industrious, Barnes must affect an air of leisure.

Notice that Jake draws a life lesson from the encounter with Cohn. One frequently unnoticed aspect of *The Sun Also Rises*, and of Hemingway's writing in general, is its subtle didacticism. Jake tells us not just what he does but his reasons for doing so and the broader implications for men's conduct. It is a popular misconception, fueled largely by Hemingway's own writing on the art of fiction, that Hemingway's style is one of bare reportage. As spare and concrete as his account may be, Jake constantly editorializes. He positions the reader as one who might learn from his example, and his use of the second-person "you" drives this relationship home. In this respect, *The Sun Also Rises* is closer in spirit to Franklin's work than it might at first seem. Franklin would be quite comfortable telling an anecdote and then reflecting, as Jake does, "It is very important to . . . ." The actions he takes and the lessons he draws from them would be quite different from those of Jake, but his approach to moralizing in general would not be. To borrow the title of one of Franklin's earlier works, *The Sun Also Rises* is a study in "the art of living."

One could argue, of course, that Barnes is a highly functioning drunk, and that he takes Cohn to the bar not only to get rid of him but to furnish an excuse for having a drink. While this may well be true, look at what Barnes does after having his drink and returning to his office: "The Editor and Publisher and I worked hard for two hours. Then I sorted out the carbons, stamped on a by-line, put the stuff in a couple of big manila envelopes and rang for a boy to take them to the Gare St. Lazare" (12). Barnes's desire for a drink may be genuine, but so is his desire to "work hard." If anything, the drink fuels the work. The hard-drinking, hardworking man who adopts a cynical pose that hides his fundamentally Puritan character would become a staple of American fiction, film, and popular culture. This is particularly true of the detective novel, in which three generations of private eyes, from Raymond Chandler's Philip Marlowe through Robert B. Parker's Spenser, owe their very existence to the pattern Hemingway established with Jake Barnes.

Barnes's attitude toward working and drinking reverses the logic of Prohibition and of the temperance movement that gave rise to it. In America, where alcohol was outlawed for much of the 1920s, one worked openly and hid one's drinking. In Paris, however, Barnes does just the opposite. The temperance movement was grounded in part on the assumption that drinking hurt the productivity of the American worker. Ben Franklin, who was an early advocate of temperance, certainly thought this to be true. Working at a printing press in England during his own stint as an expatriate, Franklin finds himself surrounded by drinkers: "I drank only Water; the other Workmen, near 50 in Number, were great Guzzlers of Beer . . . I thought it a detestable custom" (50). Many of Franklin's fellow workers drink on and off over the course of the day. Franklin argues that abstaining from drink makes him not only physically stronger than his companions but better able to save money and hence to improve his situation in life. He tries to convince one of the workers, who is in the habit of drinking five pints of beer during the workday and even more after work, to become temperate. The effort fails, and Franklin recalls: "He drank on however, & had 4 or 5 shillings to pay out of his Wages every Saturday Night for that muddling Liquor; an Expense I was free from. And thus these poor Devils keep themselves always under" (50). For Franklin, the cardinal virtues by which he lived are intertwined: temperance, industry, and thrift all beget and support one another. Jake Barnes represents not a refutation of Franklin's value system but a subversion of it. Like Franklin, Jake places great value on having a profession and being industrious in one's work. Yet Barnes must disguise his industry so that he can function in a dissolute age.

It is worth comparing Jake Barnes and the youthful protagonist of Franklin's autobiography not only with each other but with the authors who created them. Franklin's youthful avatar is perhaps more single-minded and wholly virtuous than Franklin himself was at any given stage of his life. Kenneth Silverman explains that the real Franklin was "less easy to characterize" than his "earnest young protagonist." This is particularly true when it comes to temperance and moderation: "Unlike his abstemious hero, the real Franklin sometimes 'drank more than a Philosopher ought,' as he put it, and in later life grew heavy and suffered from gout as a result of his love of rich food and wine; indeed his writings teem with food imagery" (in Franklin xiii).

In some key respects, therefore, Franklin's account of himself reflects the values he believes one should live by rather than the ones he *did* live by. The youthful Franklin of the autobiography is as much an ideal as a man. The gaps between Franklin's real life and the version of that life that he created in the *Autobiography* underscore the value he places on temperance, thrift, and other virtues. Because at times the man lacked self-discipline, the author must exercise self-censorship. What Franklin omits from his self-portrait can tell us as much as what he includes.

One can identify a similar process of idealizing and fictionalizing if one triangulates among Hemingway's character in *The Sun Also Rises*, Hemingway as a character in his memoir *A Moveable Feast*, and those aspects of Hemingway's life in Paris that he did not mention or emphasize in either account. As with Franklin's life and autobiography, Hemingway's "editing" of his own life story shows him presenting his own conduct in the light of the principles he espoused. *A Moveable Feast*, Hemingway's 1964 memoir of life in Paris, serves as a fascinating counterpoint to *The Sun Also Rises*. The young Hemingway's novel and the old man's memoir mine the same material: the expatriate life in Paris of the 1920s. In the opening chapter of *A Moveable Feast*, "A Good Café on the Place St.-Michel," Hemingway writes what might be the definitive romantic vision of a writer at work. The author walks through winter rain to a café, where he settles in and gets to work:

> It was a pleasant café, warm and clean and friendly, and I hung up my old waterproof on the coat rack to dry and put my worn and weathered felt hat on the rack above the bench and ordered a *café au lait*. The waiter brought it and I took out a notebook from the pocket of the coat and a pencil and started to write. I was writing about up in Michigan and since it was a wild, cold, blowing day it was that sort of day in the story. (5)

This image of the writer at work is, in its own way, a distinctly American fantasy. Most people who start keeping a journal or who try penning a short story flirt with the idea that they, too, resemble a Hemingway protagonist. The tremendous appeal of the writing life may lie in its combining two American archetypes: those of the hardworking Puritan and the rugged individualist. The writer works as steadily and with as much dedication as any of his forebears, yet he answers to no one but himself. In Hemingway's sketch, moreover, the writer's success is assured: we not only know that Hemingway will become a great writer, but we also recognize the very story he is writing (it is "The Three-Day Blow," which he would publish in his first collection). The café is therefore the ideal site for a writer to frequent: it is neither home nor office, but simply, to use one of Hemingway's famous titles, a clean, well-lighted place where he can work undisturbed.

The reader of *The Sun Also Rises* may be surprised to find Hemingway, at the conclusion of "A Good Café on the Place St.-Michel," returning home to his wife, Hadley. Jake Barnes, of course, is single—and doomed to be so by his debilitating war injury. This is one of many striking differences between Hemingway and his protagonist, differences that are all the more interesting in the context of a novel that might otherwise be considered a roman à clef. Like Franklin, Hemingway carefully cultivated his image, creating a version of himself in his novels and his memoirs that was based as much on his ideals as on his real life. What Hemingway chose to censor or exclude from his accounts of life in Paris may therefore speak directly to his value system.

One topic on which Hemingway is particularly unreliable is that of his income. Both Jake Barnes and the Hemingway of *A Moveable Feast* seem to support themselves through their writing. Hemingway, like Jake, worked for a wire service, sending stories back to America. Yet in point of fact, the income Hemingway earned as a reporter did less to cover his family's expenses than did the interest earned on his wife's trust fund (Reynolds 179). Hemingway simply would not have been able to set himself up in Paris or to continue living there without Hadley's financial support. This might come as a blow to those who have too credulously embraced Hemingway's vision of the writer as self-sufficient man. Some of the mystique of the Hemingway hero—be he Jake Barnes or the author's version of himself—lies in his rugged independence, and some of this mystique leaches away when one knows that Hemingway himself was not, in fact, as autonomous as he wished and claimed to be.

Being supported by one's wife simply did not fit into Hemingway's conception of how a man ought to conduct and govern himself, and therefore was not acknowledged in his fiction or his memoir. Much as Franklin did in his autobiography, Hemingway in his memoir simply excluded or elided those details of his younger life that did not fit neatly into his value system. Despite his lifelong self-imposed exile from the American Midwest in which he grew up, Hemingway lived according to a set of values that were quintessentially American. His expatriate life in Paris was characterized not by the sad debauchery that so many of the characters in *The Sun Also Rises* seek but by a steady application to his chosen trade. What Hemingway says and what he chooses not to say about his work and his sources of income reveal a man who believes profoundly in the Franklinesque vision of the self-made man.

Hemingway rejected the American society whose values and principles he nevertheless lived by. Richard Wright, on the other hand, was rejected by American society, despite his possessing so many of the character traits that are supposed to be quintessentially American. Wright's 1945 autobiography *Black Boy* serves as a counterpoint both to the representations of life in the 1920s that Fitzgerald and Hemingway crafted and to Franklin's vision of America as a land of opportunity. Born in 1908, Wright came of age in the segregated Jim Crow South, and his passage to adulthood involved identifying and negotiating the great limitations that systematic racial oppression placed on him. His autobiography ends with his leaving the South in 1928, having survived childhood and adolescence in a place that is worlds away from Gatsby's New York or Hemingway's Paris. Wright, like Franklin, Gatsby, and the Hemingwayesque hero, is a self-made man. Yet he must "make it" within the confines of a society that is bent on keeping him from succeeding. Reading *Black Boy* complicates one's vision of Ben Franklin's success: although Franklin was a remarkably disciplined and visionary man, he operated within economic, social, and legal structures that enfranchised him and that rewarded his discipline and vision. America was a free and open society for a white man like Franklin. For African Americans, however, from Franklin's time down to Wright's, a different set of rules applied. To succeed and to better himself, Wright needed to mask or subvert the very qualities of industry, thrift, and ambition that Franklin had popularized.

As a child, Wright saw a stark object lesson in the limits that white America placed on African Americans' industry and success. For a brief time, Wright and his mother lived with his Uncle Hoskins and Aunt Maggie. A successful saloon-keeper, Wright's uncle lives in comfort and provides well for his extended family. Wright recalls, "At mealtime Aunt Maggie's table was so loaded with food that I could scarcely believe it was real. It took me some time to get used to the idea of there being enough to eat; I felt that if I ate enough there would not be anything left for another time" (50). Long accustomed to going to bed hungry and waking up to a house without food, Wright eats all he can. Still, he cannot break himself of the "habit of stealing and hoarding bread" (51); the idea of having enough food is still alien to him. Although Hoskins is a success story, he must sleep with a loaded gun within reach. Wright's mother confides that "men had threatened to kill him, white men" (53). One day they follow through on the threat, gunning Hoskins down at the saloon. Wright explains:

> I learned afterwards that Uncle Hoskins had been killed by whites who had long coveted his flourishing liquor business. He had been threatened with death and warned many times to leave, but he had wanted to hold on a while longer to amass more money. . . . Aunt Maggie was not even allowed to see his body nor was she able to claim any of his assets. . . . This was as close as white terror had ever come to me and my mind reeled. (54-55)

Hoskins's story stands in sharp contrast to Ben Franklin's. Both men built businesses of their own that provided for themselves and their families, but Franklin operated within a society that safeguarded his basic human rights. He faced competition and adversity, but always on the even playing field of a free market; Franklin never seemed to be in danger of physical violence or intimidation. The Declaration of Independence, which Franklin would sign, proclaimed that all men are created equal and hold an inalienable claim to "life, liberty, and the pursuit of happiness." Yet Hoskins, as an African American business owner in the Jim Crow South, is afforded none of these rights. It is his very success that makes him a target, and he meets with violence precisely because he has built up a business that other men envy.

Wright's experience of hunger and his survivor's habit of secreting food provides another telling counterpoint to Franklin's account of himself. As an adolescent, Franklin experimented with vegetarianism, and throughout his autobiography he speaks of his abstemiousness regarding food. Franklin sees it as a virtue to eat less than those around him. Wright, however, eats little out of necessity. His disbelief at Uncle Hoskins and Aunt Maggie's well-appointed table indicates just how central hunger has been to his childhood. Sometime later, he will try to sell his prized dog for a dollar in order to buy food. As a schoolboy, he claims never to be hungry at lunch, when the truth is that he cannot afford to pay for it. In fact, Wright's original title for *Black Boy* was *American Hunger*, a phrase that speaks both to his physical hunger and to his yearning for a different kind of life. Reading Franklin's and Wright's autobiographies together, one may begin to see Franklin's attitude toward food as an abstraction. He is able to be moderate in his eating precisely because he has the security of knowing that food will always be available to him. Knowing, too, that Franklin ate more heartily in real life than his youthful version of himself does, one may come to see his preoccupation with abstemiousness as romanticizing hunger in a way only a man who never has to go hungry could.

If Franklin's coming-of-age involves his taking advantage of expanding opportunities, Wright's involves negotiating a series of constricting threats and limitations. After visiting his grandmother, an African American woman with light skin, Wright asks his own mother a series of questions about race and skin color. "What am I?" he inquires. "They'll call you a colored man when you grow up," his mother says (49). Wright's mother knows the realities of racial segregation in a way that her son cannot yet understand. Her comment goes to the heart of the racist and segregationist mind-set: race will be the primary lens through which her son is viewed. As an African American, he will have to operate within a set of societal limitations that are bent on keeping him from succeeding to the fullest of his abilities. One often-cited example of Wright's negotiating these limitations is found in his strategy for checking books out of the public library. He forges a note to present to the librarian: "*Dear Madam: Will you please let this nigger boy*—I used the word 'nigger' to make the librarian feel I could not possibly be the author of the note—*have some books by H. L. Mencken*?" (246). As a young man, Ben Franklin spent much time, energy, and money getting his hands on books so that he might educate himself. When he was established in life, he founded America's first library system so that others would be able to borrow books easily. Ironically, an American living two hundred years after Franklin must struggle even harder to borrow books from the very institution that Franklin founded.

Nor is it only white America that limits Wright. In 1923, at the age of fifteen, Wright publishes his first short story in an African American newspaper, and his family and classmates greet this act with hostility and suspicion. When Wright tells his grandmother that the piece is "a story I made up," she responds, "Then it's a lie" (167). His classmates insist that he must have copied it out of a book. He reflects: "If I had thought anything in writing the story, I had thought that perhaps it would make me more acceptable to them, and now it was cutting me off from them more completely than ever" (167). Wright wants something that no one around him, black or white, seems to recognize as valid. He writes:

> I knew that I lived in a country in which the aspirations of black people were limited, marked-off. Yet I felt that I had to go somewhere and do something to redeem my being alive.
>
> I was building up in me a dream which the entire educational system of the South had been rigged to stifle . . . the dreams that the state had said were wrong, that the schools had said were taboo. (169)

To draw meaningful conclusions about both Franklin's idea of America as a land of opportunity and the broader context of American life in the 1920s, one must take into account the systematic racism of the Jim Crow South. Wright's successful bid to remake himself as a man and as an artist, despite the formidable opposition of the society in which he lived, both indicts and validates the American Dream.

Works Cited

Fitzgerald, F. Scott. *The Great Gatsby*. New York: Charles Scribner's Sons, 1925.

Franklin, Benjamin. *The Autobiography and Other Writings*. Ed. Kenneth Silverman. New York: Penguin Books, 1986.

Hemingway, Ernest. *The Sun Also Rises*. New York: Charles Scribner's Sons, 1926.

____________. *A Moveable Feast: Sketches of the Author's Life in Paris in the Twenties*. New York: Charles Scribner's Sons, 1964.

Melville, Herman. *Israel Potter: His Fifty Years of Exile*. 1855. Charleston, SC: BiblioBazaar, 2006.

Reynolds, Michael. *Hemingway: The Paris Years*. New York: W. W. Norton, 1999.

Wright, Richard. *Black Boy (American Hunger): A Record of Childhood and Youth*. 1945. New York: HarperCollins, 1993.

CRITICAL READINGS

Medical Electricity and Madness in the Eighteenth Century: The Legacies of Benjamin Franklin and Jan Ingenhousz

Sherry Ann Beaudreau and Stanley Finger

After experiencing a powerful electric shock, the Dutch chemist Jan Ingenhousz wrote to Franklin, describing the effect: "I feld the most lively joye in finding . . . my judgment infinitely more acute. It did seem to me I saw much clearer the difficulties of every thing." Franklin's ever-curious mind could not neglect a development this exciting, and he conducted a number of investigations into how electricity might have medical and psychological applications.

Sherry Ann Beaudreau and Stanley Finger are interested in Franklin the scientist, but their approach is different, owing, perhaps, to their own disciplinary backgrounds: both come from departments of psychology. Their firsthand knowledge of neuroscience gives them a distinctive point of view on Franklin's interest in "medical electricity." Beaudreau and Finger reexamine this episode in Franklin's career, looking backward to precursors and forward to successors, and work "to set the record straight." They assert that "the history of electroshock therapy for the severely mentally ill did not begin in the 20th century or even a century earlier": it was Franklin and his contemporaries who did the pioneering work. — J.L.

January 17, 2006, marks the 300th anniversary of Benjamin Franklin's birth (for biographies, see Brands 2002; Isaacson 2003; Van Doren 1938). Among his many achievements, Franklin is often cited for his scientific acumen, particularly for his research and insights on the nature of electricity (Cohen 1941). What is not as well known is that Franklin also conducted experiments to determine whether electricity could cure palsies, blindness, and hysteria (see Finger 2006). Even less well recognized is that Franklin and Jan Ingenhousz, an enlightened

Dutch physician who championed smallpox inoculations and conducted pioneering experiments in photosynthesis, suggested applying electricity directly to the head as a cure for melancholia (for more on Ingenhousz, see Conley and Brewer-Anderson 1997; Reed 1947-48).

In this article, we shall trace the history of Ingenhousz's idea that cranial electricity might help "mad" patients. We shall then examine some of the case reports that appeared soon after Ingenhousz and Franklin requested clinical trials.

Advent of Therapeutic Electricity

The use of devices that could produce electricity by friction is usually traced to Otto von Guericke of Magdeburg, who constructed a rotating sulfur globe to study the Earth's gravitation (Hackmann 1978). In 1672, Guericke reported that his rotating sphere, when rubbed, might attract or repel small objects. In the opening decades of the 18th century, Francis Hawksbee turned to glass to construct even better devices for generating sparks, making thin pieces of brass "dance" and even inducing a glow in a nearby glass globe (Hawksbee 1709). The next step was taken by Stephen Gray (1731), who showed, among other things, that electricity from glass instruments could be transmitted over wires.

To many people, electricity was largely a philosophical amusement (see Schaffer 1983, 1993; Sutton 1995). They flocked to see how a boy safely electrified by Gray or one of his followers could attract objects and throw sparks, or how an electrically charged man could set a glass of brandy ablaze. By mid-century, however, the idea that electricity might have a welcome place in medicine was beginning to be given serious consideration by physicians (Heilbron 1979; Licht 1967).

In many ways, the new interest in medical electricity was a logical outgrowth of efforts to understand the nature and properties of electricity, then an exciting part of experimental natural philosophy. It was aided by various technological innovations that made administering electrical therapy easier, and by its appeal to a heterogeneous group of people, including physicians, apothecaries, and instrument makers, who recognized its market potential (Bertucci 2003). Simon Schaffer (1993), who examined the lay and professional appeal of electricity in the mid-18th century, as well as its politics, economics, theological implications, and utilitarian promises, provides this perspective:

> Electrical fire dominated London natural philosophy. . . . Public interest in the new electrical demonstrations was intense. . . . It was used by natural philosophy lecturers to swell their audiences. . . . Instrument-makers catered for an expanding market with ranges of electrical devices . . . accompanied by handbooks. . . .
>
> Electricity also intersected the concerns of the learned professions. . . . Electrical phenomena could capture an audience, satisfy customers, cure the body and save the soul. (pp. 490-91)

The first person to suggest the application of electricity to medicine was Johann Gottlob Krüger, a professor in Halle, Germany. In 1743, he told his students that "all things must have a usefulness: that is certain. Since electricity must have a usefulness, and we have seen it cannot be looked for either in theology or in jurisprudence, there is obviously nothing left but medicine" (Krüger 1744; translated in Licht 1967, p. 5). Krüger further hypothesized that electricity might do best with palsied limbs, probably because he knew how it could make even tight muscles contract.

In 1744, the year Krüger's words appeared in print, Christian Gottlieb Kratzenstein, one of Krüger's students, set out to test his professor's idea (for more on Kratzenstein, see Snorrason 1974). He cured a woman of a contraction in her little finger and helped a man with two lame (probably arthritic) fingers play his harpsichord again (Kratzenstein 1745). Joseph Priestley (1775), in his history of electricity written with Franklin's assistance, referred to Kratzenstein's writings as "the first account I have met with of the application of electricity to medical purposes" (p. 472).

Using electricity in a medical setting became easier in 1746, the year in which Petrus van Musschenbroek presented what would become known as the Leyden jar (Dorsman and Crommelin 1957). Made of glass, covered with foil, and filled with water or lead shot, the Dutchman's new device could store a charge from an electrical machine and release it on demand. Almost immediately, the Leyden jar began to be used to treat various palsies, a basket term which then referred to a number of different conditions associated with loss of movement. Researchers soon started to tout electricity as a panacea for movement disorders, as well as for many other medical conditions. With the first successful periodical, *Gentleman's Magazine*, open to medical submissions from anyone, and with most articles favoring the miraculous new cure but lacking in essential details, electricity, the most powerful stimulant yet discovered, was soon on its way to achieving fad status (Porter 1985a, 1985b).

Benjamin Franklin, who liked to see things with his own eyes, first became interested in electricity in 1743, after paying for a lecture-demonstration by Archibald Spencer in Boston. Although Franklin felt that the traveling Scottish physician's electrical demonstrations were "imperfectly performed," he helped Spencer by selling tickets and promoting his demonstrations in Philadelphia. A few years later, Franklin's Library Company received a gift of some electrical equipment from Peter Collinson, its philanthropic book purchasing agent in London and a member of the Royal Society.

By 1747, Franklin and his "leather apron" associates, who shared his interest in science, were conducting their own electrical experiments. They quickly discovered that sparks are most easily drawn to and emitted from points, a finding that led to the pointed lightning rod. They also suggested that attraction and repulsion were best explained by postulating different quantities of a single type of electricity, not two distinct varieties, as promoted by Charles François de Cisternay DuFay and Abbé

Nollet in France. Subsequently, Franklin presented ways to "capture" lightning, which helped to prove that Nature's lightning and electricity from machines are similar in their qualities, differing only in quantity. These and other findings were communicated to Collinson in England, who helped to get them published in pamphlet form in 1751. Franklin's *Experiments and Observations on Electricity* would thereafter go through many editions, making its self-educated author the best-known and most respected electrician of the Enlightenment.

Franklin, however, was not just interested in the nature of electricity. With his emphasis on utility and interest in practical medicine, he also set forth to determine if electricity really could cure patients, especially men and women left palsied by "the common paralytic disorder," meaning strokes. At the time, the nascent literature was filled with claims of remarkable successes, but also with some notable failures (Bertucci 2001, 2005; Colwell 1922; Priestley 1775).

Franklin's palsied patients included many commoners and also some of the most important people in Colonial America (Finger 2006, pp. 80-101). Among the latter, we find James Logan, who had been William Penn's secretary and was one of the most learned men in the colonies, and Jonathan Belcher, the Royal Governor of New Jersey who had previously been governor of Massachusetts. Franklin's protocol called for electrifying the palsied part with repeated but mild electrical shocks. If he could not be present to administer them himself, he sent the needed equipment with instructions to others.

After treating an undisclosed number of patients, Franklin concluded that electricity was not a cure for palsies of long duration, especially those caused by severe strokes. He penned this sober message in writing to the Royal Society late in 1757, the year he had sailed to England as agent of Pennsylvania, and his communication was presented and published in the following year. Franklin (1758) wrote that: "Patients perceiving and finding the Shocks pretty severe, they became discourag'd, went home and in a short time relapsed; so that I never knew any Advantage from Electricity in Palsies that was permanent" (p. 483).

With his strong belief in the power of experimentation and his empirical orientation to the healing arts, Franklin was careful not to generalize from his palsy cases. Indeed, he had been very successful when it came to treating a case of hysterical seizures with electricity. This case dated from 1752, and it involved a female patient identified only as "C.B." Historians speculate that C.B. was the sister of Cadwallader Evans, the medical student who worked with Franklin to treat her, and the individual who published a full report of the case in 1757 (Evans 1757; Finger 2006, pp. 104-8).

Evans wrote that C.B.'s problems began when she was 14 years old, and that "Sometimes she was tortur'd almost to madness with a cramp in different parts of the body; then with more general convulsions of the extremities, and a choaking deliquium; and, at times with almost the whole train [of] hysteric symptoms" (p. 84). From all indications, the shocks were applied to the visibly affected, tremulous and cramped parts of her body, not to her head. In an accompanying letter, C.B. wrote that "the fits were soon carried off . . . [and] I now enjoy such a state of health, as I would have given all the world for" (pp. 85-86). Interestingly, neither Franklin nor Evans ever stated why they tried electricity with C.B., or why they thought it worked.

Electrical Accidents and Melancholia

During Franklin's lifetime, the term *melancholia* was applied to severe depression, as well as to less severe, non-febrile disorders marked by sadness, tiredness, sleeplessness, fear, irritability, uneasiness, loss of appetite, self-loathing, and social isolation. To the 18th-century medical mind, melancholia was the opposite of mania and a cousin of hysteria. In earlier humoral medicine, melancholia was usually attributed to an overabundance of cold black bile (Jackson 1978). Now, with Newtonian mechanical ideas applied to physiology and pathology, melancholia was more likely to be attributed to weak, flaccid nerves, although psychological factors were beginning to be incorporated into theoretical formulations (Foucault 1965). For Franklin, the idea of treating melancholics with electrical shocks did not stem from humoral, chemical, mechanical, or even psychological theorizing. Rather, it began with some electrical accidents involving him and then Jan Ingenhousz, his close friend and faithful correspondent, whom he had first met in 1767 and who became physician to the royal family in Vienna (Conley and Brewer-Anderson 1997; Reed 1947-48).

Franklin described his first serious accident with electricity in two letters, one presumably to his brother John in 1750, and the other to Peter Collinson in 1751 (Labaree 1961-62). The massive jolt came from two fully charged six-gallon Leyden jars that were to be used to kill a turkey, and it entered his body through his hands, not his head. He equated the jolt to the combined discharges of "forty common phials," and it was so powerful that he referred to it as a "universal Blow thro'out my whole Body from head to foot." Franklin told Collinson that the universal Blow

> was follow'd by a violent quick Trembling in the Trunk, which wore gradually off in a few seconds. It was some Moments before I could collect my Thoughts so as to know what was the Matter; for I did not see the Flash tho' my Eye was on the Spot of the Prime Conductor from whence it struck the Back of my Hand, nor did I hear the Crack tho' the By-standers say it was a loud one; nor did I particularly feel the Stroke on my Hand, tho' I afterwards found it had rais'd a Swelling there the bigness of half a Swan Shot or pistol Bullet. (Labaree 1961-62, 4:113)

Hence, as a result of his first serious accident, Franklin discovered that people could survive intense shocks to the body in which electricity clearly spread to the brain. He knew that much stronger shocks could kill a man, but other than some amnesia about the event, he experienced no enduring negative effects (for more on the amnesia, see Finger and Zaromb 2006).

Still, questions went through Franklin's mind. He ended this part of his letter to Collinson with the words: "What the Consequence would be, if such a Shock were taken thro' the Head, I know not." Franklin was able to answer this question before he left for England in 1757. What he discovered in part from his second severe accident was written in a letter to John Lining, a Scottish physician and experimental natural philosopher who had settled in Charleston, South Carolina. Franklin's letter of March 18, 1755, included a description of an experiment he performed on a column of men:

> The knocking down of six men was performed with two of my large jarrs not fully charged. I laid one end of my discharging rod upon the head of the first; he laid his hand on the head of the second; the second his hand on the head of the third, and so to the last, who held, in his hand, the chain that was connected to the outside of the jarrs. . . . I applied the other end of my rod to the prime-conductor, and they all dropt together. When they got up, they all declared they had not felt any stroke, and wondered how they came to fall; nor did any of them hear the crack, or see the light of it. (Labaree 1961-62, 5:525)

Franklin also wrote that he

> had seen a young woman, that was about to be electrified though the feet (for some indisposition) receive a greater charge through the head, by inadvertently stooping forward to look at the placing of her feet, till her forehead (as she was very tall) came too near my prime-conductor: She dropped, but instantly got up again, complaining of nothing.

Between these two descriptions, Franklin noted: "You suppose it a dangerous experiment, but I had once suffered the same myself, receiving by accident, an equal stroke through my head, that struck me down, without hurting me." Franklin did not, however, provide the details of the accident that sent a jolt of electricity directly through his own head, remarking only that such a jolt causes a person to "sink down doubled, or folded together as it were, the joints losing their strength and stiffness at once, so that he drops on the spot where he stood, instantly."

Franklin described his second accident in considerably more detail almost three decades later. The stimulus was a letter he had received from Ingenhousz. Inspired by Franklin, who had nominated him for foreign membership in England's Royal Society, Ingenhousz conducted many hands-on experiments with electricity. And like Franklin, he also had his mishaps.

In 1783, Ingenhousz informed Franklin about a frightful accident he had just experienced. Not only did it knock him unconscious, but he awoke very confused and feared that he might "remain for ever an idiot." After a good night's sleep, however, he felt that he had more than recovered:

> My mental faculties were at that time not only returned, but I feld the most lively joye in finding, as I thought at the time, my judgment infinitely more acute. It did seem to me I saw much clearer the difficulties of every thing, and what did formerly seem to me difficult to comprehend, was now become of an easy Solution. I found moreover a liveliness in my whole frame, which I never had observed before. (Packard Humanities Institute 2003, vol. 40, u. 209, 2)

Ingenhousz specifically asked Franklin for more information about his own electrical accidents. But with his other responsibilities in France (including his work on the commission investigating Mesmer), and often incapacitated by the pain caused by his gout and large bladder stone, Franklin did not write back until April 29, 1785. He then directed Ingenhousz to the fifth edition of his *Experiments and Observations on Electricity*, which contained his 1751 letter to Peter Collinson. It also contained his 1755 letter to Lining, briefly mentioning his second accident, about which he now wrote:

> I had a Paralytick Patient in my Chamber, whose Friends brought him to receive some Electric Shocks. I made them join Hands so as to receive the Shock at the same time, and I charg'd two large Jars to give it. By the Number of those People, I was oblig'd to quit my usual Standing, and plac'd myself inadvertently under an Iron Hook which hung from the Ceiling down to within two Inches of my Head, and communicated by a Wire with the outside of the Jars. I attempted to discharge them, and in fact did so; but I did not perceive it, tho' the charge went thro' me, and not through the Persons I entended it for. I neither saw the Flash, heard the Report, nor felt the Stroke. When my Senses returned, I found myself on the Floor. I got up, not knowing how that had happened. I then again attempted to discharge the Jars; but one of the Company told me they were already discharg'd, which I could not at first believe, but on Trial found it true. They told me they had not felt it, but they saw I was knock'd down by it, which had greatly surprised them. On recollecting myself, and examining my Situation, I found the Case clear. A small swelling rose on the Top of my Head, which continued sore for some Days, but I do not remember any other Effect good or bad. (Smyth 1906, pp. 308-9)

Thus, Franklin explained once again that electricity could be applied to the head without putting a person in danger, and that it did not have significant long-term effects that might prevent a person from returning to work. He did not state anything, however, about feeling elated the next day, which was also of great interest to Ingenhousz.

At the end of his letter of 1783, Ingenhousz had informed Franklin that

> This experiment, made by accident, on my self, and of which I gave you at the time an account, has induced me to advise some of the London mad-Doctors, as Dr. Brook, to try a similar experiment o[n] mad men, thinking that, as I found in my self, my mental faculties impro[ved] and as the world well knows, that your mental faculties, if not improved [by] the two strooks you received, were certainly not hurt, by them, it might perhaps be[?] a

remedie to restore the mental faculties when lost. (Packard Humanities Institute 2003, vol. 40, u. 209, 2)

Franklin clearly appreciated the findings and reasoning behind what Ingenhousz was suggesting, the potential significance of his novel idea, and the need for clinical trials. He therefore further informed Ingenhousz in his return letter that he "communicated that Part of your Letter to an Operator, encourag'd by Government here [in France] to electrify epileptic and other poor Patients, and advis'd his trying the Practice on Mad People according to your opinion" (Smyth 1906, pp. 308-9).

Hence, what Ingenhousz and Franklin viewed as a new way to treat severely melancholic and other mentally ill patients was put into circulation, or at least into wider circulation, at this time. Prior to the mid-1780s, mild electrical shocks to the head had been tried with some patient groups. John Wesley (1760), for instance wrote in his *Desideratum* that cranial shocks had been used with some success to treat headache, "fits" (seizures), and hysteria. But other than saying the shocks were light, he provided minimal details about the cases cited in his book and did not single out melancholia as disorder to be treated with cranial electricity. Further, he was vague about various forms of madness and how they should be treated in his popular *Primitive Physic*, including those editions updated in 1780 (e.g., Wesley 1791). Notably, he praised electricity along with valerian root for "Nervous Disorders," whereas under the heading "Lunacy," he merely noted "electricity: tried" and added nothing more, leaving readers of these two undefined and unillustrated categories to wonder just where on the body it should be applied and precisely for whom it should work. Interestingly, Wesley fully recommended agrimony and rubbing the head with vinegar and ground ivy for "Lunacy," specifying in one of his more informative sentences that ivy "generally cures melancholy."

In retrospect, it seems reasonable to conclude that electrical treatments for melancholia and other forms of lunacy were not widely used, if used at all, in England and France, when Ingenhousz and Franklin called for clinical trials. These two men were exceptionally well read and well connected, and much more likely than not, they would have known if experiments of the type they were proposing had been published in books and journals or were sanctioned and ongoing. Instead, and perhaps most revealing, they presented the idea of treating melancholia with cranial shocks as novel and clearly worthy of proper evaluation.

Because the suggested use of cranial electricity for severe melancholia and other forms of madness was endorsed by two of the greatest scientific minds of the Enlightenment, and also based on experiential findings rather than loose speculation, the idea might have been further disseminated by word of mouth. Although Ingenhousz informed Franklin in his 1783 letter that he "could never persuade any one" to test the new treatment, and Franklin wrote back to Ingenhousz in 1785 that he had not yet heard back from the French electrical operator he had contacted, publications describing how cranial electricity was used to treat deeply melancholic patients now began to circulate.

Early Clinical Trials and Successes

John Birch founded and ran the electrical department at St. Thomas's Hospital in London. In 1792, he described how he successfully treated two melancholic patients using electricity applied to the head. Birch's case reports appeared in a letter to instrument maker George Adams, who included the letter in the fourth edition of his *Essay on Electricity* (1792).

Birch stated that for over a decade he had been conducting electrical experiments on patients who were not responding to conventional medicines. More importantly, he wrote that he first began to use cranial electricity to treat melancholia in 1787. His first case was a "porter of the India warehouses," who had a history of melancholia and whose current condition appeared to be "induced by the death of one of his children." Birch (1792) explained:

> He had been two months afflicted when I first saw him. He was quiet, would suffer his wife to lead him about the house, but he never spoke to her; he sighed frequently, and was inattentive to every thing that passed. I covered his head with a flannel, and rubbed the electric sparks all over the cranium; he seemed to feel it disagreeable, but said nothing. On the second visit . . . I passed six small shocks through the brain in different directions. As soon as he got into an adjoining room, and saw his wife, he spoke to her, and in the evening was cheerful, expressing himself, as if he thought he should soon go to his work again. I repeated the shocks in like manner on the third and the fourth day, after which he went to work: I desired to see him every Sunday, which I did for three months after, and he remained perfectly well. (pp. 561-63)

Birch's second melancholic case was a singer who had tried to commit suicide. After receiving "about six" shocks "through the head" everyday for a fortnight, this patient experienced "a refreshing sleep, from which he awoke a new being: that he felt sensible of the powers of electricity every day after it's application, being capable of mental exertions immediately. . . . he said . . . no one but himself could have an adequate idea of the sudden change the first electric shocks wrought in his mind" (pp. 564-65).

Although successful with these two patients, it remains unclear if the shocks used and only vaguely described were strong enough for a therapeutic effect on mood, raising the possibility of a placebo effect. In a third case, however, Birch increased the strength of the shocks to levels that might have been physiologically therapeutic, but he observed no improvement. This patient was a 26-year-old man with "moping melancholy," possibly a low-grade, chronic depressive disorder, sometimes referred to as *dysthymia* in the modern literature. He experienced shocks "as far as prudence would direct." By day three, this patient reported nothing more than a mild headache for an hour after the procedure. Birch subsequently "dismissed the patient, in the same unhappy state he had so long suffered" (p. 566).

Giovanni Aldini also attempted to cure melancholia with cranial electricity (Bourguignon 1964; Parent 2004). Aldini first worked under the tutelage of his uncle Luigi Galvani, and in 1798 was appointed Professor of Physics at University of Bologna. Five years later, he published a treatise that included many experiments with medical electricity, and in 1804 an expanded, French version of this book was published. In his fourth commentary, "Application of Galvanism on Madness, and Other Illnesses of a Different Nature," included in both books, he described two successful cases from Bologna.

Aldini's first patient, a 27-year-old farmer by the name of Louis Lanzarini, "fell into a state of deep melancholy" and was sent to the public hospital of St. Ursula in 1801. When questioned, he gave laconic and confused answers, suggestive of what we would today diagnose as schizophrenia of the disorganized type, or schizoaffective disorder, a diagnosis also consistent with his age at symptom onset and family history of mental illness. Aldini proceeded to administer cranial electricity to Lanzarini, and noted that he responded well to his electrical treatments and even began to associate the galvanic instruments with feeling better:

> We . . . conceived the idea of shaving the head above the suture of the parietal bone. . . . The patient then touched with one of his hands the bottom of the pile, and at the same time an arc was established from the summit of the pile to the metallic armature placed on the head. By this arrangement the action of the Galvanism was rendered more moderate; the patient endured it for a long time, and seemed to be greatly relieved by it. . . . On his leaving the hospital I carried him to my house, that he might be fitted by proper nourishment for resuming his former occupations. He remained with me eight days . . . during which time he was exceedingly tractable, and performed his duty with great care and attention. . . . After this period, I obtained a regular report respecting his behavior and state of his health . . . and I learned . . . that he continued to enjoy good health, and to exercise his usual employment. (Aldini 1803, pp. 117-19)

Aldini also presented the case of a laborer with less severe symptoms, whose treatment and progress were similar to Lanzarini's. Yet Aldini was conservative in his claims, knowing that two successful clinical cases were not enough for firm conclusions, and cautioning that cranial treatments did not seem to work "in cases of raving madness," meaning mania.

A third early administrator of cranial electrotherapy was T. Gale, a relatively unknown but seemingly well-meaning evangelical physician who practiced in New York State. In *Electricity, or Ethereal Fire, Considered* (1802), Gale wrote:

> If the electric shock can be applied in the first stages of madness, before indirect debility takes place, it may be immediately removed; . . . I have found, by experience, that gentle shocks through every part of the system upon the nerves, and through the stomach, and down the back of the head, upon the top of the head, through the brain to the feet, have assisted in restoring a person to the use of reason. (p. 125)

Gale described three patients suffering from melancholia. The first was a young woman who might have had postpartum-onset major depression with psychotic features (paranoid type). The woman was breast-feeding during the summer of 1795, when she began to ignore her baby and stopped eating. Gale noted that "her mother was the only person she would correspond with . . . she was terrified at the sight of her husband, with whom she had lived in perfect cordiality until she became insane. . . . She was emaciated almost to a skeleton; deep dejection of spirits, gloomy and melancholy" (p. 127). Consequently, the young woman was given some "very light shocks," which induced her to smile the next day. After four or five weeks of additional electrical treatments, "all that gloominess of mind was dispelled, and . . . she was able to unite with her husband again in keeping house" (p. 127).

Gale was also successful in treating a suicidal man. This individual had been in a delirium for several years and had even cut his own throat. He exhibited excellent recovery after just two sessions with what Gale considered to be moderate to fairly strong electrical shocks, although Gale did not quantify the amount of electricity applied.

Gale's third case was a man who might have had a reactive psychosis, based on how he had become delusional after being cheated out of a large amount of money. Gale reported that:

> His family had become much alarmed. . . . he told them that the devil said he must kill a daughter of his. . . . I charged the machine as high as I thought he could bear, and live through. . . . I passed the shock upon him, which almost knocked him to the floor. Passed the shock from the top of his head to the feet. . . . I gave six or seven more, but lighter. He went home, and was more composed in his mind the next day, as I was informed; but it was necessary to bring him again. . . . I gave him a second electrification and they took him home, and it was not long before he had the right use of his mind, was composed and well. (pp. 129-30)

Giving Credit Where It Is Due

Did Birch, Aldini, and Gale come up with the idea of using electrical shocks to the head to treat melancholia and other forms of madness from Ingenhousz or Franklin? Although Franklin was praised by most everyone for his groundbreaking work on electricity, these three men did not cite Ingenhousz or Franklin, or any other person for that matter, for this therapeutic idea. Nevertheless, citing sources, especially if the information were not published in a book or journal, was not the norm during the 18th century. Thus, the absence of citations cannot be construed to mean that Ingenhousz and Franklin did not influence the clinical trials that followed. Indeed, it seems fairly likely that the requests made by Ingenhousz and Franklin to the London and Paris operators were heard in the 1780s, and that others ventured in as the idea spread orally and good results began to appear in print. Birch is highly significant in this context, both because he was one of the best-known electrical operators in London and because he stated that he began treating melancholic patients with electricity in 1787. As for Aldini, he was well read, traveled extensively, and was in contact with experimental natural philosophers throughout Europe. In contrast, nothing seems to be known about Gale, other than that his writing would indicate that he was following the emerging literature as best he could.

The exact strength of shocks recommended by Ingenhousz and Franklin may never be known, although fundamental to Franklin's medical approach was the premise that the caregiver must never do anything that might seriously harm or endanger the patient (Finger 2006). Hence, Franklin, along with the other electrotherapists in this era, would have hoped to administer mild to moderate shocks, with treatments extending across several sessions. Also knowing that this protocol would dissipate fear in their patients, it is unlikely that the 18th-century therapists set forth to administer convulsive jolts that would cause falling and unconsciousness.

In this context, a distinction has to be made between electrotherapy for the mentally ill as practiced by Birch, Aldini, and Gale, and its reemergence with Ugo Cerletti's work in Italy in the 1930s. Cerletti was guided by the idea that seizure disorders might somehow offer protection against schizophrenia, and he conducted his first electroconvulsive shock trials on a schizophrenic man brought to him in 1938 by a local police commissioner (Accornero 1988; Cerletti 1950). This individual, who seemed to be schizophrenic, appeared to be much improved after receiving the strong therapy, and soon practitioners in Italy and then elsewhere were praising electroconvulsive therapy as a medical marvel (Golla, Walter, and Fleming 1940; Kalinowsky 1939). Cerletti and his followers seemed unaware of what Ingenhousz and Franklin had suggested, or what Birch, Aldini, and Gale had done, when they began their transcranial shock treatments. Furthermore, because they did not know about or cite the earlier literature, the belief grew that "the first application of electroshock in human beings occurred in April of 1938, in a room of the Clinic for Mental and Nervous Diseases in Rome, then under the direction of Professor Ugo Cerletti" (Accornero 1970, p. 41).

On the 300th anniversary of Benjamin Franklin's birth, it seems proper to set the record straight. The history of electroshock therapy for the severely mentally ill did not begin in the 20th century or even a century earlier. Its history with electrical machines can be traced to the 18th century. Additionally, when Ingenhousz and Franklin called for clinical tests of cranial electroshock therapy with melancholic and other mentally ill patients, they did not base their work on theory (e.g., the role of amnesia). Rather, what they proposed was based on personal experiences: Franklin discovered that cranial shocks could be administered safely, and Ingenhousz had felt unusually elated and mentally sharper the morning after he had a serious electrical accident.

Neither Ingenhousz nor Franklin had any idea about how strong the cranial shocks they called for would have to be to produce beneficial effects with severely melancholic or perhaps other mad patients. This would have to be worked out. They also seemed to be little concerned about underlying mechanisms that might help explain why electricity could work. Methodological, physiological, and theoretical issues such as these would become much more important in the 20th century, with the rediscovery of cranial shocks as a viable therapy for mentally ill patients. For Franklin, whose medicine was driven by facts, the most important thing by far was to get clinically relevant findings—outcomes that could better help people in need.

Note

Some of the material covered in this article, and more on Franklin's thoughts about the use of electricity in medicine, can be found in Finger 2006.

References

Accornero, F. 1988. An eyewitness account of the discovery of electroshock. *Convulsive Ther* 4:41-49.

Adams, G. 1792. *An essay on electricity*, 4th ed. London: Hindmarsh.

Aldini, G. 1803. *An account of late improvements in galvanism*. London: Wilkes and Taylor.

Bertucci, P. 2001. The electrical body of knowledge. In *Electric bodies*, ed. P. Bertucci and G. Pancaldi, 43-68. Bologna: Università di Bologna.

Bertucci, P. 2003. The shocking bad: Medical electricity in mid-18th-century London. *Nuova Voltiana* 5:31-42.

Bertucci, P. 2005. Sparking controversy: Jean Antoine Nollet and medical electricity south of the Alps. *Nuncius* 20:153-87.

Birch, J. 1792. A letter to Mr. George Adams. In *An essay on electricity . . . by George Adams*, 4th ed. London: Hindmarsh.

Bourguignon, A. 1964. *La découverte par Aldini (1804) des effets thérapeutiques de l'électrochoc sur la mélancolie*. Paris: Masson.

Brands, H. W. 2002. *The first American*. New York: Anchor Books.

Cerletti, U. 1950. Old and new information about electroshock. *Am J Psychiatry* 107:87-94.

Cohen, I. B. 1941. *Benjamin Franklin's experiments*. Cambridge: Harvard Univ. Press.

Colwell, H. A. 1922. *An essay on the history of electrotherapy and diagnosis*. London: Heinemann.

Conley, T. K., and M. Brewer-Anderson. 1997. Franklin and Ingenhousz: A correspondence of interests. *Proc Am Philos Soc* 141:276-96.

Dorsman, C., and C. A. Crommelin. 1957. The invention of the Leyden jar. *Janus* 46:275-80.

Evans, C. 1757. A relation of a cure performed by electricity. *Med Obser Inquir* 1:83-86.

Finger, S. 2006. *Doctor Franklin's medicine*. Philadelphia: Univ. of Pennsylvania Press.

Finger, S., and F. Zaromb. 2006. Benjamin Franklin and shock-induced amnesia. *Am Psycholog* 61(3):240-48.

Foucault, M. 1965. *Madness and civilization*. New York: Vintage Books.

Franklin, B. 1751. *Experiments and observations on electricity*. London: E. Cave.

Franklin, B. 1758. An account of the effects of electricity in paralytic cases. *Phil T Roy Soc* 50(2):481-83.

Gale, T. 1802. *Electricity, or ethereal fire, considered*. Troy, MI: Moffitt & Lyon.

Golla, F. L., W. G. Walter, and G. W. T. H. Fleming. 1940. Electrically induced convulsions. *Proc R Soc Med* 33:261-67.

Gray, S. 1731. A letter to Cromwell Mortimer. *Phil T Roy Soc* 37:18-44.

Guericke, O. von. 1672. *Experimenta nova (ut vocantur) Magdeburgica*. Amsterdam: Jansson-Waesberg.

Hackmann, W. D. 1978. *Electricity from glass*. Alphen aan den Rijn: Sijthoff & Noordhoff.

Hawksbee, F. 1709. *Physico-mechanical experiments on various subjects*. London.
Heilbron, J. 1979. *Electricity in the seventeenth and 18th centuries*. Berkeley: Univ. of California Press.
Isaacson, W. 2003. *Benjamin Franklin*. New York: Simon & Schuster.
Jackson, S. W. 1978. Melancholia and the waning of humoral theory. *J Hist Med Allied Sci* 33:367-76.
Kalinowsky, L. B. 1939. Electric-convulsion therapy in schizophrenia. *Lancet* 2:1232-33.
Kratzenstein, C. G. 1745. *Schreiben von dem Nutzen der Electricität in der Arzneywissenschaft*. Halle: Hemmerde.
Krüger, J. G. 1744. *Zuschrift an seine Zuhörer, worinnen er Gedancken von der Electricität mittheilt und Ihnen zugleich seine künftigen Lectionen bekannt macht*. Halle: Hemmerde.
Labaree, L. W., ed. 1961-62. *The papers of Benjamin Franklin*, vols. 4-5. New Haven: Yale Univ. Press.
Licht, S. [H.] 1967. History of electrotherapy. In *Therapeutic electricity and ultraviolet radiation*. 2nd ed., ed. S. Licht, 1-70. Baltimore: Waverly Press.
Packard Humanities Institute. 2003. *Papers of Benjamin Franklin*. Prepublication CD-ROM 102.
Parent, A. 2004. Giovanni Aldini: From animal electricity to human brain stimulation. *Can J Neurol Sci* 31:576-84.
Porter, R. 1985a. Lay medical knowledge in the eighteenth century: The evidence of the *Gentleman's Magazine*. *Med Hist* 29: 138-68.
Porter, R. 1985b. Laymen, doctors and medical knowledge in the eighteenth century: The evidence of the *Gentleman's Magazine*. In *Patients and practitioners: Lay perceptions of medicine in pre-industrial society*, ed. R. Porter, 283-324. Cambridge: Cambridge Univ. Press.
Priestley, J. 1775. *History and present state of electricity, with original experiments*, 3rd ed. London. Repr. New York: Johnson Reprint Corporation, 1966.
Reed, H. S. 1947-48. Jan Ingenhousz. *Chron Bot* 11:288-391.
Schaffer, S. 1983. Natural philosophy and public spectacle in the 18th century. *Hist Sci* 21:1-43.
Schaffer, S. 1993. The consuming flame: Electrical showmen and Tory mystics in the world of goods. In *Consumption and the world of goods*, ed. J. Brewer and R. Porter, 489-526. London: Routledge.
Smyth, A. H. 1906. *The writings of Benjamin Franklin*, vol. 9. New Haven: Yale Univ. Press.
Snorrason, E. S. 1974. *C. G. Kratzenstein and his studies on electricity during the 18th century*. Odense: Odense Univ. Press.
Sutton, G. 1995. *Science for a polite society: Gender, culture, and the demonstration of enlightenment*. Boulder: Westview Press.
Van Doren, C. 1938. *Benjamin Franklin*. New York: Viking Press.
Wesley, J. 1760. *The desideratum*. London: Flexney.
Wesley, J. 1791. *Primitive physic*. Philadelphia: Parry Hall.

Franklin and the Revolutionary Body

Betsy Erkkila

In telling the horrid story of the "Tryal of a Man and His Wife" for murder, Franklin, Betsy Erkkila argues, "suggests both a new conceptualization of the body as a source of agency and responsibility in the eighteenth century and the constitutive role that the unruly body would come to play in defining enlightenment notions of the natural, the human, the rational, and the universal." And yet that project was ultimately a failure—or, at least, incomplete—for, despite "Franklin's efforts to subject the body to regimes of discipline and control, his *Autobiography* is grounded in a reconceptualization of the self as fleshly, worldly, fluid, and ungodly." — J.L.

> While my Care was employ'd in guarding against one Fault, I was often surpris'd by another. Habit took the Advantage of Inattention. Inclination was sometimes too strong for Reason.
>
> —Benjamin Franklin, *Autobiography*

On 24 October 1734, Benjamin Franklin's *Pennsylvania Gazette* carried his report of the "Tryal of a Man and His Wife" for the murder of their fourteen-year-old daughter, who was turned "out of Doors," exposed to the elements, fed on her own excrement, and left to die. "Instead of supplying her with Necessaries and due Attendance," Franklin wrote, "they treated her with the utmost Cruelty and Barbarity, suffering her to lie and rot in her Nastiness, and when she cried for Bread giving her into her Mouth with a Iron Ladle, her own Excrements to eat, with a great Number of other Circumstances of the like Nature, so that she languished and at length died."[1] Presenting further details of the trial and the jury's verdict of "only *Man-slaughter,*" Franklin attributes the "hitherto unheard-of Barbarity" of their "Crimes" to the excesses of drink: "But this is not the only Instance the present Age has afforded, of the incomprehensible Insensibility **Dramdrinking** is capable of producing" (*M*, 234).

The story is remarkable in its bodily excess, its pairing of appetite and excrement, and its lack of a religious perspective. As Franklin reports it, this is a story about a man and a woman possessed not by the devil but by the excesses of their own bodily desire, as signified by the habit of dramdrinking. I drink therefore I am. The emphasis on human rather than divine agency is underscored by their punishment: "They were sentenced to be burnt in the Hand" (*M*, 234). More "terrible and shocking" than this outward "Punishment," however, is their inner recognition of their own abjection: "the inward Reflection upon their own enormous Crimes" (*M*, 234).

Published a year after Franklin undertook his "Project of arriving at moral Perfection" in July 1733, at a time when he had given up his occasional attendance at Presbyterian services, the report is part of Franklin's general effort in the 1730s to use the newly emerging power of the print press in America to clean up both private character and public space by writing against the excesses of drink, alehouses, fairs, gaming, and other idle pursuits.[2] The story suggests both a new conceptualization of the body as a source of agency and responsibility in the eighteenth century and the constitutive role that the unruly body would come to play in defining enlightenment notions of the natural, the human, the rational, and the universal. As a sign of the excesses of the intemperate body, drinking is associated not only with the violation of the parent/child bond, but with the unnatural, the savage, and the monstrous. The couple "had not only acted contrary to the particular Laws of all Nations, but had even broken the Universal Law of Nature; since there are no Creatures known, how savage, wild, and fierce soever, that have not implanted in them a natural Love and Care of their tender Offspring, and that will not even hazard Life in its Protection and Defence" (*M*, 234).

I begin with this story of the intemperate body because I want to argue that in the life, work, and reception of Benjamin Franklin, it is on the level of the body and its potential excess that the American Revolution was fought.[3] Later in 1771, when Franklin undertook the story of his rise from poverty to public power that became known as *The Autobiography*, it is the body and its "Inclinations" that drive his narration (*A*, 28). Whereas Thomas Jefferson and Tom Paine appealed to abstract human rights and John Adams invoked historical precedent and English canon law, Franklin narrated the Revolution on the level of the body and the individual human life, as an on-going struggle between "Reason" and "Inclination" (*A*, 66). Against what Lemay and Zall have called "the Poor Richard caricature of Franklin," I want to suggest that for all of Franklin's efforts to subject the body to regimes of discipline and control, his *Autobiography* is grounded in a reconceptualization of the self as fleshly, worldly, fluid, and ungodly.[4] This transformation in body image and self-image was part of a broader set of religious, economic, and political transformations that came in the eighteenth century with the challenge to the traditional authority of church and state; the rise of commerce, the market, and the print public sphere; and the proliferation of an enlightened political language of reason, liberty, rights, and human happiness.[5]

Although Franklin's narrative is usually read as a unified work called the *Autobiography*, this title—which it did not receive until 1868, when John Bigelow published all four parts of the narrative for the first time in a volume entitled *Autobiography of Benjamin Franklin*—has tended to shift attention away from the different historical and national contexts in which it was written: England in 1771; France in 1784; and Philadelphia between 1788 and 1790. These different historical, spatial, and temporal frames split the narrative from itself, giving it a fragmented, discontinuous, and disjunctive quality that belies the unity and self-coherence of the individual life that the generic form and title—*The Autobiography*—are meant to encode. While Franklin's biographers and his critics have continued to read his *Autobiography* back into his life, it is important to recognize the artfulness of his narrative and the ways its various parts are shaped by the exigencies of the different historical and cultural moments in which they were written.

I. Bodily Acts

Franklin's narrative begins as a "private" letter to his illegitimate son, William Franklin, who was himself the probable offspring of one of the illicit bodily acts of Franklin's youth. The letter was written from an English country estate in July and August of 1771, at a time when Franklin still believed that the future of the British empire lay in America and that it would be a grave error for the Crown to lose the colonies through the lack of foresight of a few foolish ministers.[6] Franklin's desire to narrate the "Circumstances of *my* Life" as a model "fit to be imitated" by "my Posterity" (*A*, 1) appears to be part of an effort to take control of his life, his story, and his future at a time when the old world appeared to be coming apart at the seams. Associated with the "Pleasure" of ancestral "Anecdotes" (*A*, 1), the gratification of personal "*Vanity*" (*A*, 2), and the "Inclination so natural to old Men" of always talking about "themselves" (*A*, 1), Franklin's "Recollection" (*A*, 1) is presented as a form of bodily resurrection, a means of achieving immortality through the materiality of writing and letters.

The story begins as one of familial and ancestral attachment to England, a country world of artisans and farmers ordered by the filial values of dutiful obedience to father and God. In the New England world of early eighteenth-century Boston, where Franklin was born in 1706, sons were still expected to follow the work and will of their fathers. "Be to thy parents an Obedient Son" / "Adore the Maker of thy Inward part," Franklin's Uncle Benjamin had written in a poem sent to Franklin when he was four years old (*A*, 4). But Franklin—or at least his body—grew another way. Over and over in this early part of his narrative, Franklin's bodily impulses—his likes, dislikes, and "Inclinations"—put him at odds with the traditional authority of father, family, church, and state. When he is taken home, at age ten, "to assist [his] Father in his Business, which was that of a Tallow Chandler and Soap-Boiler," Franklin resists: "I dislik'd the Trade and had a strong Inclination for the Sea; but my Father declar'd against it" (*A*, 6).

"To prevent the apprehended Effect" of Franklin's "Hankering for the Sea," his Father has him "bound" and indentured to his brother James, who is a Boston printer (*A*, 10). Allowed to follow his "Bookish Inclination" (*A*, 9), Franklin is relatively successful as a printer's apprentice. In 1721, his brother begins publishing the *New England Courant*, one of the earliest newspapers in the colonies; and in 1722, Franklin goes to print for the first time disguised as a woman, Silence Dogood, the anonymous author of the first essay series in America. But there are tensions between the two brothers: "Tho' a Brother, he considered himself as my Master and me as his Apprentice" (*A*, 15), Franklin writes, in words that already suggest a transformation in the older filial order of hierarchy and deference in which both sons and apprentices were expected to submit to the constituted authority of family and master. When his brother, who is "passionate," beats him, Franklin's body rises in protest. "Under the Impressions of Resentment, for the Blows his Passion too often urg'd him to bestow upon me," Franklin writes, "I took upon me to assert my Freedom" (*A*, 16, 17). He decides to break with his father, his master, and the traditional structures of New England authority by fleeing the province.

Franklin's act of resistance is grounded not in abstract rights or political principle but in the body and the intimacy of the family relation. In fact, Franklin adds a manuscript note to his statement, "my Brother was passionate and had often beaten me," that stresses the relation between his childhood experience of being physically abused by his brother and his later principled resistance to tyranny: "I fancy his harsh and tyrannical Treatment of me, might be a means of impressing me with that Aversion to arbitrary Power that has stuck to me thro' my whole life" (*A*, 16).

Franklin's note offers an explicit example of the ways the political perspective of 1771 gets read back into his account of his early life. Narrated through the lens of the imperial crisis of 1771, at a time when Lord Hillsborough, the secretary of state for the colonies, had refused to recognize Franklin's credentials as an agent of Massachusetts, and Parliament continued to insist on its right to tax and legislate for the colonies, Franklin's story represents a transformation in the relations of father and son, master and apprentice, minister and parishioner, government and subject that anticipates even as it is shaped by the revolutionary impulses that would lead to the break with England in 1776.[7] Although in 1771 Franklin is still one of the King's men, his story of his break away from father, master, minister, and state already embodies the revolutionary concepts of personal liberty, the naturalness of separation, and the natural rights of every *body* that would receive their fullest political formulation a few years later in Paine's *Common Sense* and the Declaration of Independence.

Franklin's emphasis on separation and agency rather than submission and dependence corresponds with an increasing concern not only with ancestry, progeny, and descent but also with bodily constitution, health, cleanliness, and the care of the body.[8] Fascinated with the culture and discipline of the body, Franklin, like the emergent middle classes his narrative represents, had a particular taste for self-help books. At sixteen, he writes, "I happen'd to meet with a Book written by one Tryon, recommending a Vegetable Diet"; this encounter results in his refusal "to eat Flesh" (*A*, 12). Like Franklin's movement away from his father's work as a boiler of animal fat toward the culture of print, books, letters, and polite conversation, his attempt to rid his body of animal fat is part of a more general narrative movement away from the desires of the body, undertaken in an effort to assert the activity of mind and head over the lower body parts. Franklin's refusal "to eat Flesh" saves him time and money for study; it also enables him to make "greater Progress" in his studies, "from that greater Clearness of Head and quicker Apprehension which usually attend Temperance in Eating and Drinking" (*A*, 13).

But while the first part of Franklin's narrative is driven by the desire to subdue the body to regimes of reason, discipline, and control, what stands out in Franklin's story and the stories of others he recounts is the continual triumph of the lower over the upper body parts. This is particularly evident in the struggle "between Principle and Inclination" that Franklin experiences on his flight from Boston when the smell of Cod coming "hot out of the Frying Pan" causes him to give up his "Resolution of not eating animal Food" (*A*, 28). "[O]n this occasion," Franklin recalls, "I consider'd with my Master Tryon, the taking every Fish as a kind of unprovok'd Murder, since none of them had or ever could do us any Injury that might justify the Slaughter. All this seem'd very reasonable" (*A*, 28). In the contest between "Principle and Inclination" that ensues, the senses—smell, appetite, taste, and the desires of the body—prevail. Conceiving of the world as a kind of cosmic stomach in which large fish eat "smaller Fish," Franklin concludes that "if you eat one another, I don't see why we mayn't eat you. So I din'd upon Cod very heartily and continu'd to eat with other People, returning only now and then occasionally to a vegetable Diet" (*A*, 28).

What is striking about this scene of bodily consumption is that it inverts the moral and progressive logic of the tale Franklin seeks to tell about the need to control the appetites and inclinations of the body in order to achieve worldly success. Rather than "Reason" and "Principle" controlling the body, they themselves become instruments of the appetitive body. The body wags the mind. Or as Franklin puts it: "So convenient a thing it is to be a *reasonable Creature*, since it enables one to find or make a Reason for everything one has a mind to do" (*A*, 28). The passage is the first in which Franklin suggests the instability of "Reason" as the ground of the enlightened self and the new secular order he seeks to embody. If one can "find or make a Reason for everything one has a mind to do," and if what one has "a mind to do" is driven by the desires of the body, where exactly is the rational ground for an enlightened social order in this narrative? Though presented humorously, this scene of the body's triumph over reason and mind represents a major moment of crisis in Franklin's narrative and in the political grammar of reason, rights, liberty, and happiness on which the American Revolution would be founded. Whereas Jefferson's *Notes on the State of Virginia* (1787), like his original version of the Declaration of Independence, is haunted by the specter and contradiction of the enchained slave, Franklin's *Autobiography* returns obsessively to the prospect of a world driven by the irrational compulsions of the body.

Franklin's account of his arrival in Philadelphia has entered the national imaginary as the scene of American origins—the story of the rise of the self from an "unlikely Beginning" (*A*, 20) to fortune and fame. The bodiliness and materiality of Franklin's arrival, however, is left out of later mythologizations. "Dirty," hungry, and poor, his pockets "stuff'd out with Shirts and Stockings," Franklin appears in the figure of a grotesque Rabelaisian body as he marches up Market Street eating "three great Puffy Rolls": "a most awkward ridiculous Appearance," thought his future wife, Deborah Read, as he passed by her house "with a Roll under each Arm, and eating the other" (*A*, 20). Associated with dirt, materiality, the senses, and the appetites, and suspected for his "youth and Appearance" of being "some Runaway" (*A*, 21), Franklin enters Philadelphia in the guise of the low other or mass body against whom he would seek to define the virtue, industry, and refinement of an emergent middle class of urban tradesmen, shopkeepers, and clerks.

Franklin's story of his rise and success as a printer is grounded in his struggle to master the unruly impulses of the body. The city as Franklin presents it is a dangerous place, full of passions, self-interest, secrets, and masquerade. Images of liquidity, instability, and risk abound, from the "drunken Dutchman" who "fell overboard" on the boat to Philadelphia (*A*, 17), to the "Croaker" who warned that "Philadelphia was a sinking Place" in the very year that Franklin opened his "new Printing-House" (*A*, 47), to the many who sink or swim amid the fluctuations of the market economy. Like the increased social interest in the art of swimming that went hand-in-hand in the eighteenth century with transformations in the market and new conceptions of the body, Franklin's mastery of the art of swimming—his ability to perform "Feats of Activity both upon and under Water" in accord with Thévenot's illustrations—becomes emblematic of his ability to negotiate the fluid conditions of the market through artful control of the body (*A*, 39).[9]

Franklin's emphasis on the labor and habits of the body as the source of character, credit, and virtue represents a transformation in body image, a new conceptualization of the body as separate, independent, responsible, and self-regulating. This transformation is particularly evident in Franklin's account of his trip to England (1724-26), where he undertakes to change the work patterns of the old world—its concepts of time, labor, leisure, and pleasure—by changing the habits of the body. As "the Water-American" who drinks "only Water" during working hours, Franklin seeks to wean English workmen of the "detestable Custom" of drinking beer all day long that they "might be *strong* to labour" (*A*, 36). Franklin's temperate and self-regulating "Water-American" registers on the level of the body the increasing conflict between the American colonies and the British empire. Reversing the image of the American colonies as the receptacle for the idle and criminal of England, Franklin presents America as the future of the British empire in accord with the ideas he sets forth in *Observations concerning the Increase of Mankind* (1751).[10]

As a figure of rational and temperate self-control, Franklin's "Water-American" anticipates in the body and *as* body the language of "Reason," "Liberty," and the "Rights" of Englishmen that Franklin would use in his 1729 *Pennsylvania Gazette* editorial describing the "warm Contest" between Governor Burnet and the Massachusetts Assembly over the principle of colonial consent, the "mutual Dependence between the *Governor* and the *Governed*" (*A*, 50-51). "Their happy Mother Country will perhaps observe with Pleasure," Franklin wrote, that "her SONS in the remotest Part of the Earth, and even to the third and fourth Descent, still retain that ardent Spirit of Liberty, and that undaunted Courage in the Defence of it, which has in every Age so gloriously distinguished BRITONS and ENGLISHMEN from all the Rest of Mankind" (*A*, 51). Although Franklin is still speaking as a loyal subject of "the Crown of *Great-Britain*" (*A*, 50), his words already give voice to the political construction of America and the Americans as the cocky sons of liberty, some forty years before their historical formation.[11]

Through rigorous regimes of industry, culture, temperance, and frugality, Franklin seeks to present himself as a model body of the rising middle class and the rising glory of America. And yet, as in the struggle between "Reason" and "Inclination" that marks Franklin's break away from the structures of New England patriarchy, there is an underlying fluidity and instability in the body upon which he seeks to found his character, his credit, and his worldly success. Franklin's emphasis on his own bodiliness and materialism—what he calls his "Giddiness and Inconstancy" (*A*, 56)—and his refusal to postulate a single truth, or God, or human nature beyond the desires of the body lead him to suggest that in the new market economy "Appearance" (*A*, 54)—or bodily affect—may be all.

Referring to the formation of his printing-house as his "public Appearance in Business" (*A*, 45), Franklin seeks to secure "Credit and Character" as a "Tradesman" through the manipulation of public image and bodily affect:

> I took care not only to be in *Reality* Industrious and frugal, but to avoid all *Appearances* of the Contrary. I dressed plainly; I was seen at no Places of idle Diversion; I never went out a-fishing or shooting; a Book, indeed, sometimes debauch'd me from my Work; but that was seldom, snug, and gave no Scandal: and to show that I was not above my Business, I sometimes brought home the Paper I purchas'd at the Stores, thro' the Streets on a Wheelbarrow. (*A*, 54)[12]

The public-ness and commonness of the bodily image Franklin cultivates is complemented by his work in "Public News" and the popular medium of print and his support of causes popular with "the common People" (*A*, 53), such as paper currency and the consent of the governed.[13] If on the one hand Franklin's self-description suggests the ways the Franklinian body extends itself outward, structuring public space and the fundamental habits and categories that organize the modern world, on the other hand it suggests a breakdown in the distinction between private and public, inside and outside, "*Reality*" and "*Appear-*

ance." Franklin and his "*Appearances*" do not mask an inner self, or soul, or reality: he is the body and its various public effects.

Troubled by the materialism, bodiliness, and godlessness of his youth, he resolves to practice certain religious and moral principles because they might be useful as forms of bodily and social control and as a means of achieving social order and human happiness.[14] And yet, despite Franklin's resolve, his "abominable" (*A*, 34) and godless perspective continues to manifest itself in the body of his text. Alluding to his secular and utilitarian understanding of biblical revelation, he writes:

> And this Persuasion, with the kind hand of Providence, or some guardian Angel, or accidental favorable Circumstances and Situations, or all together, preserved me (thro' this dangerous Time of Youth and the hazardous Situations I was sometimes in among Strangers, remote from the Eye and Advice of my Father) without any *willful* gross Immorality or Injustice that might have been expected from my Want of Religion. (*A*, 46)

As in the struggle between "Reason" and "Inclination" that inaugurates Franklin's story, by refusing to locate the self definitively within any larger structure of authority beyond itself and by refusing to privilege reason and self-coherence as the ground of self, Franklin once again suggests that the body and its desires may be the prime movers of the individual and social world. This body is neither classically republican nor classically liberal but revolutionary in its refusal to postulate any ground outside the utilitarian and the social as its ultimate mechanism of regulation and control. Franklin's by-words are not spirit, law, or even human reason, but passion, self-interest, utility, and "the Felicity of Life" (*A*, 46).

At the end of the first part of his narrative, Franklin reflects on his inability to contract a good marriage because the printer's trade was "generally thought a poor one" (*A*, 56). "In the mean time," he writes, "that hard-to-be-govern'd Passion of Youth, had hurried me frequently into Intrigues with low Women that fell in my Way, which were attended with some Expense and great Inconvenience, besides a continual Risk to my Health by a Distemper which of all Things I dreaded" (*A*, 56). Franklin presents his common law marriage to Deborah Read on 1 September 1730 as both an economic partnership and an escape from the excesses of the body.[15] But what he fails to say is that his illegitimate son William—to whom his narrative is addressed—was probably the offspring of one of these "Intrigues with low Women" who frequently fell in his way. William was born in 1730, the same year Franklin married Read. Both historically and in his narrative, young Franklin is a figure of the "hard-to-be-govern'd" body that post-Revolutionary American writers and early nineteenth-century male purity reformers would come to fear. His story of the arrival of the male adolescent in the city is one to which the culture would return obsessively in the nineteenth century. In fact, even Walt Whitman recognized Franklin's historical precedence when he named his 1842 temperance novel *Franklin Evans; or The Inebriate: A Tale of the Times*.

II. Revolution and the Body

The first part of Franklin's narrative breaks off in 1731 at the very moment when he begins to extend his private bodily regime outward to "the common Tradesmen and Farmers" through what he calls "my first Project of a public Nature, that for a Subscription Library" (*A*, 57). When Franklin returns to "the Account of [his] Life" (*A*, 62) in 1784, the American Revolution has ended, and he is in France after aiding in the negotiation of the peace treaty with Britain, which was signed 3 September 1783. Franklin never finally gets to an account of the American Revolution in his narrative, which breaks off open-endedly in 1757.[16] But while the Revolution is not present as part of the manifest content of Franklin's narrative, it is present as the political or narrative unconscious of Franklin's "Life"—as a scene of social crisis, bloody contest, and challenge to traditional structures of authority in family, society, church, and state. Like Jefferson's *Notes on the State of Vir-*

ginia, the second part of Franklin's narrative represents an attempt to come to terms with the bloody wounds and excess of the Revolutionary War. But whereas Jefferson's *Notes* focuses on the need to revise Virginian and ultimately American law in accord with republican principle, Franklin's post-Revolutionary "Account" of his life focuses on the need to achieve mastery and control of the body.

The second part of Franklin's narrative is preceded by a note that distinguishes between the familial and private address of the first part of his manuscript, and its succeeding pages, which were "written many Years after" and "intended for the Public." "The Affairs of the Revolution," Franklin writes, "occasion'd the Interruption" (*A*, 57). The Revolution makes itself felt first as a formal break in Franklin's narrative, and then as a transformation in the narrative frame and focus of his story: from private letter to public address; from himself as a model for his "Posterity" to himself as a model for every body—especially the newly mobile bodies of young men in the city; from the story of his youthful rise to "Affluence" and "Reputation" (*A*, 1) to an increasingly concerted focus on himself as an embodiment of the moral idealism of the American Revolution.

In the letters that Franklin includes as a preface to the second part of his narrative, both Abel James in America and Benjamin Vaughan in England urge him to take control of the contested and potentially dangerous meanings of the American Revolution by completing and publishing the "history" of his life (*A*, 59). "I know of no Character living," writes James, "who has so much in his Power as Thyself to promote a greater Spirit of Industry and early Attention to Business, Frugality and Temperance with the American Youth" (*A*, 58). In Vaughan's view, too, Franklin's life might serve as a means of modeling and controlling human character and subjectivity in the post-Revolutionary period. While Vaughan emphasizes the role Franklin's life will play as an "efficacious advertisement" for America and "the manners and situation of *a rising* people," its most important function will be "the forming of future great men" (*A*, 59). "Invite all wise men to become like yourself," Vaughan writes, imagining a nation and indeed a world not of self-made men but of men imprinted in the self-regulating image of Benjamin Franklin (*A*, 60).

As the historical frame for Franklin's post-Revolutionary account of his life, what is striking about Vaughan's letter is its darkness: its anxiety about a potentially "vicious and detestable" human nature, its fear of "civil broils" and a general collapse of social order, and its closing vision of a world "darkened by anxiety, and too much injured by pain" (*A*, 61-62). Rather than appeal to either God or law as a higher source of authority and control, in Vaughan's letter the defense of the American Revolution, the stability of the American nation, and the future of the human race come to depend on Franklin's ability to embody all three in a temperate, virtuous, and well-regulated life.

At first, Franklin appears to script his public "performances" (*A*, 62) of his life in accord with Vaughan's moralistic directives. The second part of his narrative is focused almost wholly on the body, as Franklin undertakes an "Account" of what he calls his "bold and arduous Project of arriving at moral Perfection" (*A*, 66). "I would conquer all that either Natural Inclination, Custom, or Company might lead me into," Franklin writes of his youthful struggle to clear the body of faults (*A*, 66). But he soon realizes the "Difficulty" of becoming "completely virtuous": "While my Care was employ'd in guarding against one Fault, I was often surpris'd by another. Habit took the Advantage of Inattention. Inclination was sometimes too strong for Reason" (*A*, 66).

Reflecting even as he helps to constitute a new conception of human nature as malleable, manageable, and (perhaps) perfectible rather than fixed, fallen, and given, Franklin seeks to formulate a "Method" (*A*, 66), a kind of early "how to" guide on the art of attaining virtue. He reduces the "moral Virtues" to thirteen, enters them in a little account book, and systematically sets about breaking bad habits and acquiring good ones by striving to "Master" one virtue at a time (*A*, 67-68). "Temperance" heads the list, followed in descending order by "Silence," "Order," "Resolution," "Frugality," "Industry," "Sincerity,"

"Justice," "Moderation," "Cleanliness," "Tranquility," "Chastity," and "Humility." Each virtue is accompanied by a moral aphorism. Under "TEMPERANCE," Franklin writes: "Eat not to Dulness. Drink not to Elevation." "CLEANLINESS" bears the injunction: "Tolerate no Uncleanness in Body, Clothes or Habitation." For "CHASTITY," Franklin writes, "Rarely use Venery but for Health or Offspring" (*A*, 67-68). Like "Temperance," which enables the "Head" to maintain "constant Vigilance" and "Guard" (*A*, 68) against the incursions of the body, Franklin's art of virtue marks a shift in the eighteenth century from an external to an internal discipline of the self through the regulation of every "Pleasure, Appetite, Inclination or Passion, bodily or mental" (*A*, 67).

Franklin's struggle to subject the body to an internal discipline of temperance and industry suggests the ways reason and liberty lock arms with repression and regulation in the emergence of modernity, liberalism, and the modern body.[17] But while Franklin has been read as an embodiment of rationalism, modernity, and what Weber calls the "spirit of capitalism . . . in almost classical purity," this now canonical reading fails to take account of the fluid, discontinuous, and split nature of Franklin's written "performances" of himself.[18] There is little historical evidence that Franklin's moral account book—what he called "this little Artifice" (*A*, 73-74)—had any existence beyond its print representation in his post-Revolutionary narrative of his life.[19] Although critics have tended to assume a coincidence between Vaughan's didactic letter and Franklin's focus on self-regulation in the second part of his narrative, a close reading reveals a volatile body and an ironic, shape-shifting persona that resist young Franklin's moral idealism and his rationalizing regime. There is in fact an increasing temporal dissonance between the young man who aspires and the old man who narrates—between the working class body of Franklin the shopkeeper and printer in Philadelphia in the 1730s and the cosmopolitan and elite body of Franklin who drank, flirted, and flourished in France in the 1780s.[20]

Read in the context of the post-Revolutionary moment, what is most striking about Franklin's account of his "Project of arriving at Moral

Perfection" is its failure. "I was surpris'd to find myself so much fuller of Faults than I had imagined," Franklin writes (*A*, 71). Punning on traditional religious notions of holiness, his book is indeed "holy" in the sense that it is "full of Holes" as a mark of the body's excess (*A*, 71). Although Franklin avows that he was "made a better and a happier Man" by his "Endeavour" to achieve "Perfection" (*A*, 73), he finally gives up his "Plan for Self-examination" entirely because—he confesses slyly—he was "employ'd in Voyages and Business abroad with a Multiplicity of Affairs, that interfered." "But," he adds, "I always carried my little Book with me" (*A*, 71). Like the drunken Dutchman in the first part of Franklin's narrative, who falls overboard carrying a copy of *Pilgrim's Progress*, there is an ironic disjunction between the moral idealism of Franklin's book of virtues and the inclinations of his historical body. Engaged in "a Multiplicity of Affairs," his body is, in effect, too busy either to pursue the course of virtue set forth in his book or to write a book on "the ART *of Virtue*" to help others be virtuous (*A*, 74).

Franklin refracts his own story and the story of the American Revolution through the story of a man who sets out to make a perfectly bright axe but, fatigued by the bodily labor of turning the wheel, gives up the struggle: "*I think I like a speckled Axe best*" (*A*, 73). Written from the vantage of the post-Revolution, Franklin's narrative appears to be split between the moral idealism of the founding and an uneasiness with the lofty ideals and abstractions of the Revolution. On the one hand Franklin owes "the constant Felicity of his Life down to his 79th Year" to his youthful "Endeavour" to achieve "Perfection"; on the other hand he appears to agree with the "many" who "have given up the Struggle, and concluded that *a speckled Axe was best*": "For something that pretended to be Reason was every now and then suggesting to me, that such extreme Nicety as I exacted of myself might be a kind of Foppery in Morals, which if it were known might make me ridiculous" (*A*, 73). The passage, which is doubly uncertain, of both the project to achieve moral perfection and of reason—or "something that pretended to be Reason"—as the ground for perception and judgment, suggests a darker prospect on self, revolution, body, and body politic than we are accustomed to reading in Franklin's exemplary American life.

The second part of Franklin's "History" (*A*, 76) concludes with the on-going dialectics of the Revolution represented not as a power struggle in the public sphere but as a struggle on the level of the body to disguise and quell the "natural Passion" of "*Pride*." "In reality there is perhaps no one of our natural Passions so hard to subdue as *Pride*," Franklin writes. "Disguise it, struggle with it, beat it down, stifle it, mortify it as much as one pleases, it is still alive, and will every now and then peep out and show itself" (*A*, 76). What Franklin's story suggests is not so much the origin of the modern rational self but the difficulty, the physical labor, struggle, and "violence to natural Inclination," of putting a fully rational, coherent, and virtuous self and body into place (*A*, 75). This difficulty suggests larger anxieties and misgivings about a body politic, a new government, and a New World founded on the notion of a rational and virtuous subject and citizenry. In fact, the unruliness of the body and the "natural Passion" of "*Pride*" "peep out" even in the midst of Franklin's "List of Virtues" when he writes under "HUMILITY": "Imitate Jesus and Socrates" (*A*, 68).

III. Constitution and the Public Body

Whereas the second part of Franklin's narrative focuses on personal bodily virtue, the third and longest section turns with a heightened sense of political urgency to public virtue and the social body. While this move reflects Franklin's historical turn toward what he called "public-spirited Projects" (*A*, 102) and "public Affairs" (*A*, 85) in the thirties, forties, and fifties, his emphasis on public virtue and the social body in the final sections of his narrative is also shaped by the political debates and social anxieties surrounding the creation of the Constitution of the United States and an American "Union" grounded in the constituted authority of "We the People." Franklin returned to his narrative in August 1788, a month after New York had approved the new Constitution and Congress, under the Articles of Confederation, had initiated its own dissolution by calling for national elections to be held in January 1789. He continued to work on and revise his narrative until his death in April 1790, during the very years when statesmen, the American public, and America's friends and enemies abroad vigorously contested the constitution and implementation of a new—and newly powerful—form of national republican government.[21]

For Franklin the problem of reconciling liberty and social union, self-interest and public interest, personal wealth and the commonwealth addressed by Madison especially in *The Federalist* (1787-88) was not a problem of law, of "energetic" national government, or a written Constitution but a problem of bodily constitution, of personal virtue and morality extended outward into the public sphere. As a delegate to the Constitutional Convention, which met in Philadelphia between 25 May and 17 September 1787, Franklin pressed for structures of governance that would increase rather than decrease popular representation: a plural executive; a single legislature grounded in popular rather than state representation; and no absolute executive veto over the legislature. "It is of great consequence that we should not depress the virtue and public spirit of our common people," he said, speaking against limiting suffrage to freeholders.[22]

In his speech at the close of the Convention in September 1787, Franklin confessed that he found fault with "several parts" of the Constitution, which had failed to incorporate most of his proposals regarding popular representation. An assembly of wise men, he observed, inevitably assembles "all their Prejudices, their Passions, their Errors of Opinion, their local Interests, and their selfish Views."[23] The Constitution was in effect an attempt to balance within a national body of laws the particular interests, passions, and prejudices of its framers: its flaws represented the imperfect constitutions of its framers writ large.[24] As such, the success or failure of the Constitution would depend finally not on the form of the government but on the virtue of the people: it "can only end in Despotism as other Forms have done before it," Franklin said, "when the People shall become so corrupted as to need Despotic Government, being incapable of any other" (*S*, 1140).

Although the American Revolution had been fought against tyrannical power, Franklin was less concerned during the period of the Constitutional founding with excess of corruption in the rulers than he was with excess of corruption in the people. "But, after all, much depends on the people who are to be governed," Franklin wrote of the new form of American government in May 1789. "We have been guarding against an evil that old States are most liable to, *excess of power* in the rulers; but our present danger seems to be *defect of obedience* in the subjects."[25] Franklin's anxiety about the possible corruption and "defect of obedience" in newly empowered American subjects—an anxiety that may have been prompted by Shays's rebellion in Massachusetts in 1787 and by the uprisings led by John Franklin (no relation to Benjamin) on the Pennsylvania frontier in the mid-80s in the name of popular sovereignty and "the sacred rights of mankind"—manifests itself in the heightened moral tone and emphasis on public virtue in the third part of his narrative.[26]

While Franklin signed the Constitution because he believed "a General Government necessary for us" (*S*, 1140), the narrative that he wrote and revised in the wake of the Constitutional founding continues to locate the possibility of public order and social happiness in personal and public virtue and in non-state forms of social organization from the Junto and the Library Company to the Fire Company, the American Philosophical Society, the University of Pennsylvania, and the Hospital of Philadelphia. In recounting the story of his rise from "Poverty and Obscurity" to "a State of Affluence" (*A*, 1) in the first sections of his narrative, Franklin uses the lure of riches to solicit the virtue of the masses. "[N]o Qualities were so likely to make a poor Man's Fortune as those of Probity and Integrity," Franklin writes of his "Art of Virtue" in the second part of his narrative (*A*, 75). But in the third part, Franklin stresses the importance of wealth not as an end in itself—as Weber and others have argued—but as a means of securing private and public virtue. The "Proverbial Sentences" of *Poor Richard's Almanac*, Franklin writes, were intended to inculcate "among the common People" the lesson of "Industry and Frugality, as the Means of procuring Wealth and thereby securing Virtue, it being more difficult for a Man in Want to act always honestly" (*A*, 79). It is this emphasis on wealth as a means to virtue—especially public virtue and benevolence—that shapes the final sections of Franklin's history.

By the early forties, Franklin's business had become sufficiently profitable for him to "disengage" from "private Business" and turn his attention to "public Affairs" and natural philosophy: "I flatter'd myself that, by the sufficient tho' moderate Fortune I had acquir'd, I had secur'd Leisure during the rest of my Life, for Philosophical Studies and Amusements" (*A*, 100). But, Franklin hastens to add, "the Public now considering me as a Man of Leisure, laid hold of me for their Purposes; every Part of our Civil Government, and almost at the same time, imposing some Duty upon me" (*A*, 100). This public trajectory of Franklin's life reverses the popular image of Franklin as the purveyor of the capitalist ethos of money for money's sake popularized by nineteenth-century Romantic writers and later by D. H. Lawrence, Weber, and others. Franklin's history is not finally about *the way to wealth* but about *the way to public virtue.*

In representing himself as a model of public virtue, Franklin turns in the third part of his narrative from an account of private bodily virtue as the ground of fortune to a chronological catalogue or public account of his various public projects and roles—from more local activity as Clerk of the Pennsylvania Assembly in 1736 and Postmaster of Philadelphia in 1737 to his increasingly inter-colonial and transatlantic service as representative to the Albany Congress in 1754 and representative of colonial grievances in England in 1757. The model of the temperate, virtuous, and chaste body extends outward in the final sections of Franklin's narrative to structure social space, public institutions, civic order, the body politic, and New World history. The body as enlightenment grid becomes a model for ordering urban space: "Our City," Franklin writes, was "laid out with a beautiful Regularity, the Streets large, straight, and crossing each other at right Angles" (*A*, 104). The goal of personal enlightenment manifests itself publicly and materially in what Franklin calls "the Idea of enlightening all the City" by placing lamps on city streets (*A*, 105). And the private virtues of "ORDER" and "CLEANLINESS" have their public counterpart in Franklin's battle with the mud, dust, dirt, and mire of city streets—his efforts literally to clean up people, houses, goods, and the marketplace through a subscription campaign for "the Cleanliness of the Pavement that surrounded the Market" and "a Bill for Paving the City" (*A*, 105). This desire to rid the city of dirt and excrement is accompanied by a similar impulse to clean up, order, and regulate the mass body through the creation of public institutions for the instruction, management, correction, and "Cure" of the body (*A*, 102). Among Franklin's most successful "political Maneuvers," he remembers the founding of the Hospital of Philadelphia, "for the Reception and Cure of poor sick Persons" "free of Charge for Diet, Attendance, Advice and Medicines" (*A*, 102, 103).

It is perhaps because Franklin was more concerned with the potential excess of the public body than with particular forms of national government that he was less concerned than others about whether the colonies lived under a constitutional monarchy as part of the British empire or under a constitutional republic as part of an American nation. Along with his catalog of public projects and public service, the final sections of Franklin's history provide a detailed account of his efforts to reconcile the conflicting interests of the colony and the Pennsylvania proprietors for the general good of preserving the British empire. Commenting on the rejection of his Albany Plan of Union, which had been approved by the Albany Congress in 1754 as a plan for uniting the colonies in a form of inter-colonial governance, Franklin continues to defend its terms. The colonial Assemblies "thought there was too much *Prerogative* in it; and in England it was judg'd to have too much of the *Democratic*," Franklin writes:

> The different and contrary Reasons of dislike to my Plan, makes me suspect that it was really the true Medium; and I am still of Opinion it would have been happy for both Sides the Water if it had been adopted. The Colonies so united would have been sufficiently strong to have defended themselves; there would then have been no need of Troops from England; of course the subsequent Pretense for Taxing America, and *the bloody Contest it occasioned, would have been avoided. But such Mistakes are not new; History is full of the Errors of States and Princes*. (*A*, 110; my emphasis)

The American Revolution as a "Mistake," an "Error of States and Princes," a "bloody Contest" that might have been avoided if Franklin's Albany Plan of Union had been adopted by England and the colonies—the passage not only expresses Franklin's regret at the "bloody Contest" and break with the British empire but his possible fear of more "bloody Contest" in the aftermath of the Revolution. This fear is suggested in his narrative by the specter of the drunken and half-naked "Bodies" of the Indians on the borders of the colonies (*A*, 102) and historically by what Franklin called "our present danger"—the "defect of obedience in the subjects," which might include blacks, women, workingmen, the disaffected, and the disenfranchised, who had already begun to contest the constituted orders of white masculine authority in the same revolutionary terms that Franklin's history embodies.[27]

And yet, despite the melancholic regret of the Revolution that broods over Franklin's narrative and keeps the Revolution from ever happening as an event in his history, the final section also accentuates Franklin's increasing definition of himself and his historical body against Britain. Within the time frame of his narrative Franklin is still a loyal British subject, but the figure he represents from the vantage of the post-Revolution and the national founding is an increasingly rebellious American. Rather than reverting to the virtuous figure of the "Water-American," this nationalist Franklin constitutes himself in the image of the historical figure who arrived in France in 1776 sporting a trapper's fur cap and the public persona of the backwoods American philosopher.

Critical of the simultaneous arrogance and incompetence of British General Braddock in his disastrous march on Fort Duquesne before the French and Indian War, Franklin identifies with the "raw American Militia" and the "Savages" against what Braddock calls "the King's regular and disciplin'd Troops" (*A*, 119). "This whole Transaction," Franklin writes, "gave us Americans the first Suspicion that our exalted Ideas of the Prowess of British Regulars had not been well founded" (*A*, 120). Aligning himself with the French against the British, Franklin contrasts the oppressive and abusive behavior of Braddock, who had "plundered and stripped the Inhabitants" in his march through the "Settlements" in 1755, with the behavior of the French during the American Revolution: "How different was the Conduct of our French Friends in 1781, who during a March thro' the most inhabited Part of our Country, from Rhode Island to Virginia, near 700 Miles, occasion'd not the smallest Complaint, for the Loss of a Pig, a Chicken, or even an Apple!" (*A*, 120-21). Telescoping events of the 1750s through the lens of the 1780s, in Franklin's narrative the American Revolution had, in effect, already begun.[28]

In the brief fourth section of his narrative, which was written between November 1789 and his death on 17 April 1790, Franklin adumbrates the image of the rebellious lower class colonial Other that is imposed upon him by the Pennsylvania proprietors. When he arrives in England in 1757 as a representative of what he calls "the Good of the People" against "the Proprietary Interest" (*A*, 134), Franklin notes that after an initial unproductive meeting, Thomas Penn and the proprietaries refuse to deal with him because they consider him improper, dishonest, and "Rude" (*A*, 144). Rather than respond to Franklin's "Paper" detailing "the Heads of our Complaints in Writing," the proprietaries send a lengthy address to the Pennsylvania Assembly, "reciting my Paper, complaining of its want of Formality as a Rudeness on my part . . . adding that they should be willing to accommodate Matters, if the Assembly would send over *some Person of Candor* to treat with them for that purpose, intimating thereby that I was not such" (*A*, 144).

It is here that Franklin's narrative breaks off suddenly without a period in 1757, with Franklin being constituted in the image of the "Rude" and low class colonial American, with the on-going contest between the colonies and the British empire that would lead eventually to the bloody break with England, and with the politically charged word "Execution" (*A*, 146).

IV. Embodying Franklin

The process of constituting both Franklin and America as the low bodily Other of the British imperial imaginary was carried on historically in Franklin's famous scene in the Cockpit of the Privy Council in 1774, when he was publicly shamed by Alexander Wedderburn as the secret agent and most visible American representative of colonial rebellion. Wedderburn concludes his attack on Franklin's character by comparing him with the figure of the "bloody African" in Edward Young's popular tragedy, *The Revenge* (1721), which was modeled on Shakespeare's *Othello*: "I ask, my Lords, whether the revengeful temper attributed, by poetic fiction only, to the bloody African; is not surpassed by the coolness and apathy of the wily American?" Determined to remind Franklin in "his new self-created importance" that he is "a subject" of British "law," who "moves in a very inferior orbit," Wedderburn's personal attack, which took place only nine days after news of the Boston Tea Party reached England, suggests the ways Franklin's own body would become implicated in the contests around the American Revolution on both sides of the Atlantic.[29]

"The Life of Dr. Franklin was a Scene of continuall discipation,"

John Adams wrote of Franklin's years as an American diplomat in France.[30] It was Franklin's bodiliness and his commonness that made Adams edgy and anxious about his potentially ill effects on "the rising generation of this country."[31] "Franklin's fame was universal," Adams wrote. "His name was familiar to government and people, to kings, courtiers, nobility, clergy, and philosophers, as well as plebeians, to such a degree that there was scarcely a peasant or a citizen, a *valet de chambre*, coachman or footman, a lady's chambermaid or a scullion in a kitchen, who was not familiar with it, and who did not consider him as a friend to human kind" (*JA*, 245). For Adams, as for others in the eighteenth and early nineteenth century, Franklin embodied the American Revolution in its most radical, "democratical," populist, and leveling dimensions. "His plans and his example," Adams wrote, "were to abolish monarchy, aristocracy, and hierarchy throughout the world" (*JA*, 248).

Although Weber would later identify Franklin with the "Protestant Ethic" and the "worldly asceticism" of the capitalist spirit and D. H. Lawrence would accuse him of trying to put the mystery and "dark forest" of sex "into a barbed wire paddock," the image of Franklin as puritanical capitalist and moral prude was largely a creation of the nineteenth century, especially the Gilded Age, when Franklin began to emerge as the very emblem of the rational, disciplined, and well-managed capitalist body.[32] But while the nineteenth century would seek to clean up, domesticate, and depoliticize Franklin's image in accord with the moral and economic needs of the Age of Jackson and, in the post-Civil War period, an increasingly aggressive capitalist economy, the eighteenth century knew and feared a very different Franklin. In the words of William Cobbett writing in *The Life and Adventures of Peter Porcupine* (1796), Franklin was "a fornicator, a hypocrite, and an infidel."[33] His name and his image were associated during the Revolutionary and post-Revolutionary years with the excesses of the Revolutionary body—its passions, its commonness, its materiality, its godlessness, and its on-going acts of popular resistance. It was this unruly body—

autonomous, fleshly, ungodly, free—that Franklin's personal history simultaneously narrates, calls forth, and, like his political contemporaries, fears.

Notes

For Larry Ziff, for everything.

1. Benjamin Franklin, reprinted under the title "The Murder of a Daughter," in his *Writings*, ed. J. A. Leo Lemay (New York: Library of America, 1987), 234. Hereafter cited parenthetically in the text and abbreviated *M*.

2. *Benjamin Franklin's Autobiography*, ed. Lemay and P. M. Zall (New York: W. W. Norton and Company, 1986), 66. Hereafter cited parenthetically in the text and abbreviated *A*. During the 1730s, Franklin published several pieces on drinking in the *Pennsylvania Gazette*: "Death of a Drunk," 7 December 1732; "On Drunkenness," 1 February 1732/33; "A Meditation on a Quart Mug," 19 July 1733; and "The Drinker's Dictionary," 13 January 1736/37 (all can be found in Franklin's *Writings*, ed. Lemay). See also Robert D. Arner, "Politics and Temperance in Boston and Philadelphia: Benjamin Franklin's Journalistic Writings on Drinking and Drunkenness," in *Reappraising Benjamin Franklin: A Bicentennial Perspective*, ed. Lemay (Newark: Univ. of Delaware Press, 1993), 52-77.

3. In his influential study of the rise of the bourgeois print public sphere in America, Michael Warner argues that for Franklin and others "print—not speech—is the ideal and idealized guardian of civic liberty, as print discourse exposes corruption in its lurking holes but does so without occupying a lurking hole of its own" (*The Letters of the Republic: Publication and the Public Sphere in Eighteenth-Century America* [Cambridge: Harvard Univ. Press, 1990], 82). See also Jürgen Habermas, *The Structural Transformation of the Public Sphere: An Inquiry into a Category of Bourgeois Society*, trans. Thomas Burger (Cambridge: The MIT Press, 1991). Whereas Warner emphasizes the abstract, universalizing, and disembodying effects of print culture, I want to focus on the ways the struggle to regulate the body and public space underwrites and enables the emergence of a bourgeois public sphere and a republican print discourse of reason, liberty, and disinterested truth. If Franklin aspired to what Warner calls "print rationality" and "civic virtue" (82), it is the "lurking holes" of corruption and bodily compulsion that command his attention and ground his definitions of civic liberty, public virtue, progressive rationalism, and modern subjectivity. Moreover, while Franklin seeks to present himself as the abstract and generalizing voice of *Plain Truth*, he and the print medium were themselves frequently associated with the bodiliness and materiality of the streets, the city, commerce, the lower orders, popular

culture, and what Peter Oliver called Franklin's black "Art" of "forcing the Press often to speak the Thing that was not" (*Peter Oliver's Origin & Progress of the American Revolution*, ed. Douglass Adair and John A. Schutz [Stanford: Stanford Univ. Press, 1961], 79).

4. Lemay and Zall, in their headnote to the *Autobiography*, 257.

5. "The human body is always treated as an image of society," writes the symbolic anthropologist Mary Douglas; "there can be no natural way of considering the body that does not involve at the same time a social dimension" (*Natural Symbols: Explorations in Cosmology* [New York: Vintage Books, 1973], 70). See also Douglas, *Purity and Danger: An Analysis of the Concepts of Pollution and Taboo* (Boston: Routledge & Kegan Paul, 1966). For major studies of the socially symbolic and constructed meanings of the modern body, see Michel Foucault, *The History of Sexuality: An Introduction*, trans. Robert Hurley (New York: Vintage Books, 1990); Pierre Bourdieu, *Distinction: A Social Critique of the Judgement of Taste*, trans. Richard Nice (Cambridge: Harvard Univ. Press, 1984); Norbert Elias, *The History of Manners*, vol. 1 of his *The Civilizing Process*, trans. E. Jephcott (New York: Pantheon, 1978); and Thomas Laqueur, *Making Sex: Body and Gender from the Greeks to Freud* (Cambridge: Harvard Univ. Press, 1990).

6. On 3 January 1760, Franklin wrote to Lord Kames "that the Foundations of the future Grandeur and Stability of the British Empire, lie in America" (in *The Papers of Benjamin Franklin*, ed. Leonard W. Labaree, 34 vols. [New Haven: Yale Univ. Press, 1959-], 9:5). In a letter to the Massachusetts House Committee of Correspondence dated 15 May 1771, Franklin observed that while "one may clearly see, in the system of customs to be exacted in America by a act of Parliament, the seeds sown of a total disunion of the two countries," he still hoped that "both countries might thence much longer continue to grow great together, more secure by their united strength, and more formidable to their common enemies" (in *Papers*, 18:102, 104). It was not until he left England in March 1775 and arrived back in Philadelphia that he came to feel that a "separation" was "inevitable" (Franklin to David Hartley, 3 October 1775, in *Papers*, 22:217).

7. In *Writing in the New Nation: Prose, Print, and Politics in the Early United States* (New Haven: Yale Univ. Press, 1991), Larzer Ziff writes of the pre-Revolutionary years: "literature together with civil institutions such as church and family embodied the conditions of revolution before they were abstracted into political creeds and then embodied in political institutions" (32). For a study of transformations in family relations during the Revolutionary period, see Jay Fliegelman, *Prodigals and Pilgrims: The American Revolution Against Patriarchal Authority, 1750-1800* (New York: Cambridge Univ. Press, 1982).

8. In *The History of Sexuality*, Foucault attributes this "intensification of the body" in the mid-eighteenth century neither to the asceticism of the new work ethic and the rise of capitalism nor to the desire of the ruling classes to repress the pleasures of others but to "techniques for maximizing life" by focusing on "the body, vigor, longevity, progeniture, and descent of the classes that 'ruled'" (123).

9. Melchisédec Thévenot, *L'Art de nager* (Paris, 1696); a translation entitled *The Art of Swimming* was published in London in 1699.

10. See also Franklin's satirical proposal that American rattlesnakes be sent to the "Mother Country" in response to the British policy of exporting "Convicts" to America for "*the* IMPROVEMENT *and* WELL PEOPLING of the Colonies" (*Pennsylvania Gazette*, 9 May 1751, in *Writings*, ed. Lemay, 359-61).

11. Perhaps recognizing the ways this editorial, dated 9 October 1729, anticipated contests between the colonial Assemblies and the Crown that would lead to the American Revolution, Franklin later inserted the editorial into the first part of his *Autobiography*.

12. Franklin's printing business was formed as a partnership with Hugh Meredith in 1728. By borrowing money from friends, he was able to buy out Meredith in 1730 and set up on his own.

13. Franklin's pamphlet *A Modest Enquiry into the Nature and Necessity of a Paper-Currency* was published anonymously on 3 April 1729. His editorial on the "Contest" between Governor Burnet and the Massachusetts Assembly over the "mutual Dependence between the *Governor* and *the Governed*" appeared in the *Pennsylvania Gazette* on 9 October 1729.

14. Franklin looked upon religion as socially useful rather than true. See, for example, "Reasons Against Satirizing Religion" (1757), in which he argues that "weak and ignorant Men and Women . . . have need of the Motives of Religion to restrain them from Vice, to support their Virtue, and retain them in the Practice of it till it becomes *habitual*, which is the great Point for its Security" (in *Writings*, ed. Lemay, 748).

15. See also Franklin's letter in the form of an essay entitled "Old Mistresses' Apologue" (1745), in which he advises a young man to marry as a means of regulating the violence of sexual desire: "I know of no Medicine fit to diminish the violent natural Inclinations you mention," Franklin writes; "Marriage is the proper Remedy. It is the most natural State of Man" (in *Papers*, 3:30).

16. For an eloquent analysis of Franklin's textual deferral and containment of the Revolution in the *Autobiography*, see Christopher Looby, *Voicing America: Language, Literary Form, and the Origins of the United States* (Chicago: Univ. of Chicago Press, 1996), 99-144.

17. "Enlightenment is totalitarianism," write Max Horkheimer and Theodor W. Adorno in *Dialectic of Enlightenment* (trans. John Cumming [New York: Continuum, 1995], 6). See also Michel Foucault's classic study of the politics of discipline and incarceration in *Discipline and Punish: The Birth of the Prison* (trans. Alan Sheridan [New York: Vintage Books, 1979]).

18. Max Weber, *The Protestant Ethic and the Spirit of Capitalism*, trans. Talcott Parsons (London: Allen & Unwin, 1930), 48.

19. There is no extant copy of this moral account book among Franklin's papers. According to Lemay and Zall, Pierre J. G. Cabanis testified that Franklin had his "little Book" with him in France (*A*, 70 n. 3). In a footnote to his early nineteenth-century edition of Franklin's narrative, William Temple Franklin, Franklin's grandson, claimed that he had a copy of Franklin's book, dated 1 July 1733, in his possession (*Memoirs of the Life and Writings of Benjamin Franklin*, 6 vols. [London: Henry Colburn, 1817-18], 1:131n). However, no further record of Franklin's "little Book" exists except in his account of his life.

20. "Frugality is an enriching Virtue; a Virtue I never could acquire in myself," Franklin wrote from France on 24 June 1782 (Franklin to Miss Alexander, in *Writings of Benjamin Franklin*, ed. Albert Henry Smyth, 10 vols. [New York: 1905-07], 8:459). According to his biographer, Carl Van Doren, Franklin lived lavishly at his residence in Passy, where he had nine servants and a cellar stocked with some 1200 bottles of wine and rum (*Benjamin Franklin* [New York: Penguin Books, 1991], 636-37). He also carried on amorous, though probably never consummated, affairs with several French women, including most notably Madame Brillon and Madame Helvétius. See Claude-Anne Lopez, *Mon Cher Papa: Franklin and the Ladies of Paris* (New Haven: Yale Univ. Press, 1966).

21. In *The Federalist* (1787-88), Alexander Hamilton, James Madison, and John Jay defend the new Constitution as the only means of preserving "the UNION" against "Dangers from Foreign Force and Influence," "Dangers from War Between the States," and "Domestic Faction and Insurrection" (in Hamilton, Madison, and Jay, *The Federalist Papers* [New York: The New American Library, 1961]). Others, like Thomas Jefferson, looked upon the Constitution's lack of a Bill of Rights as an ominous sign for the direction of the country. When Richard Henry Lee proposed that a Bill of Rights be inserted, his proposal was defeated by what he called "a coalition of monarchy men, military men, aristocrats and drones whose noise, impudence and zeal exceeds all belief" (quoted in John M. Blum, Edmund S. Morgan, and others, *The National Experience: A History of the United States to 1877* [New York: Harcourt Brace Jovanovich, Inc., 1981], 135). These debates became even more heated with the outbreak of the French Revolution on 14 July 1789. For a discussion of the attempt to undo the more radical effects of the American Revolution during the period of the Constitutional founding, see Gordon S. Wood, *The Creation of the American Republic, 1776-1787* (Chapel Hill: The Univ. of North Carolina Press, 1969), 430-564. See also Stanley Elkins and Eric McKitrick, *The Age of Federalism* (New York: Oxford Univ. Press, 1993).

22. *The Records of the Convention of 1787*, rev. ed., ed. Max Farrand, 4 vols. (New Haven: Yale Univ. Press, 1986), 2:204. See also Franklin's opposition to conservative revisions in the Pennsylvania constitution, which was the most democratic to come out of the American Revolution. Writing against a proposal to create a bicameral legislature with an Upper House representing "Property" and a Lower House representing the "Population," Franklin asked: "Why is this Power of Controul, contrary to the spirit of all democracies, to be vested in a Minority, instead of a Majority?" In fact, "why is Property to be represented at all?" "Private Property," Franklin wrote, "is a Creature of Society, and is subject to the Calls of that Society, whenever its Necessities shall require it, even to its last Farthing." Reaffirming a populist definition of American rights and liberties, Franklin asserts: "the important ends of Civil Society, and the personal Securities of Life and Liberty, these remain the same in every Member of the society; and the poorest continues to have an equal Claim to them with the most opulent, whatever Difference Time, Chance, or Industry may occasion in their Circumstances" ("Queries and Remarks Respecting Alterations in the Constitution of Pennsylvania," in *Writings*, ed. Smyth, 10:58-60).

23. Franklin, "Speech in the Convention at the Conclusion of its Deliberations," in *Writings*, ed. Lemay, 1140. Hereafter cited parenthetically in the text and abbreviated *S.*

24. The new government was like a game of chance, Franklin wrote to Dupont de Nemours on 9 June 1788, shortly before the Constitution had been approved: "The players of our game are so many, their ideas so different, their prejudices so strong and so various, and their particular interests, independent of the general, seeming so opposite, that not a move can be made that is not contested; the numerous objections confound the understanding; the wisest must agree to some unreasonable things, that reasonable ones of more consequence may be obtained; and thus chance has its share in many of the determinations, so that the play is more like *tric-trac* with a box of dice" (in *Writings*, ed. Smyth, 9:659).

25. Franklin to Charles Carroll, 25 May 1789, in *Writings*, ed. Smyth, 10:7.

26. For a discussion of the contests over western lands surrounding John Franklin's resistance and eventual arrest see Van Doren, 756-59.

27. During the Revolution, Franklin's daughter, Sarah Bache, was actively involved in efforts to extend the meanings of political engagement for women. Although Franklin continued to press for eliminating property as a requirement for suffrage on both the state and the national level, for him, as for other revolutionary founders, the common people meant white men. In the years before his death, he appears to have felt the historical urgency of addressing the glaring social contradiction of slavery that had been left unresolved in the Constitution. One of his last public acts before he died was to sign a memorial to Congress for the abolition of slavery. When Congress refused to rule on the question of slavery, Franklin wrote his fierce parody in defense of Christian enslavement, *Sidi Mehemet Ibrahim on the Slave Trade*, which was published under the name "Historicus" in the *Federal Gazette* on 25 March 1790, only a month before his death.

28. During the Revolutionary years, Franklin became increasingly angered by the superior attitude of the British to American colonial subjects. At the time of the Stamp Act crisis he wrote to Lord Kames: "Every Man in England seems to consider himself as a Piece of a Sovereign over America; seems to jostle himself into the Throne with the King, and talks of *OUR subjects in the Colonies*" (25 February 1767, in *Papers*, 14:65). When Lord Howe suggested the possibility of pardoning the Americans for their offenses following the Declaration of Independence on 4 July 1776, Franklin responded: "Directing Pardons to be offered to the Colonies, who are the very Parties injured, expresses indeed that Opinion of our Ignorance, Baseness, and Insensibility which your uninform'd and proud Nation has long been pleased to entertain of us" (Franklin to Lord Howe, 30 July 1776, in *Papers*, 22:518).

29. "Wedderburn's Speech Before the Privy Council," 29 January 1774, reprinted in Franklin, *Papers*, 21:50, 59.

30. "Autobiography of John Adams, Part II" (1806), entry dated 27 May 1778, in *The Diary and Autobiography of John Adams*, ed. L. H. Butterfield, 4 vols. (Cambridge: Belknap Press of Harvard Univ. Press, 1961), 4:118.

31. John Adams, *The Boston Patriot*, 15 May 1811, reprinted in *A*, 244. Hereafter cited parenthetically in the text and abbreviated *JA*.

32. Weber, 196n; D. H. Lawrence, *Studies in Classic American Literature* (1923; rpt. New York: The Viking Press, 1964), 19. Within an increasingly bourgeois order committed to sexual monogamy and sex for reproduction or not at all, even Franklin's

definition of "Chastity"—"Rarely use Venery but for Health or Offspring"—had to be suppressed when Jared Sparks published his edition of Franklin's narrative in 1840 (see *The Works of Benjamin Franklin*, ed. Jared Sparks, 10 vols. [Boston: Hilliard, Gray & Co., 1836-40], 1:107). In the nineteenth and early twentieth century, Franklin's "Old Mistresses' Apologue" (more commonly known as "Advice to a Young Man on the Choice of a Mistress"), in which he details the sexual advantages of older over younger women, was regarded as so "indecent" (Labaree, headnote, in *Papers*, 3:29) that the State Department kept it under lock and key after the United States government purchased Franklin's papers in 1882. According to the editors of Franklin's *Papers*, "no nineteenth century editor or biographer . . . dared to print it" (Labaree, headnote, 3:29). See also Louis B. Wright, "Franklin's Legacy to the Gilded Age," *Virginia Quarterly Review* 22 (1946): 268-79.

33. William Cobbett, cited in Richard D. Miles, "The American Image of Benjamin Franklin," *American Quarterly* 9 (Summer 1957): 121. According to Miles, this characterization of Franklin was "reprinted and handed around in the little circle of hostility which survived Franklin in Philadelphia" (121). Later in the work of Van Wyck Brooks and others, Franklin would come to define the very essence of the "Low Brow," the non-literary, and the anti-aesthetic whose work could only enter the transcendent realm of American literature by being attached to the "High Brow" of Jonathan Edwards through the figure of Emerson. As Brooks writes, Emerson "perfectly combined the temperaments of Jonathan Edwards and Benjamin Franklin;—the upper and the lower levels of the American mind are fused in him and each becomes the sanction of the other" (*America's Coming of Age* [New York: B. W. Huebsch, 1915], 80).

Feeling or Fooling in Benjamin Franklin's "The Elysian Fields"

A. Owen Aldridge

One of Franklin's short works, usually known as "The Elysian Fields," has long been read as an example of the author's characteristic wit. It is an imaginary "dialogue of the dead," a favorite satirical literary form of the eighteenth century, addressed to the learned Anne Catherine Helvétius. In this text, though, lies a tantalizing biographical conundrum: Franklin proposes an erotic attachment. Was he serious? And how can we hope to know?

A. Owen Aldridge explains that, throughout the first two-thirds of the twentieth century, a style of interpretation known as the New Criticism reigned in the English departments of American universities, in which it was almost an article of faith that biography was off-limits to literary critics. New Critical interpretations were focused on the words of the text itself, without regard for context. Aldridge, however, is not convinced that such interpretation is the best way to approach this critical conundrum. His essay therefore provides both careful close reading and a thorough consideration of biographical contexts. After sorting through all the evidence, he concludes "that the work plainly solicits either a sexual liaison or a marriage"—and, more to the point, that the "bagatelle" (a playful but trivial literary performance) is much more than "a piece of light flirtation." The essay ends up being a consideration of the way different schools of interpretation can reach different conclusions about the same text. — J.L.

One of the best known of Franklin's writings in a lighthearted vein belongs to the somewhat anomalous classical literary genre of the Dialogues of the Dead. No copy of the original manuscript exists, but when published in Melchior Grimm's *Correspondance littéraire* in June 1780, it was entitled merely "Lettre de M. Franklin à Madame Helvétius." Later editors have given it a title referring to its classical background,

"The Elysian Fields," and have classified it among several other pieces as a "bagatelle." Belonging to a group of exercises Franklin wrote in French as a means of improving his ability in the use of that language, his accomplishment aroused sufficient pride for him to print it on his private press and probably to contrive at having it reprinted and circulated by Grimm immediately after its composition. It has since been widely regarded as a worthy sample of Franklin's wit and humor.

Madame Anne Catherine Helvétius, widow of the celebrated philosopher, was Franklin's neighbor in Paris, and they became close friends and frequent visitors at each other's dwelling. Franklin's letter ends with an unmistakably frank entreaty for her to become either his wife or his mistress. The only ambiguity confronting historical scholars, literary critics, or general readers is deciding whether he was serious in making his liaison-proposal or writing merely for their common amusement. Most modern interpretations, under the influence of American New Criticism of the first half of the twentieth century, which bases literary judgments on textual rather than on biographical evidence, have suggested that Franklin was playing a game. But textual evidence taken by itself equally supports the opposite conclusion that he was sending a serious message—offering either marriage or sex for pleasure. Consideration of the cultural background and Franklin's personality makes the latter conclusion almost mandatory.

The editors of the Franklin *Papers* at Yale University give scant background evidence concerning this significant biographical document, significant even though classified under the category of a bagatelle, and, therefore, they do not attempt to decide whether Franklin was merely indulging in fanciful play-acting or attempting to promote an amorous relationship. They ask, however, whether the work was "a genuine proposal of marriage" or "nothing more than a piece of light flirtation" (Franklin 31: 322-27). Both a reexamination of the text itself and a reconsideration of the biographical and historical background lead to the conclusion that Franklin was sending a serious message even though utilizing a lighthearted instrument to do so.

Since Franklin's epistle to Mme. Helvétius is well known and readily available, I shall make my summary brief. One night after she has refused an offer of marriage from Franklin out of loyalty to her deceased husband, Franklin dreams that he is in the Elysian Fields. When asked if he wishes to see there anyone in particular, he mentions philosophers and is told that Socrates and Helvétius live close by. Franklin opts for Helvétius, whom he had previously admired but never met. Helvétius treats him with great courtesy, indicating that his reputation had preceded him, and then unleashes a barrage of questions concerning contemporary conditions in France. When Franklin expresses surprise that Helvétius has not inquired about his widow and volunteers the information that she still loves him and for that reason has refused several offers of marriage, including one from Franklin himself, Helvétius replies that for many years he had also regretted the absence of his late spouse, but had finally decided that in order to console himself he had taken another wife, who loves him infinitely and seeks only to give him pleasure. After Franklin is given some words of advice on how he should continue his courtship, the new Mme. Helvétius enters and Franklin immediately recognizes her as his former American wife. He attempts to reclaim her as his "Euridice," but she coldly replies that she had been faithful to him for nearly 50 years, but has now formed a new connection that will last an eternity. Franklin, annoyed by this refusal, returns to the world of the sun and the actual Mme. Helvétius.

It has not been previously noticed that Franklin's bagatelle mixes classical myths, confusing two quite separate supernatural worlds. In his introductory sentences, Franklin dreams that he has ascended to the Elysian Fields, but in his concluding ones he describes Mrs. Franklin as his "Euridice." The original Elysian Fields, which appeared in literature in Homer's *Odyssey*, represent a paradise inhabited by the distinguished or the good. Eurydice, however, did not go to the Elysian Fields, but crossed the River Styx to Hades, the underworld. Her lover, Orpheus, while seeking her, is given permission to take her back to earth provided that he does so without looking back, but he fails to adhere to this condition and she vanishes forever. Franklin reinforces this reference to the nether world by indicating that he is leaving Mrs. Franklin to return to the good world and see once more the sun. In the classical legend established by Virgil, it is the male, Orpheus, who is responsible for the permanent separation; in Franklin's version it is the female, Euridice.

The fundamental meaning of Franklin's bagatelle depends in great measure on the interpretation of the last three words in the original French version: "Me voici, Vengeons." If the closing verb is translated as simply the noun "Revenge!" as in *Mon Cher Papa* by Claude-Anne Lopez, one of the editors of the *Papers*, the letter can be considered as merely a playful gesture (Lopez 267). But if it is translated in the imperative mood, that of the original French, it means "Let us revenge ourselves" or "Let us get our revenge." The letter must then of necessity be regarded as containing a realistic proposition.

The editors of the Franklin *Papers* lean to the hypothesis that the work is "nothing more than a piece of light flirtation" on the basis of an article by Dorothy Medlin that discredits "the long-accepted theory that Franklin and Turgot were serious rivals for the widow's hand, and that Mme. Helvétius fled to the countryside in June, 1780, to escape the Doctor's [Franklin's] persistent proposals" (Medlin 42-58). Medlin's article thoroughly refutes the theory of Turgot's involvement, but it offers no additional evidence whatsoever concerning Franklin's motivation in writing. His actual letter, moreover, begins with the clear assertion that he has already made a formal marriage proposal. The editors seem to reason that if Mme. Helvétius had really been driven away, the soliciting would have been serious, but since she remained at home, it could be considered as harmless play. Logically, however, the discovery that she had not been driven away does nothing to promote this hypothesis. The possibility of serious intention is not in the least weakened.

Essentially, no more fundamental knowledge about Franklin's basic motivations has emerged from Franklin's day to the present. Those most closely involved in the episode, the members of Franklin's closely knit household in Paris, amused themselves by passing around his letter and other suggestive proposals as though parts of a Samuel Richardson-type epistolary novel. The majority of twentieth-century commentators, like the editors of the *Papers*, have interpreted these missives as some kind of harmless game. More recently, however, some critics have regarded the work as an erotic message, whether intended to bring about a marriage or merely a casual liaison. This interpretation is founded upon Franklin's personality and previous history. A French scholar, Daniel Royot, has published a percipient article on humor and sex in Franklin's writings in which he observes that his "Old Mistresses' Apologue" and "Polly Baker," on the one hand, and Madame Brillon and Madame Helvétius, on the other, bear witness to an interplay of hard-core and soft-core evocations (Royot, "Long Live," 308). He interprets "The Elysian Fields" as "playfully provocative," comprising an invitation to "wife-swapping," and reflecting "a style of mental masturbation unfamiliar to sophisticated libertines for whom connubial faithfulness to the living or the dead was not a major concern" (312). Royot also points out that "*bagatelle*" originally meant "libertinage" or "love-making" (308) and that the phrase "à la papa," widely used in Franklin's day, meant "the missionary position." This French scholar offers no precise interpretation of Franklin's motivation in "The Elysian Fields," however, other than the general reflection that he obtained great personal satisfaction from the libertine atmosphere of aristocratic French society.

For a balanced opinion on the matter, the personal character and reputation of the two principal figures must be taken into consideration. Franklin throughout his entire life revealed a sexual preoccupation and activity extending considerably beyond the bonds of marriage. Previous discussants have overlooked the circumstance that during his residence in London, long before meeting Mme. Helvétius and while his own wife was still alive, he had entertained the prospect of entering into a marriage made possible by the death of the wife of an acquaintance. In his *The Craven Street Gazette*, a parody of a newspaper gossip column written for the amusement of the daughter of his London landlady, Franklin reports that he had been informed by one of his gentleman friends that "an amiable and delectable companion whose friendship they shared in common . . . had made a vow to marry absolutely him of the two whose wife should first depart this life" (Franklin 17: 233). Franklin and his friend experienced various and similar mental agitations: "Vanity at the preference given them over the rest of mankind; affection to their present wives, fear of losing them, hope, if they must lose them, to obtain the proposed comfort; jealousy of each other in case both wives should die together." In his memoirs, moreover, Franklin reveals several illicit sexual contacts, and he is known to have fathered an illegitimate son, who in turn had an illegitimate son. The latter accompanied Franklin to Paris, where he followed this example of his progenitors. The most barren period in Franklin's biography, that of the London years between 1757 and 1775, has revealed very little concerning his social life. It his known, however, that during the 1770s, Franklin became a close friend of Sir Francis Dashwood, frequently visiting the latter's country estate at Medmenham, home of a notorious secret society labeled the Hell Fire Club. Along with prostitutes and other female visitors, the members engaged in community sex and heavy drinking. Their excesses inspired a couplet by the contemporary poet Charles Churchill that provides an idea of the ambiance Franklin there encountered:

> Whilst womanhood, in habit of a nun,
> At Mednam lies, by backward monks undone.
> (Aldridge, *Nature's God*, 167-68)

This background certainly does not prove that Franklin ever sought or obtained sexual relations of one kind or another, but neither does it support the theory that his two epistolary proposals were designed as merely vicarious stimulants. When Franklin wrote his bagatelle to Mme. Helvétius, he was 74 years old, an age at which many men retain their active sexual powers. Franklin's delight in all aspects of feminine companionship showed no signs of decreasing when he entered the atmosphere of French enlightenment society. His earlier work "Old Mistresses' Apologue," moreover, specifically itemizes reasons for having sex with elderly women.

The probable attitude of Mme. Helvétius toward Franklin's invitation also needs to be considered realistically. During the period when it was generally believed that she had temporarily abandoned her residence in order to escape from Franklin's ardor, there may have been some warrant in portraying her as either a sexual tease or a superannuated bluestocking, but now that it has been shown that such a flight did not take place, these hypotheses can no longer be admitted. Eyewitness accounts from John Adams and his wife, Abigail, indicate that Mme. Helvétius not only accepted but encouraged Franklin's attention. Nearly all of the critics who treat "The Elysian Fields" quote Abigail's scandalized reaction to her appearance and her behavior toward Franklin, but few, if any, have cited John Adams's related comments on her way of life. According to Abigail, when Franklin entered the room, Mme. Helvétius kissed him twice on each cheek and once on the forehead, and at table locked her hand into Franklin's and threw her arm carelessly about his neck. After dinner she reclined upon a settee, showing "more than her feet" (Adams, *Family Correspondence*, 5: 436-37). Royot comments that this description places her "in the prurient posture of an odalisque surrounded by depraved young abbots" ("Long Live" 312). Abigail closes her letter, moreover, with a joke, omitted in most citations, comparing Franklin to the biblical King David as not averse to the latter's example, "for if embraces will tend to prolong his life and promote the vigor of his circulation, he is in fair way to live the age of an antediluvian." John Adams wrote in his autobiography that after Mme. Helvétius became a widow there were "three or four handsome Abby's who daily visited the House and one at least resided there, so that she might not be "without the Society of Gentlemen." He continues, "These Ecclesiasticks, . . . I suppose have as much power to Pardon a Sin as they have to commit one" (*Diary* 4: 58). Here Adams anticipates Royot's phrase concerning "an odalisque surrounded by depraved young abbots." In another passage Adams suggests that Franklin did not limit his amorous attentions to Mme. Helvétius. "At the age of seventy odd," having "neither lost his love of Beauty nor his taste for it," he "called Mademoiselle [*sic*] De Passy his favourite and his flame and his Love and his Mistress, which flattered the Family and did not displease the young Lady." After she married a certain Marquis de Tonnerre, another lady of the circle cried out in Franklin's presence, "Helas! Tous les Conducteurs de Monsieur Franklin, n'ont pas pu empeche le Tonnere de tomber sur Mademoiselle de Passi." [Alas! All the lightning rods of Monsieur Franklin have not prevented the Marquis of Thunder from descending upon Miss Passy] (*Diary* 4: 64).

Related evidence exists in a letter of John Adams on Franklin's womanizing in France in which he remarks, "You may depend on this, the moment an American minister gives a loose to his passion for women, that moment he is undone." Claude-Anne Lopez quotes this letter in an article that has nothing to do with Mme. Helvétius. In a footnote she expresses her personal opinion that Adams was here describing Franklin's sexual urge: "Considering that Franklin was seventy-seven when this passage was written, it betrays at least a grudging admiration of his enduring powers" ("Was Franklin" 149, 152 n. 22).

Franklin in one of his other missives to Mme. Helvétius has the flies in her bedroom suggestively reporting, "nous avons consommés gaiement nos petits Amours sous son Nez" [We have gaily consummated our little loves under her nose] (Lopez, *Mon Cher*, 262). After returning to the United States, he wrote to her affirming that he was "awaiting the celestial kiss which I firmly hope to give you one day." This proclamation was characterized by Pierre Cabanis, one of Franklin's younger associates in Paris, as his "swan song" (Aldridge, *Franklin and His French*, 210).

Although no infallible interpretation of Franklin's psychological goals in "The Elysian Fields" can ever be realized, the preceding evidence demonstrates that the work plainly solicits either a sexual liaison or a marriage and that Franklin would have been delighted to have either one. But whether he hoped to gain either erotic or marital success, his letter to Mme. Helvétius has considerably more vigor and substance than that associated with "a piece of light flirtation." In the absence of more conclusive evidence, it should at least be denominated a well-meant plea for reciprocal endearment, if not a sincere invitation to elderly lovemaking.

Works Cited

Adams, John. *Adams Family Correspondence*. Vol. 5. Ed. Richard A. Ryerson. Cambridge, Mass.: Harvard Univ. Press, 1933.

___________. *Diary and Autobiography*. Vol. 4. Ed. L. H. Butterfield. Cambridge, Mass.: Harvard Univ. Press, 1961.

Aldridge, A. Owen. *Benjamin Franklin and Nature's God*. Durham, N.C.: Duke Univ. Press, 1967.

___________. *Franklin and His French Contemporaries*. New York: New York Univ. Press, 1957

Franklin, Benjamin. *The Papers of Benjamin Franklin*. Vol. 17. Ed. W. B. Willcox. New Haven: Yale Univ. Press, 1973.

___________. *The Papers of Benjamin Franklin*. Vol. 31. Ed. Barbara B. Oberg. New Haven: Yale Univ. Press, 1995.

Lopez, Claude-Anne. *Mon Cher Papa: Franklin and the Ladies of Paris*. New Haven: Yale Univ. Press, 1966.

___________. "Was Franklin Too French?" *Reappraising Benjamin Franklin*. Ed. J. A. Leo Lemay. Newark: Univ. of Delaware Press, 1993.

Medlin, Dorothy. "Benjamin Franklin's Bagatelles for Madame Helvétius." *Early American Literature* 15 (1980): 42-58.

Royot, Daniel. "Benjamin Franklin as Founding Father of American Humor." *Reappraising Benjamin Franklin*. Ed. J. A. Leo Lemay. Newark: Univ. of Delaware Press, 1993.

___________. "Long Live *La Différence*: Humor and Sex in Franklin's Writings." *Finding Colonial America: Essays Honoring J. A. Leo Lemay*. Ed. Carla Mulford and David S. Shields. Newark: Univ. of Delaware Press, 2001.

Benjamin Franklin's *Autobiography* and the Credibility of Personality

Jennifer Jordan Baker

Jennifer Jordan Baker, one of the most learned and penetrating scholars of early American literature writing today, illuminates an aspect of Franklin's writing that has too often been neglected. She argues that it is impossible to make sense of Franklin's world without an understanding of the economic situation his country faced.

Baker's reading of Franklin's credit and his credibility looks at the way he fashions his personal identity against the background of an incipient country trying to establish its own national identity. She puts it well: "As both a tale of his own rise to wealth and social prominence as well as a more speculative archetype of the success *other* Americans might achieve, the *Autobiography* ultimately operates as a financial instrument—a national letter of credit endorsed by Franklin himself—that attests to the economic promise of America." — J.L.

After reading the first installment of Benjamin Franklin's memoirs, Benjamin Vaughan concluded that his friend's life story would offer a fitting paradigm of American upward social mobility. "All that has happened to you," he wrote to Franklin in 1783, is "connected with the detail of the manners and situation of a *rising* people" (*Autobiography* 59). Vaughan's insistence that Franklin's was a prototypical story of success and self-making suggested that the memoir was representative of the American experience. While the limitations of this prototype are clear to the modern reader—Vaughan spoke specifically of a "rising people" of Euro-American males with access to economic opportunities not available to others—critics have recognized nonetheless a presumption of representativeness in this text. In the words of Mitchell Breitwieser, Franklin "aspires to representative personal universality," creating a rhetorical personality by cultivating "characteristics he felt were in accord with what the age demanded" (Breitwieser 171). Franklin's *Autobiogra-*

phy, according to William Spengemann, attempts to "represent the conclusions of his experience as being universally true and hence applicable to every life, rather than peculiar to his own case" (55).[1]

Recent criticism especially has located this concept of representativeness in the economic and political culture of early America. Michael Warner has maintained that Franklin effaces the particularities of his own personality in order to achieve a "republican impartiality"—refuting his own personal authority and embodying, through writing, the legitimacy of a public statesman. Grantland Rice argues that Franklin, by producing and circulating written representations of himself, suppresses the idiosyncrasies of his personality in favor of a disembodied self constituted in print; this "objectified self" (realized in letters, public proposals, treatises, newspaper articles, and, of course, the autobiography itself) takes its cues, he emphasizes, from a burgeoning capitalist economy in which the exchange of goods and money replaces interpersonal relationships.

A different concept of representativeness, I would argue, is at work in this text. In the third section of the *Autobiography*, Franklin recalls that, upon his retirement from the printing business, he repeatedly lent his own name to governmental financial schemes and projects for public improvement. His memoir, by implication, is one of those projects that bears this valuable endorsement. As both a tale of his own rise to wealth and social prominence as well as a more speculative archetype of the success *other* Americans might achieve, the *Autobiography* ultimately operates as a financial instrument—a national letter of credit endorsed by Franklin himself—that attests to the economic promise of America. As with the later public projects that depend upon the visibility, rather than the effacement, of Franklin's name, the efficacy of this national voucher derives from his personal authority. In this sense, the *Autobiography* is representative not as a generic tale of an ordinary American experience but rather as a story of *exemplary* success that uses Franklin's experience to advocate, like a celebrity endorsement, the possibilities of American life.

This representativeness, in fact, takes as its model a philosophy of public credit through which prominent individuals might help ensure the strength of governmental credibility. According to a notion that circulated during the colonial era and later during Alexander Hamilton's tenure as treasury secretary, governmental credit instruments, though technically vouchers for civic fiscal reliability, might be supported by individuals willing to sign instruments and thus lend their names for public credit (I speak of this *theory* of patronage because, in practice, such support was not necessarily successful in countering economic downturns). In the *Autobiography*, an elder Franklin uses his name to support paper financial instruments, and this model applies to his endorsement of all public projects. Having established himself as financial representative, moreover, Franklin encourages the reader to read his *Autobiography* with a speculative spirit. Through early tales of his own rise by means of credit, Franklin emphasizes how vital it is for creditors to support fledgling entrepreneurs; and so these stories illustrate, by implication, the importance of the reader's willingness to credit Franklin's representation of the American experience.

While Franklin does, in the earlier phases of his career, create and exploit an abstract, generalized persona for his own advancement, once he achieves civic prominence, the success of his endorsements ultimately depends upon the particularities of his experience. This is not to say that the later, more visible incarnation is any less a rhetorical persona but rather that it is different in that it trades on Franklin's name. It must, like a bill of credit, assume a measure of personal authority in order to work effectively. Franklin's individual credibility, in other words, enhances the credibility of America.

Franklin drew a figural relation between his own biography and that of the nation; according to Christopher Looby, he rehearses in the story of his own life "both the past and the (predicated) future of America" (Looby 110). Franklin wrote the four parts of the *Autobiography* over the two decades from 1771 to 1790, and the maturation and independence chronicled in the text parallels America's own coming of age. To this thinking I would add that there is, in particular, an analogy drawn between Franklin's own rise on credit as a budding entrepreneur in the first half of the text and the enterprising use of public credit for funding community development in the second half. With this shift, Franklin's role changes: in the first two installments of the memoir, he relies on the willingness of patrons to grant him credit; in the third and fourth parts, Franklin, having benefited from those who invested in him when he was young, lends his patronage to fledgling public projects.

Franklin signals the fact that the *Autobiography* itself is such a project in the opening of part 2, where he inserts personal letters from Abel James and Vaughan, written in 1782 and 1784, respectively. These letters reinforce Franklin's narrative transition from familial letter (an epistle to his son, William) to a document "intended for the public" (57). In particular, the letters emphasize that his memoir itself is a public project that could benefit the new nation. Vaughan's letter, for example, predicts that Franklin's story will not only promote desirable qualities in young businessmen (industry, frugality, and the patience to await one's advancement) but also "tend to invite to [America] settlers of virtuous and manly minds" (59). Vaughan adds, "And considering the eagerness with which such information is sought by them, and the extent of your reputation, I do not know of a more efficacious advertisement than your Biography would give" (59). While Vaughan claims that the *Autobiography* is representative in the sense of being typical of—or "connected to"—the "rising people" of America, his very term "advertisement" suggests another process at work: the publicizing of an extraordinary story designed to arouse desire and patronage. Vaughan's letter identifies the memoir's potential to boost economic confidence and to promote America in the eyes of prospective immigrants; moreover, the letter serves as a fitting prelude to the more publicly oriented sections of the *Autobiography*, in which Franklin—as a protagonist within the narrative and as author of the autobiographical advertisement—works to promote civic ventures.

In part 3, these activities as civic spokesman begin to differ markedly from his earlier public service. In the first two sections, Franklin recalls that in his earlier years he tended to submit project proposals anonymously or under the auspices of a group so as not to arouse suspicions of his own interests: "The Objections, and Reluctances I met with in Soliciting the Subscriptions, made me soon feel the Impropriety of presenting oneself as the Proposer of any useful Project," he writes, explaining his decision to put himself "as much as [he] could out of sight" (64). This strategic self-effacement exemplifies how Franklin, as the critical tradition maintains, uses depersonalized print media to construct a universal, archetypal life. Another well-known illustration of this self-effacement, which comes about a third of the way into part 3, is Franklin's anonymous proposals for an academy. He writes, "I stated their Publication not as an Act of mine, but of some *public-spirited Gentleman*, avoiding as much as I could, according to my usual Rule, the presenting myself to the Public as the Author of any Scheme for their Benefit" (99).

Critics, however, have focused on the narration of events before Franklin's retirement from his printing business, and this conclusion is simply not applicable to the latter parts of the *Autobiography*. Shortly following his anonymous proposal for an academy, Franklin's "usual rule" changes. Five paragraphs later, Franklin recalls that once he "disengag'd" himself from "private Business," a sudden change occurred: "the Public now considering me as a Man of Leisure," he writes, "laid hold of me for their Purposes; every Part of our Civil Government, and almost at the same time, imposing some Duty upon me" (100).

In the narration of events after his retirement from printing in 1748, Franklin's service entails the public endorsement of projects, and his visible connection to such projects supposedly ensures their success; indeed, after his retirement there is no mention of the self-effacement strategies that he describes earlier. As Dr. Thomas Bond discovers when he tries to establish a hospital in Philadelphia, Franklin's name has become precious currency:

> At length he came to me, with the Compliment that he found there was no such thing as carrying a public-spirited Project through without my being concern'd in it; "for, says he, I am often ask'd by those to whom I propose Subscribing, Have you consulted Franklin upon this Business? and what does he think of it? And when I tell them that I have not, (supposing it rather out of your Line,) they do not subscribe, but say they will consider of it." (102)

Recognizing that this project will benefit from his signature, Franklin subscribes, enlists other subscriptions, petitions funds from the Pennsylvania Assembly, and even pens and publishes a signed article in its support. On account of this endorsement, according to Franklin, the plan is executed and the hospital soon erected.

While Franklin's retirement from private business may not, in fact, have marked such a clear-cut transition or satisfied those adversaries who accused him of harboring ulterior motives, the text nevertheless sets up the distinction, so crucial to classical republican ideology, between his life as a man of private interests and his life as a civic statesman. His retirement, which seemingly removes him from the business world, affords him the status of "disinterested" and enhances his reputation as civic-minded (his recollection that the public "laid hold" of him for "their purposes" after his retirement effaces his individual agency and emphasizes his status as civil servant). The social prominence he attains later in life transforms his name from a liability to an asset that can be exploited for public ends.

All of Franklin's endorsements eventually follow a model in which he uses his own prominence and credibility to vouch for a project.[2] Notable among these projects are speculative issues of paper credit instruments. In the final passage of part 4, for example, Franklin recalls using his own personal credit to prevent a catastrophic repeal of 100,000 pounds of Pennsylvania currency. By co-signing a paper assuring the assembly that the local landowners will not be hurt financially by the emission, he wins their confidence in the soundness of paper currency.

Franklin, by the reputation of his name, secures its credit. "The Assembly look'd on my entering into the first Part of the Engagement as an essential Service to the Province," he writes, "since it secur'd the Credit of the paper Money then spread over all the Country; and they gave me their Thanks in form when I return'd" (146). The *Autobiography* ends, then, with this dramatic illustration that public credit depends, in part, on the credit of Franklin himself.

This attempt to buttress public paper money with personal credit was common in Franklin's time. Bills of credit bore the signatures of reputable individuals both to safeguard against counterfeiting and to increase their acceptability (even though they were, in fact, emitted by a government and implied no liability on the part of individual signers). Prominent citizens were likewise encouraged to accept paper money so as to boost its value in the eyes of buyers and sellers (readers of Cotton Mather's *Magnalia Christi Americana* might recall that Governor William Phips is applauded for his exemplary willingness to accept Massachusetts paper money). Franklin keenly understood that individuals could obtain credibility in concrete, personalized ways that an institution or government could not. Alexander Hamilton, reflecting on the U.S. petition for French war loans during the Revolutionary war, emphasized this importance of individual credibility: "I venture to assert that the Court of France will never give half the succors to this country while Congress holds the reins of administration in their own hands," he wrote in a letter to financier Robert Morris in 1781, "which they would grant, if these were entrusted to individuals of established reputation and conspicuous for probity, abilities, and fortune" (Hamilton 342).[3] Morris, a wealthy merchant who was appointed superintendent of finance in 1781, was the best-known practitioner of this personal approach to public finance. When Morris assumed his office, one historian writes, "the government's credit was shattered . . . [but] Morris's personal credit was sound, so he placed his own reputation and credit behind his acts as superintendent" (Anderson 16).

Franklin's sense of himself as financial spokesman was shaped by his more general understanding that print media could influence public credibility and monetary value. In the *Autobiography*, he points to several instances in which his own published words operated as an economic catalyst.[4] He recalls that his "well receiv'd" 1729 pamphlet on paper currency helped convince the Pennsylvania legislature to issue more money, and this emission (in addition to landing Franklin a printing contract for the currency issue) provided much-needed financial relief for the colony's debtors (53). He also writes that the reduction of the colonial trade deficit in Pennsylvania (and, as a result, the increase in metal currency available for trade in the colony) was attributed by many to his aphorisms' sage advocacy of industry and frugality in "The Way to Wealth." He recalls, "In Pennsylvania, as [the publication] discouraged useless Expense in foreign Superfluities, some thought it had its share of Influence in producing that growing Plenty of Money which was observable for several Years after its Publication" (79).

Franklin's self-appointed role as advocate of public credit in the *Autobiography* also mirrored his role as financial spokesman during the Revolutionary era. At the time Vaughan was extolling the capacity of his friend's memoir to promote America, Franklin was carrying out just this kind of promotion as minister to France. As he resumed writing his memoirs in Passy in 1784, he had just spent years using his own name to lobby the French government for crucial war loans to the United States. During this time his primary responsibility was the maintenance of America's name abroad (complicating this task were the post-war economic woes back in the United States, as the depreciation of various paper credit instruments weakened the government's credibility at home as well). "I cannot," he wrote anxiously in a letter concerning mounting French loans, "suffer the credit of our country to be destroyed" (Letter to Jackson 275).

During the Revolutionary war itself, moreover, Franklin had played a vital role as spokesman for American credit. While the Continental Congress made the refusal of legal tender a punishable offense, Franklin, who selected the mottoes for the first series of Continental dollars in the spring of 1775, understood the importance of maximizing people's confidence in their value.[5] Recognizing that Continentals were not only a source of borrowed revenue but a medium for the circulation of revolutionary rhetoric, he saw the emission as an opportunity to influence public opinion on the war. The series of ten denominations, each bearing a distinct image and Latin text, all speak, in one way or another, to the importance of the colonial cause and the promise of the American future: "SUSTINE VEL ABSTINE" ("support or leave") presents an ultimatum for the British; "DEPRESSA RESURGIT" ("Tho' oppressed it rises") predicts American victory; and "MAJORA MINORIBUS CONSONANT" ("the greater and smaller ones sound together") envisions an American consensus akin to musical harmony.[6]

Franklin understood that precisely how readers interpreted the rhetoric of bills could affect the value of those bills and, as a result, the progress of the war.[7] In September 1775, he penned an essay for the *Pennsylvania Gazette*, "Account of the Devices on the Continental Bills of Credit," to explain their meaning to the public. The essay suggests that bill readers would help determine whether the tenor (of both the projected redemption value and the mottoes' predictions) would eventually be realized. In this essay, Franklin offers a translation of the Latin phrases, an analysis of the translation and images, and a lesson on how to read a financial instrument. He assumes an innocent point of view, claiming only to give "Conjectures of their Meaning" for the simple reason that "No Explanation of the Devices on the Continental Bills of Credit [has] yet appeared" (734); however, his interpretation is clearly calculated to inspire confidence in both the bills' promises and the war effort championed by the mottoes. In the image of a busy beaver on the six-dollar note, for instance, Franklin sees a glimpse of American perseverance and financial independence from British trade regulations (Franklin would have included the timber trade among the monopolized industries). He writes,

> Another had the figure of a *beaver* gnawing a large tree, with this motto, PERSEVERANDO; *By perseverance*. I apprehend the *great tree* may be intended to represent the enormous power Britain has assumed over us, and endeavours to enforce by arms, of taxing us at pleasure, *and binding us in all cases whatsoever*; or the exorbitant profits she makes by monopolizing our commerce. Then the *beaver*, which is known to be able, by assiduous and steady working, to fell large trees, may signify *America*, which, by perseverance in her present measures, will probably reduce that power within proper bounds, and, by establishing the most necessary manufactures among ourselves, abolish the British monopoly. ("Account" 735)

Franklin makes clear that he can only *venture* an interpretation, attempting to "apprehend" what "may be intended" by the motto's representation and what will "probably" occur in the future. Despite that he cannot speak definitively about the future, Franklin nevertheless publicly extends his credit to the Revolutionary cause and, in turn, to the credit of the bills on which the rhetoric appears. Such tentative language does not undermine the colonial cause; rather, as a speculative act of imagination in a time of crisis, the analysis demonstrates, by example, the extent to which a citizen must be willing to take risks in order to keep public credit suspended.[8]

While Franklin helped craft the rhetoric of Continental bills and then penned an essay to encourage his readers to accept that rhetoric, the *Autobiography* accomplishes both tasks at once: it functions both as a credit instrument and as instructions on how to read that instrument. Franklin's tales of his early financial entanglements, in particular, illustrate the necessity of credit for the young entrepreneur and so, by implication, encourage the reader to approach Franklin's depiction of American enterprise with a similarly speculative spirit. Though Franklin enjoys a remarkable reputation at the time he writes his memoirs, the text often works to promote faith in the applicability of Franklin's life-story to other Americans or prospective immigrants.

In keeping with the text's mission to provide a conduct manual for the young tradesman, this early fiscal history teaches two important lessons: that a certain measure of start-up debt is necessary and that patient debtors and creditors can ultimately reap reward. In part 1, Franklin himself is often the unfortunate victim of loan defaults. Collins and Ralph, both chronically drunk and insolvent, eventually renege on their obligations to Franklin. And Governor Keith, who offered to write Franklin letters of credit with which to purchase start-up materials for his printing business, strings him along with deferrals: the young Franklin is "appointed to call at different times, when [the letters] were to be ready, but a future time was still named" (31), and ultimately Keith defaults on this promise altogether.[9] Franklin, though, expresses little indignation over these incidents. Recounting his trip to London, for example, he regrets his unwise decision to lend money to Ralph but emphasizes that he "lov'd him notwithstanding" and that his time in the city allowed him to acquire instead a different sort of capital, namely advantageous conversation and personal connections (40).

Franklin's sympathetic treatment of the chronically overextended here may have much to do with the fact that he is simultaneously recollecting his own early struggles with debt: in order to lend money to Collins, he himself dipped into money he was holding for Vernon—committing what he described as "one of the first great Errata" of his life—and he too needs to defer his creditor until he can acquire the funds for repayment. It is only through indebtedness, moreover, that Franklin is able to launch himself, since Meredith's father provides the funding for Franklin's first printing business, and when this backer balks on half the amount, two friends (William Coleman and Robert Grace) come forward with assistance. Praising his first printing client, George House, as a valuable patron, Franklin recalls that "the Gratitude [he] felt towards House," made him "often more ready than perhaps [he] should otherwise have been to assist young Beginners" (47). Despite the common characterization of Franklin as a self-proclaimed self-made man, he repeatedly acknowledges that his initial success could not have been possible if financial backers and customers had not been willing to invest in him. While the *Autobiography* does, as J. A. Leo Lemay writes, record a progression from dependence to independence, Franklin never loses sight of the fact that dependence—in the form of start-up loans—is the necessary first step for the entrepreneur (Lemay 352).

The young Franklin is not an irresponsible debtor like others in the *Autobiography*, and he impresses on his reader that he went to great pains to repay every loan with interest (he even repaid his brother, he writes, with a gift of new printing type for the services lost when he broke his apprenticeship and fled to Philadelphia). In the *Autobiography*, a young man grows up, makes his fortune, and pays back his start-up loans with interest; as Franklin comes of age, then, those loans mature as well. But even despite what surely would have been disapproval of Keith's irresponsibility, Franklin nevertheless identifies with the logic of the governor's promises:

> But what shall we think of a governor's playing such pitiful Tricks, and imposing so grossly on a poor ignorant Boy! It was a Habit he had acquired. He wish'd to please everybody; and having little to give, he gave Expectations. He was otherwise an ingenious sensible Man, a pretty good Writer, and a good Governor for the People. . . . (33)

With no assets, Keith has only promises to give (he is especially lacking in assets because of his ignominious character and can only give expectations of credibility; thus, not only his letter of credit but the *promise to provide* such a letter are suspect). Franklin does not condemn Keith's promises because they are, at least, an act of resourcefulness. His very use of the word "expectations," a traditional term for the projected earnings of a financial investment, suggests that Keith's optimism and promises derive from an entrepreneurial spirit.

While Franklin's rise on credit occurred during the 1720s and 1730s, his perspective in retelling the events is that of the 1770s and 1780s, and his link between credit-use and economic expansion has much in common with late-century economic thought. Mercantilism, the national economic policy that prevailed in Europe during Franklin's coming-of-age, valued, above all, economic self-sufficiency. Precious metal was the basis of value, according to mercantilism, and the goal of national policy was the accumulation of metal bullion and a favorable balance of trade (if a nation did not possess natural metal resources, then its goal was to acquire that metal wealth through international exchange). With the decay of mercantilism in mid-century, however, a new concept of a more dynamic form of wealth emerged. Neo-classical writers on political economy, including Franklin himself, emphasized that there were other forms of value, such as labor and land, that could contribute to a nation's wealth.[10] As economic historian Robert L. Heilbroner writes, the mercantilists' initial emphasis on gold began "to look a trifle naive" as new schools of thought "emphasized *commerce* as the great source of national vitality" (40). The pressing philosophical question for the new thinkers, he writes, "was not how to corner the gold market but how to create ever more and more wealth by assisting the rising merchant class in the furtherance of its tasks" (40). By using credit—that is, by undertaking a managed measure of indebtedness—the merchant class and a nation in general could create "ever more and more wealth."

Adam Smith, with whom Franklin had intellectual correspondence, offered a compelling illustration of this resourcefulness in *The Wealth of Nations* (1776). In a critique of mercantilist banking, Smith argued that a bank need *not* maintain a one-to-one ratio between gold reserves and circulating bank-notes but rather keep on hand only enough reserves to meet redemption needs and then reinvest the rest of those reserves for additional profit. Complete solvency, he emphasized, was actually the mark of a stagnant economy and, if banks could free up metal languishing as "dead stock" in the vaults, that money could do double-duty in circulation (this concept is essentially that of modern-day banking, in which the entirety of deposits are not kept but reloaned with interest). "By substituting paper in the room of a great part of this gold and silver," Smith wrote, a nation could "convert a great part of this dead stock into active and productive stock" (Smith 341).[11]

Franklin's own entrepreneurial experience required that he find substitutes for precious metal (lacking gold type for his new printing business, for example, he ultimately devises a new type made of lead), but his most resourceful substitutions for capital are loans themselves. Of course, Franklin's resourcefulness is different from what Smith describes, for he is struggling to acquire capital rather than simply get more mileage out of it; nevertheless, he shares Smith's notion that a certain measure of indebtedness can enable an individual or nation to transcend the limits of existing capital and expand economically.

Franklin brought this understanding of economic expansion to bear on his views on colonial and national finance. Because British mercantilist policy was designed to accumulate a favorable balance of trade that would have to be settled by the shipment of specie out of the colonies, Franklin saw paper as a viable alternative to metal media that might free the colonies of their trade debt to the mother country. Britain had always prohibited the colonial governments from declaring any medium "legal tender" (legally mandating its acceptance or "currency"), and, in the minds of colonists, the mother country's attempts to regulate colonial currency, via the Currency Acts of 1740 and 1751, was proof that Britain conspired to hinder their economic growth and reduce them to financial dependence.[12] In the years leading up to the Revolution, the printing of various colonial bills became symbolic of, and instrumental in, the move for political independence, and, of course, a national Continental currency, issued to pay for soldiers' salaries and military supplies, provided much of the underwriting for the risky, but potentially profitable, venture of insurrection.[13]

As he argued in his 1729 "A Modest Enquiry into the Nature and Necessity of a Paper-Currency," an essay that anticipates classical credit theory, such credit could also help individuals transcend the limitations of their initial capital.[14] Because an increased availability of credit would drive down the interest rates and provide cheaper credit to those without capital, colonial governments—for only the additional cost of the paper on which the money would be printed—could help launch the laboring classes, attract new immigrants, and stimulate exchange and real estate development.[15] If the colonies were to draw immigrants intent on advancement, he wrote, credit would have to be readily available. The title's allusion to "necessity," referring in eighteenth-century parlance to a lack of independence, emphasizes that the instruments are not only much-needed but an inevitable indebtedness. The immigrant or upstart must first rely on creditors in order ultimately to become independent.[16]

In addition to illustrating the benefits of start-up debt for the entrepreneur, Franklin's *Autobiography* also recounts stories in which the patient investor reaps rewards, thus urging the reader to credit Franklin's autobiographical voucher for American credit. Vernon's willingness to extend the terms of Franklin's loan, for example, not only enables Franklin's eventual success but garners interest for Vernon as well. Recounting the story of Thomas Denham, Franklin reiterates this point:

> He had formerly been in business at Bristol, but fail'd in debt to a Number of people, compounded and went to America. There, by a close Application to Business as a Merchant, he acquir'd a plentiful Fortune in a few Years. Returning to England in the Ship with me, He invited his old Creditors to an Entertainment, at which he thank'd them for the easy Composition they had favor'd him with, and when they expected nothing but the Treat, every Man at the first Remove found under his Plate an Order on a Banker for the full Amount of the unpaid Remainder with Interest. (39)

The account of Denham is yet another of Franklin's archetypal success stories (even making literal the figurative immigration of Franklin's arrival in Philadelphia). Once Denham achieves his American success, the patient creditors who "favor'd him" with "easy Composition" ("composition" referring here to a mutual agreement or settlement) are duly rewarded.

Such incidents entail only personal credit granted to individuals, but, in the *Autobiography*, creditors invest in new communities as well. Recalling the "croaking" Samuel Mickle, for example, Franklin applauds his own willingness to credit his surroundings:

> This Gentleman, a Stranger to me, stopped one Day at my Door, and asked me if I was the young Man who had lately opened a new Printinghouse: Being answer'd in the Affirmative, he said he was sorry for me, because it was an expensive Undertaking & the Expense would be lost; for Philadelphia was a sinking Place, the People already half Bankrupts or near being so; all Appearances of the contrary, such as new Buildings & the Rise of Rents being to his certain Knowledge fallacious, for they were in fact among the Things that would soon ruin us. And he gave me such a Detail of Misfortunes now existing or that were soon to exist, that he left me half-melancholy. Had I known him before I engag'd in this Business, probably I never should have done it. This Man continu'd to live in this decaying place, and to declaim in the same Strain, refusing for many Years to buy a House there, because all was going to Destruction, and at last I had the Pleasure of seeing him give five times as much for one as he might have bought it for when he first began his Croaking. (47)

According to historical records, Mickle was actually a real-estate developer who bought property in the city well before 1728. If Franklin embellishes the facts, he does so to craft a lesson for the entrepreneur and especially the recent immigrant: while the pessimist ignores opportunity, Franklin extends faith to his new surroundings and ultimately profits. As noted by modern editors, the encounter with Mickle took place in 1729 shortly after Franklin established his printing business but also following a short-term depression and currency depreciation. Franklin, who was apparently lucky enough not to encounter Mickle when he first arrived in Philadelphia, managed to defer his need for instant gratification despite the fact that the city was bolstered by unsecured credit and new buildings that *for the moment* housed nothing.[17] Prefacing his story with the warning that "There are Croakers in every Country always boding its ruin" (47), this episode illustrates, by Franklin's own example, that community development depends upon patronage.

This lesson that patient speculation brings profit ultimately applies to projects endorsed by Franklin's own words and signature. In part 3, Franklin composes and prints a broadside "advertisement" soliciting military supplies and services for the French and Indian War in exchange for forthcoming metal specie (as a printed promise issued in lieu of metal money, such an advertisement operates like a war-time currency); the broadside is then accompanied by a more personal letter addressed to his "Friends and Countrymen," which encourages their support for the war: a lack of morale on the part of these creditors, Franklin emphasizes, could jeopardize the financial underpinnings of the venture. One key paragraph of the attached letter attempts to entice the impoverished reader by spelling out the potentially lucrative consequences of patient investment. It reads,

> The People of these back Countries have lately complained to the Assembly that a sufficient Currency was wanting; you have now an opportunity of receiving and dividing among you a very considerable Sum; for if the Service of this Expedition should continue (as it's more than probable it will) for 120 Days, the Hire of these Waggons and horses will amount to upwards of Thirty thousand pounds, which will be paid you in Silver and gold of the King's Money. (116)

Franklin cannot say with certainty that victory is imminent (elsewhere he even admits that he harbored doubts about Braddock's campaign); however, he articulates his own faith in the "more than probable" continuation of the expedition and, by example, encourages the support of his readers.

The description of the broadside as an "advertisement" again suggests Franklin's role as a promoter of public projects. Signed twice—

"B. FRANKLIN" on the broadside and "Your Friend and Well-wisher, B. FRANKLIN" on the letter that accompanies it—these documents attempt to procure the reader's support through the credibility of its author. Suspicions of Franklin's ulterior motives apparently still plague him, as he emphasizes at the end of his letter that he has "no particular Interest in this Affair" (117); however, he likely recognizes that in this situation his name is more apt to enhance than diminish the credibility of the scheme.

This letter is one of many endorsements, monetary and otherwise, that are embedded within a larger success story that vouches for the promise of American life: the author of the war-time advertisement is also the author of the advertisement for America. Grantland Rice also sees a parallel between Franklinian self-representation and monetary mechanisms, maintaining that "Franklin's philosophy of print bears an uncanny similarity to the fin de siècle sociologist Georg Simmel's monumental study of the philosophy of money" (Rice 60). Money, according to Simmel, standardized indebtedness, making it quantifiable, numerically discharged, and *not* a function of social biases. With the introduction of money, in other words, individuals were freed from the unpredictable, idiosyncratic dependencies of social obligations. Like the money Simmel describes, Franklin's textual self-representation frees him from subjective evaluations based on social biases, according to Rice: "interpersonal relationships are evacuated of their emotional or psychological constituents," he writes, "replaced by their objectified 'values' in terms of either currency . . . or textuality" (Rice 63).

I, too, find an "evacuation of personality" and a "recession of the corporeal writer" depicted in this text. To cite one of Rice's examples, Franklin "disguises" his handwriting and submits anonymous essays to the *New-England Courant* in order to escape the prejudices of a brother who might dismiss him on the basis of youth; adapting that strategy for civic benefit, Franklin disguises his own involvement with projects in order to ensure that biases against him do not hinder their acceptance. According to the progression of the text, however, the parallel does not obtain after Franklin's retirement, for, once he enjoys prominence in Philadelphia circles, Franklin often stands to gain from such biases.

Though the Franklinian protagonist cannot fully exploit his identity until after his retirement, the equation of personal authorization and public-spiritedness is actually evident in the first pages of recollections. Recounting his family history, Franklin recalls that his ancestor Peter Folger made a point of signing a treatise condemning religious persecution precisely because he was civic-minded: "[H]is Censures proceeded from *Goodwill*, and therefore he would be known as the Author" (5). Rice finds this brand of authorship in striking contrast to Franklin's "various dependent, feminized, and masked personae" (54). But such anonymous personae, I would argue, constitute only a portion of Franklin's self-representations, and Folger's rhetorical strategy seems quite consistent with that of the *Autobiography* overall; in fact, I interpret its inclusion as a commentary on Franklin's own authoritative strategies. Though the young Franklin (as a protagonist within the narrative) cunningly disguises his name, the *Autobiography* as a whole, composed by an elder statesman three and four decades after his retirement, does not suppress the Franklinian name.

If, as I have argued, Franklin's conception of his memoir's potential public utility is shaped by a model of individually endorsed public credit, the analogy between a credit instrument and one's life story necessarily raises problems. If the *Autobiography* is an "advertisement," it is so only in Franklin's own speculative sense of the word: such advertisements promote not things that exist and wait on the shelf to be sold but rather things (military victories, American independence, financial success) that will only materialize over time. As such, it also shares with other forms of written speculation that inevitable risk that the promise on paper cannot be upheld—that the character of Franklin or his America, like currency value, can be inflated. The Franklinian persona, clanking his wheelbarrow along the cobblestone streets well into the night in order to demonstrate industry, repeatedly reminds his readers that reputation, in an economy based on credit, is an asset in itself; but that anecdote also undermines readers' confidence in the author himself, leaving them wondering what, if anything, in this life story is not simply a written management of credit analogous to that nighttime wheelbarrowing. Moreover, if Franklin himself is not credible, his endorsement of American life becomes suspect as well.

Franklin acknowledged the unsettling effects of the imaginary nature of credit, and, with regards to monetary instruments themselves, his advocacy of enterprising reading was not unconditional. Though he praised paper money as a "great instrument," he also lamented the "evil" of depreciation that would accompany excessive and mismanaged emissions (Letter 293). Creditors could support unbacked bills, but bills would eventually, at a future time, need to be redeemable for something of value—or if they remained in circulation, they would need to retain their purchasing power. And while popular opinion could sustain the fiction that the bills were, even at the moment of their issue, worth their "proclaimed" value, severe depreciation made redemption increasingly impossible and thereby rendered even the promise of its face value a lie. Arguing for provisions to curb rapid depreciation of paper money during the French and Indian War, Franklin lamented: "At present every Bill that I receive tells me a lie, and would cheat me too if I was not too well acquainted with it. Thirty Shillings in our Bills, according to the Account they give of themselves should be worth *five* Dollars; and we find them worth but *four*" ("Argument" 13). Aimed at denouncing depreciation (though not paper currency itself), Franklin's rhetoric here is a departure from his other, more optimistic writings on paper money and an acknowledgment of the capacity of instruments to misrepresent. The passage depicts nominal value as an "account" given by anthropomorphic bills and suggests the analogy between financial instruments and autobiographical representation also at work in his memoirs; the passage, moreover, warns that readers must be discriminating.

Franklin's text implicitly acknowledges that a candid equation of credit with appearance and perception inevitably unravels the reader's sense of certainty (these uncertainties of printed representation go hand-in-hand with the riskiness of a credit economy).[18] I would argue, however, that it is precisely this economic ethos that works to resolve, rhetorically at least, the problems it raises. If Franklin's relish for credit schemes inevitably raises doubts about the veracity of the *Autobiography*, it simultaneously encourages a faith in the speculative life that has been promised. In this narrative, doubts are self-fulfilling prophecies that lead to bank runs and financial collapse, and faith in his endorsement, as Franklin's own account demonstrates, keeps expectations in circulation and defers those redemptions that cannot materialize at that moment. As illustrated by Franklin's stories of war-time despair and the croaking Samuel Mickle, financial panic can sabotage potential profits. According to this financial paradigm, printed currency values and the kind of American success recalled in Franklin's memoirs are fictions for the present but may, with the reader's faith, be realized in the future.

The financial mechanisms at work in this text even make irrelevant, again at the rhetorical level, the common criticism that the *Autobiography* is thinly veiled self-promotion. Drawing from his own experience as financier, Franklin depicts a public credibility that is bolstered by his own credibility: the more reputable his own name and success story, the more viable is the American life for which he is a spokesman. By invoking a credit system that intertwines personal and civic interests, he makes self-promotion and national promotion mutually beneficial, enacting, in essence, a Franklinian pragmatism by which one could do good and do well at the same time.[19]

Notes

1. Other scholars have investigated the particular ways in which Franklin's writings might be considered characteristic of Anglo-American bourgeois culture. Franklin embodied the modern capitalist ethos, according to Max Weber, in his pragmatic transformation of industry and frugality into secular, money-making virtues. John William Ward writes that the indecipherability of Franklin's character is precisely what makes him characteristic of an age in which markers of social status were increasingly destabilized: "Franklin stands most clearly as an exemplary American because his life's story is a witness to the uncertainties about social status that have characterized our society. . . . at the beginning of our national experience, Benjamin Franklin not only puts the question that still troubles us in our kind of society, 'Who's Who?' He also raises the question that lies at the heart of the trouble: 'Who am I?'" (Ward 60-61).

2. The very word "project," which appears more than thirty times in the *Autobiography*, reinforces this speculative approach to public improvement. As John C. Van Horne writes, the term traditionally connoted financial scheming and cheating, but Daniel Defoe's *Essay Upon Several Projects* (1697) redefined projection as a potentially honest and valuable form of invention that could benefit the community. Through projection, individuals and groups could envision future public improvements, such as hospitals, bridges, and academies, and then take steps to realize them. Franklin, who cites Defoe's essay in the *Autobiography* as a key influence on his own philanthropy, celebrates his own "projecting spirit" as well as that of fellow philanthropists Thomas Bond, Gilbert Tennent and John Fothergill (Van Horne 426-27).

3. Hamilton, who did not trust all wealthy individuals to uphold civic credit purely out of public-spiritedness, believed that if private citizens were invested in the government they would be more apt to support public credit because their own assets were at stake. In this way, private credibility supports civic credibility, but civic credibility also boosts the value of individual holdings: "No paper credit," Hamilton wrote, "can be substantial, or durable, which has no funds, and which does not unite, immediately, the interest and influence of the moneyed men, in its establishment and preservation" (Hamilton 365).

4. Both the *Declaration of Independence* and the *U.S. Constitution* were written, published, and circulated, in large part, to help establish national credibility and procure much-needed European loans for the fledgling nation (such loans, it was assumed, would then strengthen public confidence in the feasibility of independence and raise currency values at home). The historian Charles Beard went so far as to argue that the *Constitution* framers were "public creditors" who had invested in the private but government-chartered Bank of North America and who hoped that the document would enhance the value of their own holdings. Other historians have since demonstrated that the theory is overwrought in attributing one motive to all framers, but Beard is essentially correct in acknowledging the interdependence of print media, public credibility and currency values. His thesis, moreover, also correctly identifies the capacity of public finance to transform individual bill-holders into public investors and to make private and civic interests ultimately inseparable. See Charles Beard, *An Economic Interpretation of the Constitution of the United States*, and for a counter-

argument see Gordon Wood, "Interests and Disinterestedness in the Making of the Constitution."

5. According to numismatist Eric Newman, Franklin culled all of the 1775 "devices" from emblem- and motto-books in Philadelphia at the time. See Newman's article, "Franklin Making Money More Plentiful," for a discussion of Franklin's work as a currency designer and printer.

6. English translations provided in parentheses are those Franklin included in his essay "Account of the Devices on the Continental Bills of Credit." My analysis of Continental bills is based on research in the print collections of the American Antiquarian Society in Worcester, Mass. For graphic reproductions of selected Continental dollars, as well as currency issued by individual colonies, see Eric Newman's *The Early Paper Money of America*.

7. These bills were secured not by material wealth but by law (a legal promise of forthcoming metal) unlike bank-notes and other instruments that *represented* metal wealth and maintained their convertibility. Although metal specie and bank-notes secured by metal had always been subject to the vicissitudes of the market-place, unbacked fiat money was particularly precarious in the eyes of buyers and sellers. Jean-Joseph Goux writes that the advent of paper instruments that were not readily redeemable brought about a "crisis of convertibility"; this crisis, moreover, implied that language, like money, was not rooted in anything absolute (Goux 18). For histories of colonial currency up to the Revolution, see Curtis Nettels, *The Money Supply of the American Colonies Before 1720* and John McCusker's introduction to *Money and Exchange in Europe and America, 1600-1775*.

8. In his analysis of the bills' "revelation," Franklin's advocacy of financial conviction bears striking resemblance to his advocacy of pragmatic religious faith. In the *Autobiography*, Franklin admits doubts as to Christ's divinity but advocates belief in Christian teachings if those teachings are socially beneficial.

9. Christopher Looby writes that Keith's deferral could serve as an emblem for the *Autobiography* as a whole because Franklin's writing enacts a similar postponement: a "real, integral Franklin," he writes, "is promised but never produced" (123). To this analysis I would add that Franklin thus depicts reading as a process that often requires an acceptance of textual deferral—a willingness to be deferred.

10. In his 1729 "A Modest Inquiry into the Nature and Necessity of a Paper-Currency," Franklin voices an early critique of this metal-based notion of value. Labor, he argues, is the basis of value, and so commodity prices are, in fact, determined by how much labor is required for their production. Moreover, he argues that, though the colonies lack metal resources, they have valuable land that might replace metal as the collateral for paper currency reserves.

11. Smith's bank-notes did not need to maintain a one-to-one solvency, but they did require a minimum measure of backing; he did not, in other words, advocate British credit instruments that were issued with no reserves. In a discussion of Pennsylvania's well-regulated and successful emission of paper money in 1722, however, Smith did identify unbacked paper money as an instrument acceptable for the enterprise of colonial settlement.

12. The benefits of paper as a cheap, plentiful medium were also undermined by the

Stamp Act of 1765, which required that all public documents be affixed with tax stamps shipped from London. The Stamp Act threatened to hinder the free circulation of communication and commerce alike, as it applied to financial instruments, as well as newspapers, pamphlets and broadsides.

13. These bills were later supplemented by other instruments, such as loan-office certificates and notes issued by the Bank of North America, a private institution with a government charter. Beginning in 1776, Congress established loan offices in several states to sell interest-bearing bonds that would mature at a future date; though these government bonds were intended to be investment securities, they often circulated as a medium (Ferguson 35). The Bank of North America and the Bank of the United States, established in 1781 and 1791, respectively, issued circulating notes. These banks were technically private, as they were secured by subscriptions of individuals like Thomas Paine and Robert Morris; however, people tended to associate the soundness of the bills with government credibility. For a comprehensive history of Revolutionary and post-war finance, see E. James Ferguson, *The Power of the Purse: A History of American Public Finance, 1776-1790* and William G. Anderson, *The Price of Liberty: The Public Debt of the American Revolution*.

14. Starting in 1690, Franklin's native Boston issued public paper money to finance military expeditions and other public expenditures; in this colony, over-emission led to severe depreciation, and the bills contributed to the debt they were designed to alleviate. In 1723, shortly after his arrival in Philadelphia, the colony of Pennsylvania introduced its own version of paper credit, lending interest-bearing bills to debtors willing to use their own lands for security. Unlike that of other colonies, Pennsylvania money was well managed and suffered little long-term depreciation.

15. Franklin considered paper money an "excellent Machine for Settling a new Country" ("Scheme" 53). The colonial landscape had yielded little silver or gold, he wrote in a defense of American paper money presented to British officials in 1767, and an "Imitation of the Bank of England, where every Bill is payable in Cash upon sight" was "impracticable" ("Legal Tender" 34). Paper currency was, in his view, a resourceful innovation, a necessary imaginative act that could compensate for the colonies' lack of metal capital.

16. See Franklin's "Dissertation on Liberty and Necessity" for his discussion of the contrast between the "necessity" of circumstances fixed and determined (especially by providential design) and the "liberty" of human transgression. For discussions of Franklin's economic ideas, see Tracy Mott and George W. Zinke, "Benjamin Franklin's Economic Thought: A Twentieth Century Appraisal" and Lewis J. Carey, *Franklin's Economic Views* (see, in particular, the chapters on "Paper Money" and "Value and Interest").

17. Editors of the Norton edition of the *Autobiography*, J. A. Leo Lemay and P. M. Zall write that Mickle was, in fact, "optimistic enough to have built a new stable only eight years earlier" (190). They also note that Franklin opened his business just after a depression and currency depreciation lasting from October 1727 to January 1728 (47).

18. Franklin does not eliminate the possibility of fictionality but rather he allows for that fictionality to take on a reality of its own. It is probably safer to say that in the

hermetic rhetorical world created by Franklin, such extratextual realities tend to be rendered irrelevant since the reader can only ever know the Franklin constituted in print. That hermetic seal, however, is occasionally punctured. Though the *Autobiography* never acknowledges a Franklin separate from the one constituted in print, Vaughan's letter raises concerns over whether the life on paper is the same as the life as lived, and even urges Franklin to counter his critics by letting "the world into the traits" of his "genuine character" (61).

19. For a discussion of the ways in which Franklin reconciles self- and civic-interests, see Michael Zuckerman, "Doing Good While Doing Well: Benevolence and Self-Interest in Franklin's *Autobiography*."

Erratum: In the spirit of Benjamin Franklin himself, I would like to correct an *erratum* that appeared in my article "Franklin's *Autobiography* and the Credibility of Personality" (*EAL* 35:3). In the *Autobiography*, Franklin recalls fashioning a makeshift printing type out of lead at a time when there were no type-foundries in the colonies. In a parenthetical comment, I concluded that part of his resourcefulness lay in his ability to design type of lead rather than of more precious metals, but, in fact, a lead alloy would have been the standard material for type at this time. Rather, Franklin is resourceful because he is able to contrive such type without the typefounder's training and tools. How exactly he is able to accomplish this task, however, is something he never fully discloses to the reader.

Works Cited

Anderson, William G. *The Price of Liberty: The Public Debt of the American Revolution*. Charlottesville: Univ. Press of Virginia, 1983.

Beard, Charles. *An Economic Interpretation of the Constitution of the United States*. New York, 1913.

Breitwieser, Mitchell. *Cotton Mather and Benjamin Franklin: The Price of Representative Personality*. New York: Cambridge Univ. Press, 1984.

Carey, Lewis J. *Franklin's Economic Views*. Garden City, N.Y.: Doubleday, Doran & Co., 1928.

Ferguson, E. James. *The Power of the Purse: A History of American Public Finance, 1776-1790*. Chapel Hill: Univ. of North Carolina Press, 1961.

Franklin, Benjamin. "Account of the Devices on the Continental Bills of Credit." *Writings*. Ed. J. A. Leo Lemay. New York: Library of America, 1987.

____________. "Argument for Making the Bills of Credit Bear Interest." *Papers of Benjamin Franklin*. Ed. Leonard Labaree. Vol. 11. New Haven: Yale Univ. Press, 1959.

____________. *Autobiography: An Authoritative Text*. Ed. J. A. Leo Lemay and P. M. Zall. New York: W. W. Norton & Co., 1986.

____________. "Dissertation on Liberty and Necessity." *Writings*. Ed. J. A. Leo Lemay. New York: Library of America, 1987.

___________. "The Legal Tender of Paper Money in America." *Papers of Benjamin Franklin*. Ed. Leonard Labaree. Vol. 14. New Haven: Yale Univ. Press, 1959.

___________. Letter to John Jay. 2 October 1780. *The Writings of Benjamin Franklin*. Ed. Albert Henry Smyth. Vol. 8. New York: Macmillan Co., 1907.

___________. Letter to Samuel Cooper. 22 April 1779. *The Writings of Benjamin Franklin*. Ed. Albert Henry Smyth. Vol. 7. New York: Macmillan Co., 1907.

___________. Letter to William Jackson. 5 July 1781. *The Writings of Benjamin Franklin*. Ed. Albert Henry Smyth. Vol. 8. New York: Macmillan Co., 1907.

___________. "A Modest Inquiry into the Nature and Necessity of a Paper-Currency." Philadelphia, 1729.

___________. "Scheme for Supplying the Colonies with a Paper Currency." *Papers of Benjamin Franklin*. Ed. Leonard Labaree. Vol. 12. New Haven: Yale Univ. Press, 1959.

Goux, Jean-Joseph. *The Coiners of Language*. Trans. Jennifer Curtiss Gage. Norman, Ok.: Univ. of Oklahoma Press, 1984.

Hamilton, Alexander. Letter to Robert Morris, 1781. *The Works of Alexander Hamilton*. Ed. Henry Cabot Lodge. Vol. 3. New York: Haskell House, 1971.

Heilbroner, Robert L. *The Worldly Philosophers: The Lives, Times and Ideas of the Great Economic Thinkers*. 6th ed. New York: Simon and Schuster, 1986.

Looby, Christopher. *Voicing America: Language, Literary Form, and the Origins of the United States*. Chicago: Univ. of Chicago Press, 1996.

McCusker, John. *Money and Exchange in Europe and America, 1600-1775*. Chapel Hill: Univ. of North Carolina Press, 1978.

Mott, Tracy, and George W. Zinke. "Benjamin Franklin's Economic Thought: A Twentieth Century Appraisal." *Critical Essays on Benjamin Franklin*. Ed. Melvin H. Buxbaum. Boston: G. K. Hall, 1987.

Nettels, Curtis. *The Money Supply of the American Colonies Before 1720*. New York: A. M. Keley, 1973.

Newman, Eric. *The Early Paper Money of America*. 3rd ed. Iola, Wisc.: Krause Publications, 1990.

___________. "Franklin Making Money More Plentiful." *Proceedings of the American Philosophical Society* 115. (October 1971): 341-49.

Rice, Grantland S. *The Transformation of Authorship in America*. Chicago: Univ. of Chicago Press, 1997.

Simmel, Georg. *The Philosophy of Money*. Ed. David Frisby. Trans. Tom Bottomore and David Frisby. 2nd ed. New York: Routledge, 1990.

Smith, Adam. *An Inquiry into the Nature and Causes of the Wealth of Nations*. 1776. Reprint. Ed. Edwin Cannan. Chicago: Univ. of Chicago Press, 1976.

Spengemann, William C. *The Forms of Autobiography: Episodes in the History of a Literary Genre*. New Haven: Yale Univ. Press, 1980.

Van Horne, John C. "Collective Benevolence and the Common Good in Franklin's Philanthropy." *Reappraising Benjamin Franklin*. Ed. J. A. Leo Lemay. Newark: Univ. of Delaware Press, 1993.

Ward, John William. "Benjamin Franklin: The Making of an American Character."

Red, White, and Blue: Men, Books, and Ideas in America Culture. Oxford: Oxford Univ. Press, 1969.
Warner, Michael. *The Letters of the Republic*. Cambridge, Mass.: Harvard Univ. Press, 1990.
Wood, Gordon. "Interests and Disinterestedness in the Making of the Constitution." *Beyond Confederation*. Ed. Richard Beeman et al. Chapel Hill: Univ. of North Carolina Press, 1987.
Zuckerman, Michael. "Doing Good While Doing Well: Benevolence and Self-Interest in Franklin's *Autobiography*." *Reappraising Benjamin Franklin*. Ed. J. A. Leo Lemay. Newark: Univ. of Delaware Press, 1993.

Death Effects:
Revisiting the Conceit of Franklin's *Memoir*

Jennifer T. Kennedy

Jennifer T. Kennedy reminds us that Franklin died before the *Autobiography* was complete, and that his most famous work speaks to us posthumously. That great work also served, paradoxically, to keep him alive: "Franklin," writes Kennedy, "appears to have found in his autobiography the mechanism for an endless proliferation of himself." In Kennedy's consideration of Franklin the printer confronting death, printing itself is not production so much as *reproduction*, and writing itself is a kind of repetition. This repetition leads her into a sophisticated meditation on the ghostly traces. "If Franklin's narrative haunts American literature," she writes, "Franklin himself is also haunted by his own life, by his past lives." — J.L.

I think Pennsylvania a good country to *dye in*, though a very bad one to *live in*.
—Franklin[1]

According to John Adams, Benjamin Franklin died of his own theory. Biographers often quote from the scene in Adams's diary in which he describes the discomfort he felt on sharing a room with Franklin, when Franklin insisted they keep the window open all night.[2] Franklin believed that fresh air was essential to health and that keeping windows open at night would prevent, rather than cause, colds. The anecdote is used, often enough, to portray a grumpy Adams entangled by Franklin's eccentric genius. What is less often quoted is Adams's last word. On hearing of Franklin's death, Adams concluded that the cold night air had finally killed him, and he made a little-noticed notation in his diary to the effect that Franklin "fell a Sacrifice at last, not to the stone, but to his own Theory; having caught the violent Cold, which finally choaked him, by sitting for some hours at a Window, with the cool Air blowing upon him" (1:3, 419). In fact, Franklin's decline was more gradual than Adams would have it—he spent the last year of his life in bed and up until his final days was apparently at work on his memoirs. In the definitive *Genetic Text* of what became known as *The Autobiography of Benjamin Franklin*, Leo Lemay and P. M. Zall note, "The last paragraph, on page 220, is written in such a slanting hand (evidently while Franklin was sitting in bed) that it could even have been penned in early April 1790. Franklin died the evening of April 17, 1790, at age 84."[3] If Franklin did not die of his own theory, he did die writing a document that was in many ways a theory of death.

The possibility of an afterlife, figured in comparatively secular terms, was one of Franklin's cherished themes. Franklin relates in the memoirs how he and his friend Osborne had "a serious Agreement, that the one who happen'd first to die, should if possible make a friendly Visit to the other, and acquaint him how he found things in that separate State" (*Writings* 1245). Osborne never fulfilled his promise, but Franklin was able to imagine a variety of returns for himself in his letters, including the one described in his famous love letter to Madame Helvétius. After she had rejected his marriage proposal in 1778 on the grounds that she must remain faithful to her dead husband, Franklin wrote to her, "I went home, and, believing myself dead, found myself in the Elysian Fields." Franklin then describes how, in the Elysian Fields, he met Madame Helvétius's husband and determined that he was now happily remarried. On discovering this fact, Franklin recounts, "I suddenly decided to leave these ungrateful spirits, to return to the good earth, to see again the sunshine and you. Here I am! Let us revenge ourselves!" (*Writings* 924-25). Thus, Franklin returns from the hereafter a more faithful lover than Monsieur Helvétius, who is content to remain dead. When Adams sealed his triumphant outrage at Franklin after his death, he composed a dialogue of the dead in which Franklin finds himself ignored through eternity by the likes of Rousseau.[4] But here Franklin ultimately manages to trump Adams, for he had envisioned his own eternal life so piquantly in his bagatelles that Adams's wish fulfillment fantasy goes unremembered by history, whereas Franklin's frolic in the Elysian Fields with his beloved Madame Helvétius is the stuff of myth. In this essay, I will explore the ways in which the conceit of the memoir provides Franklin with yet another form of visitation, one in which the word affords access to an instantaneous posthumousness.

It has often been noted that Franklin presents himself as a kind of "representative personality" in his *Memoir*,[5] and current scholarship emphasizes the extent to which the *Memoir* itself is about representation. The interest within colonial studies in the emergence of print culture has made Franklin, as America's premier printer, the focus of renewed interest as a cultural figure; and critics with a theoretical background, such as Michael Warner, Christopher Looby, and Larzer Ziff, have drawn attention to Franklin as a literary figure who highlights his own linguistic self-fashioning.[6] Both schools have been attracted to the conceit of the *Memoir*, which Franklin describes in textual terms as a second "Edition" of his life. But the famous passage in which he introduces the conceit is also notable for its surreptitious metaphor of posthumousness and shows that Franklin had found ways of dying in theory long before Adams had him dying of his theories: "[W]ere it offer'd to my Choice, I should have no Objection of a Repetition of the same Life from its Beginning, only asking the Advantage Authors have in a second Edition to correct some Faults of the first. So would I if I might, besides corr the Faults, change some sinister Accidents & Events of it for others more favorable, but tho' this were deny'd, I should still accept the Offer" (*Writings* 1307). He goes on: "However, since such a Repetition is not to be expected, the Thing most like living one's Life over again, seems to be a *Recollection* of that Life; and to make that Recollection as durable as possible, the putting it down in Writing" (*Writings* 1307). Franklin appears to have found in his autobiography the mechanism for an endless proliferation of himself. And while Franklin has come to be so strongly identified with the current investigation of eighteenth-century print culture that it is almost impossible to imagine him in any other way than as America's archetypal printer, it is important to remember that this was, in fact, the myth Franklin constructed for himself. Franklin scholarship seems doomed to reprint it for him endlessly. His admonition, "Fear not death; for the sooner we die, the longer shall we be immortal" (*Writings* 1217), while not necessarily universally good advice, seems to apply well in his own case. But the conceit of the *Memoir* is more subtle. In the *Memoir*, Franklin is concerned about the preservation of his fantasy afterlife, and this is a fundamentally literary concern. He asks the paradoxical question: How durable is death? and uses the *Memoir* to answer it.

Despite the attention that the conceit of the *Memoir* has received for its printing metaphor,[7] the safeguard against eternity that Franklin describes is not a printed text, but a handwritten one: the *Memoir* itself, which was not published in his lifetime. The image of the "second Edition" is thus not totally assimilable with the idea of the reproducible, representative Franklin, template for a nation. Indeed, Franklin's *Memoir* possesses both a certain haunting singularity and a disturbing mutability. The fragility of the original made it possible for Franklin's son to suppress it—as indeed, according to Jefferson, Franklin may have feared he would[8]—and contributed to the irony that it appeared first in America as a translation of a pirated French version. Franklin's *Memoir* thus went into several editions before the "original" appeared and it was ahead of itself in the world just as Franklin was ahead of himself when he imagined himself dead and repeating his life, in the year 1771. Whereas the focus of studies of Franklin oriented toward print culture has been on the so-called impersonality of Franklin's reproducible model of citizenship, the conceit of the *Memoir* suggests something both more personal and more profound—indeed, something more literary. While the *Memoir* presents a self-consciously pedagogical model of New World bourgeois subjectivity, Franklin is the person most anxious to follow his own example and relive his life from the beginning. In different roles and under different names, Franklin is able to kill himself off to experiment with various incarnations of the American man. But the name of "Franklin," which Franklin meditates on at length in the *Memoir*, gives him perhaps his most direct access to the afterlife: beginning with the genealogical segment of the *Memoir*, he is able to lead many different lives under his own name. And, for that matter, as he seemed to have anticipated, his famous name provides him with a lively posthumous existence to this day. Examining the first part of the *Memoir* in light of its conceit of posthumousness makes it possible to give new life to this most famous of American texts.[9] To do so is to view Franklin from outside the dominant historicist paradigm current in the study of early American literature, and to encounter death effects that have more to do with the literary than the material.

Representative Death Effects

The idea of death understood as a repetition obviously intrigued Franklin, for he wrote of it more than once. In a letter to George Whatley written in 1785, Franklin puts forward his theory of reincarnation and expands on the metaphor he first uses in the introduction to the *Memoir*, highlighting the aspect of repetition:

> You see I have some reason to wish, that, in a future State, I may not only be *as well as I was*, but a little better. And I hope it; for I, too, with your Poet, *trust in God*. And when I observe, that there is a great Frugality, as well as Wisdom, in his Works, since he has been evidently sparing both of Labour and Materials for by the various wonderful Inventions of Propagation, he has provided for the continual peopling of his World with Plants and Animals, without being at the Trouble of repeated new Creations; and by the natural Reduction of the compound Substances to their original Elements, capable of being employ'd in new Compositions, he has prevented the Necessity of creating new Matter; so that the Earth, Water, Air, and perhaps Fire, which being compounded form Wood, do, when the Wood is dissolved return and again become Air, Earth, Fire, and Water; I say, that, when I see nothing annihilated, and not even a Drop of Water wasted, I cannot suspect the Annihi-

> lation of Souls, or believe, that he will suffer the daily Waste of Millions of Minds ready made that now exist, and put himself to the continual Trouble of making new ones. Thus finding myself to exist in the World, I believe I shall, in some Shape or other, always exist; and with all the inconveniences human Life is liable to, I shall not object to a new Edition of mine; hoping, however, that the *Errata* of the last may be corrected. (*Writings* 1106)

The metaphor of the edition as well as the pun on errata is itself recycled from the *Memoir*, but in an expanded form. Here Franklin's imagination is more grandiose: the immortality he imagines for himself is specifically literary, but at the same time it is underwritten by a quasi-scientific guarantee founded on a practical observation about God. Franklin's God is as frugal and wise as Franklin could wish his own Yankee soul to be, and it is this perceived similarity to his model self that makes it possible for Franklin to hubristically extrapolate his theory of the universe. All of life, according to this vision, is an endless repetition. Franklin puts it more accessibly when he writes Thomas Bond, "Being arrived at seventy, and considering that by traveling further in the same road I should probably be led to the grave, I stopped short, turned about, and walked back again; which having done these four years, you may now call me sixty-six."[10]

To imagine a repeated life is both to cheat death (by living again) and to anticipate death (by quitting the first life).[11] A life recollected by Franklin's scheme thus resembles a half-death with the text at a ghostly third remove from life. Franklin imagines imitators: "my Posterity may like to know," he comments, "the Means he made use of to happiness, as they may find some of them suitable to their own Situations, & therefore fit to be imitated" (*Writings* 1307)—and these imitators are at yet another remove, extending Franklin's half-life into eternity. Through the device of autobiography, itself a genre that preceded its name in the eighteenth century, Franklin creates for himself a fictional death as much as a fictionalized "life."

The paradox resembles those Franklin experimented with in his *Poor*

Richard, in which comic ruminations on death form the narrative connection between editions and slyly trick the reader into believing in the fictional life of its characters by casting doubt on the assertion that one of them is dead.[12] In the first year of the almanac, 1733, Richard Saunders projects the death of his friend and rival Mr. Titan Leeds in that year, 17 October, at 3:29 p.m. In the second edition of the almanac, in 1734, Poor Richard asserts that he is unable to verify his prediction. "I cannot positively affirm whether he be dead or not" (1189), he declares, laying the groundwork for a spoof on lawyerly standards of evidence that lasts for several years of the almanac. What follows is an imagined dispute between Richard Saunders and his "dead" friend about whether he is dead or alive, a dispute that cleverly bolsters the seeming reality of Poor Richard's own fictional persona. Poor Richard expostulates, "I shall convince him from his own Words that he is dead, (*ex ore suo condemnatus est*) for in his Preface to his almanac for 1734, he says, '*Saunders adds another* GROSS FALSEHOOD *in his Almanack,* viz. *that by my own Calculation I shall* survive *until the* 26th *of the said Month October 1733, which is as* untrue *as the former*'" (*Writings* 1195). He then provides his own gloss: "Now if it be, as *Leeds* says, *untrue* and a *gross Falsehood* that he surviv'd till the 26th of October 1773 then it is certainly *true* that he died *before* that Time: And if he died before that Time, he is dead now, to all intents and Purposes, any thing he may say to the contrary notwithstanding" (*Writings* 1195). The mechanics of the spoof make use of the same device as that of the *Memoir*: as Poor Richard would have it, Leeds's own almanac was written after his (fictional) death.[13] And even as Richard exposes the posthumous almanac as a fraud, it is this element of the joke that is exploited more than any other, culminating in a letter that Poor Richard claims to have received from Leeds confirming his death that he encloses in his almanac:

> Dear Friend SAUNDERS,
>
> My Respect for you continues even in this separate State, and I am griev'd to see the Aspersions thrown on you by the Malevolence of avari-

cious Publishers of Almanacks, who envy your Success. They say your Prediction of my Death in 1733 was false, and they pretend that I remained alive many Years after. But I do hereby certify, that I did actually die at that time, precisely at the Hour you mention'd, with a Variation only of *5 min 53 sec.* which must be allow'd to be no great matter in such Cases. And I do farther declare that I furnished them with no Calculations of the Planets Motions, &c. seven Years after my Death, as they are pleased to give out: so that the Stuff they publish as an Almanack in my Name is no more mine than 'tis yours. (*Writings* 1215)

Both Poor Richard's initial prediction and the subsequent shenanigans poke fun at the spurious temporality of almanacs in general and their claims to chart uncharted time. If almanacs can speak forward from the present to the future, why should they not be able to speak back from death to the present?[14] This is not the only similarity between *Poor Richard* and the *Memoir*, both of which offer wisdom in the form of homilies and anecdotes, but it is the philosophical link. As Franklin sets it up, the *Memoir* is a kind of backwards Almanack—an almanac Titan Leeds could have written.

The self-serving nature of Poor Richard's invented correspondence is part of the joke, and it applies to Franklin's *Memoir*, which uses the cover of imagined death to recoup losses and correct "errata" as well. Titan Leeds's letter from the hereafter ends by drawing attention to the name as that which makes this kind of masquerade possible in what we might call the "separate state" of the printed word, and it is with the question of the name that Franklin commences his autobiography. Leeds's insistence that his successors have perpetrated a fraud, and that "the Stuff they publish as an Almanack in my Name is no more mine than 'tis yours" is fraught with irony. What Richard is publishing under Leeds's name is most certainly his own conscious fraud or forgotten somnambulant scribbling of the night before. But the deeper irony is that what Franklin publishes under Richard's and Leeds's names is, of course, neither of theirs. The name of Richard Saunders is stolen from English almanacs, and Titan Leeds is, in fact, the creation of Franklin's rival, Andrew Bradford. The temporal swindle at work in all autobiography—that a later self speaks in the "I" of an earlier time—is thus comically schematized in the *Poor Richard* letters in the fraudulent exchange of proper names. The static temporality of the signature that ostensibly authenticates a text also allows for the forgery of a text and for the possibility of "speech" after death, a fact that Franklin highlights in the burlesque of the almanac as much as in the introduction to the *Memoir.* In fact, it was one of Franklin's favorite ruses to attach a forged signature to his writings—from his very first literary attempt under the name of Silence Dogood to his essay under the name of The King of Prussia. But Franklin extends the eighteenth-century conventions of the unsigned essay and the pseudonym with the perpetration of his literary hoaxes, both exposing and exploiting the properties of the proper name.[15]

Franklin's Tale

Indeed, Franklin begins the *Memoir* by pairing the story of his ancestry with the story of the evolution of the proper name itself, speculating that his own surname was a word that became a proper name only after people started taking surnames:

> The Notes one of my Uncles (who had the same kind of Curiosity in collecting Family Anecdotes) once put into my Hands, furnished me with several Particulars, relating to our Ancestors. From those Notes I learnt that the Family had liv'd in the same Village, Ecton in Northamptonshire, for 300 Years, & how much longer he knew not, (perhaps from the Time when the Name *Franklin* that before was the Name of an Order of People, was assum'd by them for a Surname, when others took Surnames all over the Kingdom—*). (*Writings* 1308)

Once again, Franklin subtly unmasks the potential duplicity of the proper name by giving it a diachronic dimension that undermines its very properness (in showing that his name was once an ordinary noun). Franklin's account takes us back to an imagined moment when even his "real" name is an assumed one and creates an opportunity for Franklin to change the subject from his ancestry to his name itself. Before launching into the documentary evidence of his lineage, as Adams does in his memoir, Franklin instead inserts a curious rambling footnote that documents the history of the word *Franklin*, which he places in bold capital letters. The history of Franklin becomes the history of a name:

> *As a proof that **FRANKLIN** was anciently the common name of an order or rank in England, see Judge Fortescue, *De Laudibus Legum Angiliae*, written about the year 1412, in which is the following passage, to show that good juries might easily be formed in any part of England.
>
> "Regio etiam illa, ita respersa refertaque est *possessoribus terrarum* et agrorum, quod in ea, villula tam parva reperiri non poterit, in qua non est *miles arminger*, vel pater-familias, qualis ibidem *Franklin* vulgariter noncupatur, magnis ditatus possessionibus, nec non libere tenentes et alii *valecti* plurimi, suis patrimoniis sufficientes ad faciendum juratam, in forma pranotata."
>
> "Moreover, the same country is so filled and replenished with landed menne, that therein so small a Thorpe cannot be found wherein dweleth not a knight, an esquire, or such a householder, as is there commonly called a *Franklin*, enriched with great possessions: an also other freeholders and many yoemen able for their livelihoods to make a jury in form aforementioned."—(*Old Translation.*)
>
> Chaucer too calls his Country Gentleman, a *Franklin*, and after describing his good housekeeping thus characterizes him:
>
> "This worthy Franklin bore a purse of silk,
> Fix'd to his girdle, white as morning milk,
> Knight of the Shire, first justice at th' Assize,
> To help the poor, the doubtful to advise,
> In all employments, generous he proved;
> Renown'd for courtesy, by all beloved." (*Writings* 1309)

The fact that Franklin bothers to include both the Latin and the English translation, besides being a testament to his learning and his populism, is appropriate for a discourse on language and its mutability. Language itself allows for the repeatability of experience, the doubled life that Franklin sponsors in the *Memoir*. Here a dead language (Latin) is repeated by a translation into a living one (English). And the linguistic coincidence that there should be such a happy similarity between the late meaning of the word FRANKLIN and the character of the eighteenth-century Benjamin Franklin allows our Franklin to repeat the virtues of a whole class of people. Likewise, it is in the nature of the name that, centuries after his death, Chaucer can seem to praise Franklin: "In all employments, generous he proved / Renown'd for courtesy, by all beloved" could be a posthumous compliment.

Franklin also traces his first name back to his uncle and includes two poems sent to him by his namesake, both of which concern their name. The first is entitled, "Sent to my Name upon a Report of his Inclination to Martial Affairs," and the second is an acrostic that spells out the letters *BENJAMIN FRANKLIN* as the first letters of sixteen lines of verse. Both documents seem to deed the name of Benjamin Franklin over to its second owner and reinforce the sense that Franklin's life is a doubled or repeated one. Indeed, Franklin notes, the story of his life so closely resembles that of another one of his uncles, who died four years to the day before Franklin was born, that "had he died on the same day [. . .] one might have supposed a Transmigration" (*Writings* 1310). Descent, for Franklin, seems to be another kind of autobiography, another version of the past life relived or recalled. The name of Franklin, as much as the *Memoir* of him, appears as a vehicle for immortality.

Looby, one of the scholars who focuses on Franklin's linguistic wiles, interprets the uncle's poem via a Lacanian framework, insisting that the uncle "assumed, as the author of this poem, as the teacher of writing, and as the supplier of words, the paternal function of introducing the child into the symbolic order, initiating him into the interdependent systems of language and moral law" (*Voicing America* 113). In

Looby's cogent analysis, which has a sociological component, the law acts as a constraint, and Looby speculates that the uncle's poem initiated young Franklin into the symbolic order, "in a way that must have made a four-and-a-half-year-old boy feel, even more deeply than every child feels at that age, that he was powerless within that order" (113). The evidence that Franklin might have found the poem oppressive can lie only in the lines themselves, which sternly preach that the *B* in *BENJAMIN* stands for "Be to thy parents an Obedient Son," and the *E* stands for "Each Day let Duty constantly be Done," the *N* for "Never give Way to sloth or lust or pride," and so forth. But Franklin's inclusion of the acrostic does not necessarily suggest a perceived injury—in fact, a little of the forbidden pride seems a more likely reason to repeat the poem. The convention of the acrostic could indeed stand as a kind of cultural metaphor for language as law, but even as the visual presentation of the name suggests a kind of bondage to the social order and to the enumerated virtues, the appearance of a small gap between the name and the lines of the poem suggests a means of escape. At the very least, there are *two* ways that the text can be read—either up and down or left to right, each reading offering an alternative to the other:

B e to thy parents an Obedient Son
E ach Day let Duty constantly be Done
N ever give Way to sloth or lust or pride
I f free you'd be from Thousand Ills beside
A bove all Ills be sure Avoide the selfe
M ans Danger lyes in Satan sin and selfe
I n vertue Learning Wisdome progress Make
N ere shrink at Suffering for thy saviours sake
F raud and all Falsehood in thy Dealings Flee
R eligious Always in thy station be
A dore the Maker of thy Inward part
N ow's the Accepted time, Give him thy Heart
K eep a Good Conscience 'tis a constant Friend

L ike judge and Witness This thy Acts Attend
I n Heart with bended knee Alone Adore
N one but the Three in One Forevermore (*Writings* 1311)

Between the name and the world there is a discernible space—one that favors the name, which regains its autonomy on the left-hand margin, over the mechanism of social order, the poem, which stands cropped of its first letters. Personal identity can be written into the margin, even of a religious culture that insists that "Mans Danger lyes in Satan sin and selfe." And indeed Franklin ends the section by telling us that he inherits a lifetime of marginalia from this very uncle when he happens upon some of the uncle's papers in London and discovers "There are many of his Notes in the Margins" (*Writings* 1311). Even the poem itself offers an interesting (if conventional) slippage from the prison of *BENJAMIN*, in the image of the self divided to become its own constant "Friend," "Judge," and "Witness." The disciplined self at the end of the poem, split into its several parts, also resembles God, who is evoked not by name, but as the "Three in One." Here the uncle offers an opportunity for a species of repeated life within the self: an immediate duplication of self in the formation of Conscience, which, in turn, duplicates the structure of the divine.

The genealogy Franklin constructs in fact repeatedly evokes slippage and resistance. His family anecdote from the Reformation produces textual resistance in very literal terms with the story of a secret Bible. He explains that he learned from his Uncle Benjamin that his family was in the Reformation and were Protestants through Queen Mary and thus, "were sometimes in Danger of Trouble on Account of their Zeal against Popery" (1312). To avoid detection, "They had got an English Bible, & to conceal & secure it, it was fastened open with Tapes under & within the Frame of a joint Stool. When my Great Great Grandfather read in it to his Family, he turn'd up the Joint Stool upon his Knees, turning over the Leaves then under the Tapes" (1312). As an additional safeguard, "One of the Children stood at the Door to give notice if he saw the Apparition coming, who was an Officer of the Spiritual Court. In that Case the Stool was turned down again upon its feet, when the Bible remain'd conceal'd under it as before" (1312). This story of a secret text is a perfect introduction to Franklin's career, which was marked by a series of clandestine documents from his first stealthy contributions to his brother's newspaper, slipped underneath the printing house door in the dead of night; to his surreptitious trafficking in the explosive letters of Thomas Hutchinson; to his covert dealing in diplomatic documents in London and France. The anecdote contains elements that foreshadow the domestic drama of the Silence Dogood letters, with young Franklin standing at the door of his brother's printing house, hoping he will not be detected with his secret writings, much as the child posted at the door watches for the Apparition. The revolutionary context of the Hutchinson letters and the political element of Franklin's later diplomatic life also seem to be somehow foretold by the family story, which once again proves Franklin's character to be overdetermined by his name.

In another way the story also anticipates Franklin: it is the story of a text as an object, a three-legged Bible, which is in its way a kind of machine—a machine, in this case, for deception. Nothing could be more evocative of Franklin's conception of the literary, which, in his inventiveness, he was constantly *putting to use*. The Bible stool could easily be among the inventions designed by Franklin to aid the reader. It resembles Franklin's invention of bifocals, which make possible a double-vision that also powerfully recalls his theory of autobiography as a review of one's life.[16] Both Bible stool and bifocals provide a key to a second or secret world—that of God's word for the man who lives in a religiously restricted world and that of the printed word to the man who must wear glasses to see everyday objects. But both inventions also obfuscate vision—the Bible stool by hiding the Bible and bifocals by rendering either the long view or the near view unintelligible through the wrong half of the lens. One could also compare the Bible stool to that object of furniture that Franklin designed to aid the reader, the "Long Arm," a pine pole with a mechanical loop for removing books from high shelves, which Franklin recommended to old men who "find it inconvenient to mount a ladder or steps for that purpose, their heads being sometimes subject to giddiness, and their activity, with the steadiness of their joints, being abated by age" (*Writings* 1116). This device makes it possible for the old man to live again as he did when younger and creates a sort of mechanical self. At the same time, however, that it makes a machine function like a man (complete with "finger" and "thumb") it also, in some sense, makes the man function like a machine, or as part of a machine. In place of the old man's actions are mechanical actions, in place of his body is wood and cord. Likewise, Franklin's imagined autobiography machine is posited on the *death of the autobiographer*, who must surrender life in order to live his own life over from the start.

Franklin sees the proper name itself—or at least the surname—as a kind of invention, as his discourse on the word *Franklin* emphasizes. And Franklin relishes as well the act of inventing names for the imaginary characters he brings to life. Like the autobiography and the bifocal lens, the invented or the given name can both give and take life. Franklin's obsession with names is deeply bound up in his preoccupation with death: by sharing his name with the dead, Franklin can imagine himself as his uncle, a visitor from the dead who has "transmigrated" to the current day, or he can see himself in the centuries-old verses of Chaucer. Even his own interest in his name seems to be overdetermined by that name. In speaking of his mother's family, he describes his maternal grandfather, Peter Folgier, one of the first Settlers of New England, noting that "honorable mention is made by Cotton Mather" of him in his "Church History of that Country" as a "*goodly learned Englishman*" (*Writings* 1312). That Cotton Mather mentions his name is told before the story of Folgier's actual accomplishments, although what Franklin remembers of Folgier also has to do with his name. Franklin explains that he had occasion to read a pamphlet by Folgier that advocated religious tolerance but admits that he remembers only a few lines from it. The lines are significant, all the more so as they are the only ones Franklin recalls:

> The six last concluding Lines I remember, tho' I have forgotten the two first of the Stanza, but the Purport of them was that his Censures proceeded from *Goodwill*, & therefore he would be known as the Author,
>
> because to be a Libeler, (says he)
> I hate it with my Heart
> From Sherburne Town where I now dwell
> My Name I do put here,
> Without Offense, your real Friend
> It is Peter Folgier. (*Writings* 1313)

Although the stanza itself appears to offer an unambiguous statement of identity, Franklin produces it in such a way as to create considerable nuance. His interjection of the parenthetical phrase "says he" is, of course, intended to make it clear that it is now Folgier's lines we are reading, but their effect is curious. On first reading it can be hard to determine that this is Franklin's addition, and it is a strange addition in that at the same time it seems to draw our attention to Folgier's authorship, it intrudes Franklin himself in the text. Where Folgier is asserting his absolute claim to his text, Franklin adds a piece that is not Folgier's at all. A quite unnecessary reiteration of the poet's identity, the parenthetical repeats the strange tautology of the poem, which names the name of the writer as a name instead of simply signing off. But while it participates in the poet's doubling of the act of self-identification, the parenthetical is itself unattributed. The irony is that Franklin is quoting Folgier precisely to establish his *own* name as one tied to good family. Folgier is a peacemaker much like Franklin and anticipates Franklin's religious openness as well as his literary ambitions and public-spiritedness, thus making the recommendation a strangely solipsistic one: Folgier recommends Franklin because he is so similar to Franklin. That each of Franklin's relatives throughout the genealogical section of the *Memoir* should appear so uncannily like him (in one way or another) makes it seem as if his ancestors have a stake in Franklin as much as he has a stake in them.

If Folgier's tautological self-identification matches Franklin's contrivedly tautological genealogy, Franklin's story thrives on similar doublings. The early mention of the Franklin in the *Canterbury Tales* sets up a piquant parallel to an incident in the *Memoir*. In the "Franklin's Tale," young Aurelius pines after Dorigen, who has said she will accept his love only if he is able to clear the coast of Brittany of the dangerous rocks that endanger the safe return of her real husband, who is abroad. Aurelius hires a magician who is able to create the illusion that the beach is cleared of rocks, and he demands his beloved's hand. In the end, the true husband returns, and Aurelius cannot bear to break Dorigen's heart by calling in his promise: he repents his trickery and lets her go. Benjamin Franklin's tale is more prosaic, but it likewise involves the removal of rocks and a moral lesson.

> I was generally a Leader among the Boys, and sometimes led them into Scrapes, of wch [*sic*] I will mention one Instance, as it shows an early projecting public Spirit, tho' not then justly conducted. There was a Salt Marsh that bounded part of the Mill Pond, on the Edge of which Highwater, we us'd to stand to fish for Minews. By much Trampling, we had made it a mere Quagmire. My Proposal was to build a Wharf there fit for us to stand upon, and I show'd my Comrades a large Heap of Stones which were intended for a new House near the Marsh, and which would very well suit our Purpose. Accordingly in the Evening when the Workmen were gone, I assembled a Number of my Playfellows, and working with them diligently like so many Emmets, sometimes two or three to a Stone, we brought them all away and built our little Wharff.—The next Morning the Workmen were supriz'd at Missing the Stones; which were found on our Wharff; Enquiry was made after the Removers; we were discovered & complain'd of, several of us were corrected by our Fathers; and tho' I pleaded the Usefulness of the Work, mine convinc'd me that nothing was useful which was not honest.— (*Writings* 1314)

The specific mixture of pride and guilt revealed in the telling of the story is Franklin's own, but the predicament of triumph and regret recalls Aurelius in the "Franklin's Tale" at the moment he confronts Dorigen with the cleared beach and realizes that his happiness is her sorrow. At that moment, as the Franklin tells it, Aurelius sees his situation through the threat of death and tells Dorigen:

> if I were not so sick with love for you
> that I am dying here at your feet,
> I would tell you nothing of how woebegone I am;
> but indeed I shall die if I do not speak;
> you kill me with pain, innocent as I am.
> But although you have no pity on my death,
> consider before you break your promise. (323)[17]

Although it is of course very different from the youthful story presented in the *Memoir*, Franklin's introduction of the "Franklin's Tale" allows us to think about the intersection of Franklin's text with Chaucer's, and this passage suggests a connection between the two as texts that engage us through the imagination of death. Each of the central characters in the "Franklin's Tale," except the magician, either thinks he or she is going to die for one reason or another, or is under the threat of death, or both. Dorigen imagines her husband will die abroad, or on the rocks on the coast of Brittany; she then tells her husband, who returns home safely, that she would rather die than fulfill her promise; Aurelius in turn tells her, "I would rather be stabbed . . . than to have you fail to keep your word of honor" (331). But Aurelius is most striking for the fact that his death threat is entirely self-imposed. It is conventional for lovers to imagine themselves dying together, both in the figurative sexual sense and in the literal sense, and it is conventional for lovers to threaten each other with death-for-love, but this is certainly an unusual death-triangle. Franklin's comic version of the same triangle could be read in the bagatelle to Madame Helvétius in which he imagines himself meeting her husband in the afterworld. The *Memoir* is a more abstract version of the same thing: a vision fueled by the imagination of death, much like the impassioned speeches of the "Franklin's Tale."

Furthermore, the "Franklin's Tale," to which Franklin draws our attention, and the "Wharff" anecdote, which appears not many pages later, both figure theft and guilt through the vehicle of coastal rocks. Franklin's geography is thus doubly potent, for the anecdote makes a moral landscape of the New England coastline. When Franklin undertakes the theft of the builder's rocks, he and his friends have already helped themselves to the fish in the Highwater and defaced the marsh with their trampling feet—creating a "quagmire" with its own metaphoric resonance of culpability. Although Franklin credits himself with the idea of the robbery, he uses his friends as the commissioners of his crime and evades responsibility by carefully mentioning that there could be as many as three boys accountable for each rock. The metaphor of the "emmets" (ants) further distances Franklin from guilty agency by evoking the instinctual (and therefore blameless) collective activity of insects. Like the "Franklin's Tale," this story has a component of oedipal desire: just as the young Aurelius covets the forbidden wife of his neighbor, so Franklin strives for the adult powers forbidden by his father. And yet the same obliqueness governs each narrative. The rocks, which serve as an objective correlative for the barrier between Aurelius and his love object, also serve as temptation for young Franklin, and yet, as symbols, they have a certain inscrutability. Indeed, the heart of the story, the account of the father's censure, is rendered indirectly. What is most striking in this segment is the fact that Franklin does not refer to his father by name, even to call him simply, "my father" (although he is named earlier). Instead he is introduced here laterally, in a clause that refers back to the group of the boys' fathers: "Several of us were corrected by our Fathers; and tho' I pleaded the Usefulness of the Work, mine convinc'd me that nothing was useful that was not honest."[18] By the same technique that Franklin diffuses blame among his friends while claiming leadership, he diffuses authority among unnamed paternal figures, themselves, perhaps, performing their disciplinary function like so many emmets, while still granting his father's power over him.

The story of Franklin's "Wharff" provides a strange segue to the biography of his father, which immediately follows it. Franklin's sketch emphasizes his father's good judgment, echoing the genealogical theme of Franklins as competent judges and deepening the significance of the anecdote of the rocks and of his father's role as moral arbiter in that instance. In another way, the characterization of his father as a judge also recalls the end of the Franklin's tale, in which the Franklin proposes his story as an opportunity for his audience to judge the characters he describes:

> I think you may like to know something of his Person and Character. He had an excellent Constitution of Body, was of middle Stature, but well set and very strong. He was ingenious, could draw prettily, was skill'd a little in Music and had a pleasing Voice, so that when he play'd Psalm Tunes on his Violin & sung withal as he some times did in an Evening after the Business of the Day was over, it was extreamly agreeable to hear. He had a mechanical Genius too, and on occasion was very handy in the Use of other Tradesmen's Tools. But his great Excellence lay in a sound Understanding and solid judgment in prudential Matters, both in private and publick Affairs. In the latter indeed he was never employed, the numerous Family he had to educate and the Straitness of his Circumstances, keeping him close to his Trade, but I remember well his being frequently visited by leading People, who consulted him for his opinion. (*Writings* 1314-15)

At the same moment that Franklin introduces his father, he reintroduces his son as the interlocutor or epistolary object, thus relativizing the role of the father: "I think you may like to know something of his Person & Character." Franklin speaks of his father specifically *as* a father, engaging his own father through imagining his son's desires. And yet Franklin again avoids mentioning either the father or the son by name: the son is "you" and the father is "him." Franklin seems happier to share his name with those long dead than with those with an immediate claim to it. Indeed, congress with the dead becomes a paradoxical way for Franklin to reclaim the sovereignty of his name: he claims his name from history instead of winning it from his father—whom Franklin seems intent on depriving of a name. The failure to fully acknowledge the crime at the Wharff becomes bound in the narrative with a surreptitious removal of the father's name. But contrary to what Looby might argue, Franklin seems to think he can escape the law of the father as well as the *nom-de-père*. Indeed, on one of the few occasions his father's name does appear, it is in the epitaph that Franklin writes for him and his mother some years after his death.

The epitaph is seemingly unremarkable, and yet Franklin devotes almost as much space to reproducing it as he does to his brief biography of his father. In this way he submits his father to his own authority and writes him into the text as a dead man as much as a living one. Franklin explains that they are buried together under a stone on which he placed the following inscription: "Josiah Franklin/ And Abiah his Wife/ Lie here interred./ They lived lovingly together in Wedlock/ Fifty-five Years.—/ Without an Estate or any gainful Employment,/ By constant Labor an Industry,/ With God's Blessing,/ They maintained a large Family/ Comfortably;/ And brought up thirteen Children,/ And seven Grandchildren/ Reputably" (*Writings* 1316). Franklin takes the occasion of the tombstone as a literary one, adding, "From this Instance, Reader,/ Be encouraged to Diligence in thy Calling,/ And distrust not Providence./ He was a pious & prudent Man,/ She a discreet and virtuous Woman./ Their youngest Son,/ In filial Regard to their Memory,/ Places this Stone./ J.F. born 1655—Died 1744. Ætat. 89/ A.F. born 1667—died 1752—85" (*Writings* 1316). The marble stone that Franklin places over his father's body is a perfect sequel to the story of the purloined stones at the fishing hole. This time it is Franklin who triumphs, turning his father's tombstone into the occasion for his own display of virtue, reminding the reader of the "filial Regard" of the youngest son at the same time that it both praises and dismisses the father. Franklin transforms his father's death into another of his lessons, making the humble space of his father's life a template that any industrious reader could fill in with his own Diligence and trust in Providence. The subtle asymmetry that marks his father's death with a capital letter—he "Died" (whereas his mother merely "died")—suggests the extent to which the tombstone serves specifically to underline and rewrite the father's death. As opposed to the half-deaths that Franklin imagines for himself, the death he marks for his father is a solid one—Franklin even goes out of his way to point out that he "never knew my Father or Mother to have any sickness but that of which they dy'd" (1315), ruling out the possibility of near-death experiences. Franklin's sketch of Josiah Franklin does not bring him back to life, as his own autobiography does, but rather seals the grave.

Although Franklin repeatedly stresses his relationship with his uncles, he does not present himself as a reincarnation or a copy of his father. He suggests instead a very different model, one in which, like Rousseau's Emile, Franklin is a product of his father's experiments. Before the bifocals, then, Franklin himself was a sort of invention.[19] He describes how his brother quit the father's business, creating the expectation that young Franklin would fill his place in assisting in the tallow trade: "[T]here was all Appearance that I was destin'd to supply his Place and be a Tallow Chandler. But my Dislike for the Trade continuing, my Father was under Apprehensions that if he did not find one for me more agreeable, I should break away and get to Sea, as his Son Josiah had done to his great Vexation" (*Writings* 1316). The father has a practical and ingenious solution to the problem: "He therefore sometimes took me to walk with him, and see Joiners, Bricklayers, Turners, Braziers, &c. at their Work, that he might observe my Inclination, & endeavor to fix it on some Trade or other on Land" (*Writings* 1316). In his experiment, the father both gives Franklin the freedom necessary to keep him from craving the sea and attempts to manufacture an interest in an alternate career that he hopes will be matched to his son's inclinations. Franklin is enabled to escape taking the space of his father, his brother John, his half brother Josiah, and even the despised trade of cutler, which his father chose for him after their walks. It is in the final occupation of a printer, which his father settles him in with some misgiving, that Franklin is happiest, but although this is not his father's trade, it too is a shadow role, in that he must work for his older brother.

Ghosts

The story of Franklin's early career as a printer's apprentice, which makes up the most famous section of the autobiography, is the story of the various personae that Franklin adopted instead of his father's persona as a tallow maker. In it, Franklin details how he reincarnated himself over and over again, leaving behind so many ghosts. It is on his life as writer that he focuses our attention, and from the beginning that story, which is the story of adopted lives, is also necessarily the story of a series of mortifications. Franklin commences his writing career by establishing a correspondence with a bookish friend on the set topic of "the Propriety of educating the Female Sex in Learning" (*Writings* 1319). Although Franklin forswears his youthful disputatiousness, he makes it clear that it was the love of argument, and not conviction, that determined his position: "He [John] was of the Opinion that it was improper; & that they were naturally unequal to it. I took the contrary Side, perhaps a little for Dispute sake" (*Writings* 1319). Thus, Franklin is initiated into an unauthorized authorship, learning to write not as himself but as the contrary counterpart of someone else. For Franklin, to write is, in part, to die. The famous anecdote of Franklin's self-taught style is another example of the same thing: Franklin coaches himself in forgetting himself in order to learn to write:

> About this time I met with an odd Volume of the *Spectator*. I had never before seen any of them. I bought it, read it over and over, and was much delighted with it. I thought the Writing excellent, & wish'd if possible to imitate it. With that View, I took some of the Papers, & making short Hints of the Sentiments in each Sentence, laid them by a few Days, and then without looking at the Book, try'd to compleat the Papers again, by expressing each hinted at Sentiment at length as fully as it had been express'd before, in any suitable Words that should come to hand.
>
> Then I compar'd my Spectator with the Original, discover'd some of my Faults & corrected them. But I found I wanted a Stock of Words or a Readiness in recollecting & using them, which I thought I should have acquir'd before that time, if I had gone on making Verses, since the continual Occasion for Words of the same Import but of different Length, to suit the Measure, or a different Sound for the Rhyme, would have laid me under a constant Necessity of searching for Variety, and also have tended to fix that Variety in my Mind & make me Master of it. Therefore I took some of the Tales & turn'd them into Verse: And after a time, when I had pretty well forgotten the Prose, turn'd them back again. I also sometimes jumbled my Collections of Hints into Confusion, and after some Weeks, endeavor'd to reduce them into the best Order, before I began to form the full Sentences & compleat the Paper. (*Writings* 1319-1320)

The exercise in fact enfolds a repeated forgetting: first, a forgetting of the (untutored) self in the act of imitating the *Spectator*, then the self-imposed forgetting of the exact words of the *Spectator*, and, finally, the reciprocal forgetting of both poetry and prose. By the same token, the exercise is also an exercise in memory, but a memory founded on its own intentional mortification.[20] And here I would make a distinction between an ethic of "impersonality" and one of self-mortification, for this process makes it possible for Franklin to become a shadow author of the *Spectator*, and, indeed, to speak of "*my* Spectator" with a certain ironic pride. What emerges with the repetition of the exercise, however, is a curious situation in which Franklin is imitating himself. By the time he gets around to practicing at reassembling his own "Collections of Hints," the original he is trying to recover is *his own*.[21] Through the "Hints," Franklin invents another Franklin machine, a mechanical device by which he can recover or extend himself. Reminiscent of his uncle's shorthand, the "Hints" are a private system of communication designed for addressing the self and reassembling its consciousness. They suggest that one of the many personae that Franklin is capable of adopting is himself. The object of Franklin's game is, through an act of practiced forgetfulness, to train his memory to remember the words of the *Spectator* as if they were his own, to make himself, in short, a spectator of his own mind.

The theme of forgetting runs throughout the *Memoir*, and parallels the theme of death. Franklin's method of autobiography implies forgetting as much as remembering: he forgets the writing self in order to relive the life of the previous self. But Franklin's story itself also includes numerous acts of strategic forgetting. The most significant for Franklin's career was the accident that allowed him, first, to assume the fraudulent role of publisher of his brother's newspaper, and then to flee his brother altogether under the false pretense of having been released from his bonds. In this curious disguise, Franklin plays a character close to himself—the freed apprentice and printer that he would like to become.[22] It is an appropriate irony that Franklin *does* become the young printer that he sets himself up as in his brother's absence, in no small part because of the opportunity afforded by his playacting the part.

The story begins with its own moment of forgetting when Franklin cannot remember the political reason that his brother was imprisoned and his newspaper closed down: "One of the Pieces in our News-Paper, on some political Point which I have now forgotten, gave Offense to the Assembly. He was taken up, censur'd and imprisoned for a Month by the Speaker's Warrant, I suppose because he would not discover his Author" (*Writings* 1324). The particulars of his brother's discharge, however, Franklin remembers perfectly well: "My Brother's Discharge was accompany'd with an Order of the House, (a very odd one) *that James Franklin should no longer print the Paper called the New England Courant*. [. . .] Some propos'd to evade the Order by changing the Name of the Paper; but my Brother seeing Inconveniences in that, it was finally concluded on as a better Way, to let it be printed for the future under the Name of *Benjamin Franklin*" (*Writings* 1325). To make the scheme appear aboveboard, Franklin is released from his original indentures to his brother, while secret new ones are drawn up. Franklin takes advantage of this illicit scheme to enact a trick of his own: "At length a fresh Difference arising between my Brother and me, I took upon me to assert my Freedom, presuming that he would not venture to produce the new Indentures" (*Writings* 1325).

The story that Franklin does remember is a more potent example of what Jay Fliegelman calls the American revolution against patriarchal authority than the context Franklin omits. Franklin's brother conspires to exploit Benjamin Franklin's name for his own uses, and ends up being exploited by Franklin himself, who takes advantage of the false name he has established for himself as a free man. Thus, Franklin gambles his own treachery toward his brother against his brother's public deceit, knowing that his brother cannot sacrifice his own good name in order to reclaim the errant apprentice. He manages, therefore, to assume the identity that he had been masquerading. It is fitting, then, that what begins this sequence of events is, Franklin explains, his brother's refusal to divulge the name of an offending author in his newspaper: the secret traffic in names manages to subvert both state and family authority, bringing about a miniature domestic revolution as well as setting Franklin on his own path toward overthrowing the government.

This incident, in which Franklin so far forgets himself as to imagine he can be a freeman, is the break that makes his career possible. It is necessary for Franklin to forget his family and evade the struggle with his living kin for him to become the famous Benjamin Franklin. It is the dead who empower Franklin, and in New York, William Bradford, a local printer, tells Franklin, "My Son at Philadelphia has recently lost his principle Hand, Aquila Rose, by Death. If you go thither I believe he may employ you" (*Writings* 1326). This fateful instruction from a father to a stranger sends Franklin south to replace a dead man. When Franklin arrives, he finds the son Andrew Bradford does not need help, but he is enlisted in a spying mission when William Bradford agrees to take him to a rival printer, Keimer, who does need help. Franklin thus enters the shop where he will be employed under false pretenses: Bradford escorts Franklin because he wants an opportunity to collect intelligence on his son's rival in the local printing trade. Because Keimer does not recognize the father as a relative of his rival, Andrew Bradford, he willingly divulges his business, with Franklin accomplice to it all. Immediately on arriving in Philadelphia, then, Franklin finds himself playing a shadow role in the family romance of small-town commerce. As it turns out, when Franklin appears at Keimer's shop, he is composing the elegy for the darling son of the trade, Aquila Rose, whom Franklin was supposed to replace:

> Keimer's Printing House I found, consisted of an old shatter'd Press, and one small worn-out Fount of English, which he was then using himself, composing in it an Elegy on Aquila Rose before-mentioned, an ingenious young Man of excellent Character much respected in the Town, Clerk of the Assemble, & pretty Poet. Keimer made Verses, too, but very indifferently.—He could not be said to write them, for his Manner was to compose them in Types directly out of his Head; so there being no Copy, but one Pair of Cases, and the Elegy likely to require all the Letter, no one could help him.—I endeavor'd to put his Press (which he had not yet us'd, & of which he understood nothing) into Order fit to be work'd with; & promising to come & print off his Elegy as soon he should have got it ready, I return'd to Bradford's who gave me a little job to do for the present, & there I lodged and dieted. A few Days after Keimer sent for me to print off the Elegy. And now he had got another Pair of Cases, and a Pamphlet to reprint, on which he set me to work. (*Writings* 1331)

The literary quality of Franklin's life, which his *Memoir* exploits so well, is evident here as much as anywhere.[23] It is pure poetry that Keimer should have no room for help from Franklin because he is using his type to compose the elegy for the man Franklin was supposed to replace. Aquila Rose's place is not yet quite empty, though he is dead, and there is not yet space for Franklin in the business. Likewise, when Franklin has a business under his own name, he takes on the son of Aquila Rose as his own apprentice, completing the loop of filial substitution. Franklin's arrival also spells out the death of Keimer's venture, for Franklin will, in good time, take his place as well—so it is appropriate that Keimer should be writing an elegy when Franklin makes his entrance. The shortage of letters that makes it impossible for Franklin to work is a perfect metaphor for the shortage of space in the Philadelphia printing trade that comes to influence the fate of Keimer, Bradford, and Franklin, all in their different ways. That Franklin's life should be so rife with literary effects (or that he should so skillfully novelize it, we cannot know for certain) itself adds a literary touch: the great printer and writer has a life that makes the perfect book.

Franklin soon finds himself operating under another set of false pretenses with Keimer, because, by a seemingly fortuitous accident, Governor Keith has offered Franklin the opportunity to set up shop on his own—and Franklin keeps the offer a secret from Keimer. While Franklin waits to travel to Boston for his father's consent, he acts as if nothing has changed: "In the mean time the Intention was to be kept secret, and I went on working with Keimer as usual, the Governor sending for me now & then to dine with him, a very great Honor I thought it, and conversing with me in the most affable, familiar, & friendly manner imaginable" (*Writings* 1333). Once again, though, the deception is a double one, for the part of the humble apprentice that Franklin acts turns out indeed to be his true situation after all when it emerges that Keith's offer is itself a charade: Franklin, then, puts on an elaborate show to Keimer of being exactly who he really is, while assisting the governor in playing the part of the great man. Even the appearance of favor from the governor that vexes Keimer is false, for Franklin receives no preferment at all, and is instead sent penniless to England in search of a printing press.

During the period when Franklin waits to depart on his fool's errand, he is drawn into another scheme of deception, this one involving his friend Ralph, his eventual traveling companion. It is the reverse of his Silence Dogood trick, for here Franklin pretends to have written something he has not, instead of pretending not to have written something that he has. The continuity between the scenes, however, lies in the presentation of authorship as a pose. Ralph, impatient that his rival Osborne disparages his work, convinces Franklin to lend him his name when he presents his work to their Sunday literary club. The task for that week is to be a "Version of the 18th Psalm, which describes the Descent of a Deity" (*Writings* 1341), with all members to present their poem on their trek into the woods near the Skuylkill: "Now, says he [Ralph], Osborne never will allow the least Merit in any thing of mine but makes 1000 Criticisms out of mere Envy. He is not so jealous of you. I wish therefore you would take this Piece, & produce it as yours. I will pretend not to have had time, & so produce nothing: We shall then see what he will say to it.—It was agreed, and I immediately transcrib'd it that it might appear in my own hand" (*Writings* 1341). When Franklin reads Ralph's piece, Osborne as predicted praises it immoderately: "[W]ho could have imagin'd, says he, that Franklin had been capable of such a Performance; such Painting, such Force! such Fire! he has even improv'd the Original!" (*Writings* 1341-42). Like Franklin's exercise with the *Spectator*, this literary game is one in which originality consists of virtuous imitation. The element of friendly competition creates a new twist in which the ability to judge the relationship between copies becomes itself a virtue. The joke is that Franklin improves on the original in Osborne's unwitting estimation in more ways than one: by simply not being Ralph, Franklin raises the quality of the work in Osborne's eyes.

In Ralph's final deus ex machina Osborne is smarted, but Franklin must also descend from the role of literary deity that Osborne assigns him, and thus Ralph manages to restage the Psalm in dramatic form as well as poetic form. As Franklin has it, however, the final descent is the inevitable one that Ralph must make from poetry to prose. These descents are touched by death, as all Franklin's unmaskings are, and he ends the anecdote with obituaries:

> When we next met, Ralph discover'd the Trick we had plaid him, and Osborne was a little laught at. This Transaction fix'd Ralph in his Resolution of becoming a Poet. I did all I could to dissuade him from it, but He continu'd scribbling Verses, till *Pope* cur'd him.—He became, however, a pretty good Prose Writer. More of him hereafter. But as I might not have occasion again to mention the other two, I shall just remark here, that Watson died in my Arms a few Years after, much lamented, being the best of the Set. Osborne went to the West Indies, where he became an eminent Lawyer & made Money, but died young. He and I had made a serious Agreement, that the one who happen'd first to die, should if possible make a friendly Visit to the other, and acquaint him how he found things in that separate State. But he never fulfill'd his Promise. (*Writings* 1342)

At the moment when Franklin switches to the topic of death, there is a suggestion that the text itself has the power of death. When Franklin comments, "But as I might not have occasion again to mention the other two, I shall just remark here . . ." a relationship is established between his narrative chronology and the forward movement of time that left his friends behind. He saves them from narrative oblivion by confiscating them in their place to the separate State to which they were all condemned. The segue from the story of youthful shenanigans to the listing of the dead is an odd one—and yet the last two sentences, in which the prankster spirit is combined with the engagement with posthumousness connects the two. Even as he evokes the death of his friends with some pathos, "Watson died in my Arms a few Years after, much lamented, being the best of the Set," Franklin humorously leaves open the possibility that death is another role-playing trick: when Osborne does not "keep his promise" of a return it is the final double cross in the boyish game of exchanged identities.

When Franklin finally makes it to England on Keith's advice, he enacts his own double-cross. And, indeed, the story of the boyish schemes and the story of Keith's deception are interrelated, for both bear a Shakespearean hallmark. Franklin discovers that there is a problem with Keith while on ship, and his dilemma resembles Hamlet's in his shipboard scene. Having waited till the very last minute for Keith to provide the letters of introduction he had promised, Franklin is forced to receive them on board. When the letters don't appear even then, he extracts a promise from the captain that he will be able to examine the mailbag before they reach their destination. That the Captain kept his word to Franklin reemphasizes Keith's failure to keep *his* word. However, Franklin finds in the bag no letters, "upon which my Name was put, as under my Care; I pick'd out 6 or 7 that by the Handwriting I thought might be the promis'd Letters, especially as one of them was directed to Basket the King's Printer, and another to some Stationer" (*Writings* 1344). On attempting to deliver the letter to the stationer, Franklin meets with a surprise:

> I don't know such a Person, says he: but opening the Letter, O, this is from Riddlesden; I have lately found him to be a compleat Rascal, and I will have nothing to do with him, nor receive any Letters from him. So putting the Letter in my Hand, he turn'd on his Heel & left me to serve some Customer.—I was suprized to find these were not the Governor's Letters. And after recollecting and comparing Circumstances, I had begun to doubt his Sincerity.—I found my Friend Denham, and opened the whole Affair to him. He let me into Keith's Character, told me there was not the least Probability that he had written any Letters for me, that no one who knew him had the smallest Dependence on him, and he laught at the Notion of the Governor's giving me a Letter of Credit, having as he said no Credit to give.—On my expressing some Concern about what I should do: He ad-

> vised me to endeavor getting some Employment in the Way of my Business. Among the Printers here, says he, you will improve yourself: and when you return to America, you will set up with greater Advantage.—
>
> We both of us happen'd to know, as well as the Stationer, that Riddlesden the Attorney, was a very Knave. He had half ruin'd Mrs. Read's Father by drawing him in to be bound for him. By his Letter it appear'd, there was a secret Scheme on foot at the Prejudice of Hamilton (Suppos'd to be then coming over with us,) and that Keith was concern'd in it with Riddlesden. Denham, who was a Friend of Hamilton's, thought he ought to be acquainted with it. So when he arriv'd in England, which was soon after, partly from Resentment & Ill-Will to Keith & Riddlesden, & partly from Good Will to him: I waited on him, and gave him the Letter. He thank'd me cordially, the Information being of Importance to him. And from that time he became my Friend, greatly to my Advantage afterwards on many Occasions. (*Writings* 1344-45)

The paragraph then turns out to be about the question of keeping—and giving away—words. What Franklin looks for in the mailbag is his own name, but, failing to find this word, he takes the handwriting on the envelopes he does find as a kind of security of identity and uses it, as well as the names of the addressees, to justify his own slightly suspicious act of removing the letters. But the text of the letters, instead of introducing Franklin to the stationer, serve to introduce Franklin to Keith's real character. On the strength of his new knowledge, Franklin is then able to circulate the purloined letters as the means to destroy Keith's credit. These letters turn out to be letters of introduction indeed: they provide the entree into the London printing world that Franklin needs, despite the fact that they do not officially introduce Franklin himself. Franklin thus turns the treachery of Riddlesden, the "compleat Rascal," against Keith in his own treacherous turn. Like Hamlet, Franklin is able to make his own death sentence into someone else's mortification.

Franklin seems destined to switch places with his enemies more than once: the story of Keith, and Franklin's extended rant against Keith's conduct, is paired with two significant "errata" of Franklin's own. The first is the deferred story of his friendship with Ralph. Their friendship sours when Ralph takes Franklin's name in order to protect his future literary reputation while he labors at a lowly teaching job; and when Franklin uses the opportunity of Ralph's absence to proposition Ralph's wife. This story, which Franklin draws out over several pages, is the mirror image of the Keith story: Ralph uses Franklin's name and his pocket money for his own introduction in the world, while Franklin attempts to defraud Ralph of the woman who would take Ralph's name. What Franklin loses, like Keith, is the upper hand: "This made a Breach between us, & when he return'd again to London, he let me know he thought I had cancel'd all the Obligations he had been under to me" (1347). Here Franklin's partnership with Ralph, which again takes the form of a sharing of Franklin's name, is juxtaposed with the ignominious tale of Franklin's relationship with Deborah Read, with whom Franklin fails to share his name in marriage. Just as Keith was involved with the knave who attempted to cheat Miss Read's father, Franklin cheats the Reads—and by the same method that Keith cheated him: by failing to send letters. The stories are in fact intimately linked: "He [Ralph] seem'd quite to forget his Wife & Child, and I by degrees my Engagements with Miss. Read, to whom I never wrote more than one Letter, & that was to let her know I would not likely soon return" (*Writings* 1345). Franklin's absence is occasioned by Keith's falsity, while Franklin's betrayal of Ralph is occasioned by Ralph's absence, both of which facts contribute to Deborah Read's disappointment. Read's name is blessed with the same ironic novelistic quality that seems to pursue Franklin—for *read* is precisely what Franklin does not let Deborah do. Deborah Read is indeed "between men," to use Eve Sedgwick's phrase, for as Franklin abandons her for his interest in the love triangle with Ralph, Read ends up marrying another man, Rogers, who also deserts her. For this disaster, Franklin blames himself, noting, "This was another of the great Errata of my

Life, which I should wish to correct if I were to live it over again" (1345). However, the delinquency of Read's husband, in the final twist, allows Franklin the opportunity to give Read his name at last: "With him [Rogers] however she was never happy, and soon parted from him, refusing to cohabit with him or bear his Name It being now said that he had another Wife" (1353). Without officially dying, Franklin, then, gets the chance to relive his choice and correct his errata later in life.[24]

The unofficial death is also the theme of the affair of Franklin's career as a merchant's clerk. Here Franklin narrowly avoids an apparently satisfying life in retail through the untimely death of his mentor—an event that provides Franklin with his own foretaste of dying. The incident begins happily enough: "Mr. Denham took a Store in Water Street, where we open'd our Goods. I attended the Business diligently, studied Accounts, and grew in a little Time expert at selling.—We lodg'd and boarded together, he counseled me as a Father, having a sincere Regard for me: I respected & lov'd him and we might have gone on together very happily" (*Writings* 1354). But Denham dies, leaving Franklin a small legacy "as a Token of his Kindness for me," and abandoning Franklin "once more to the wide World" (*Writings* 1354). Franklin at the same time becomes sick: "My distemper was a Pleurisy, which very nearly carried me off.—I suffered a good deal, gave up the Point in my own mind, & was rather disappointed when I found my self recovering; regretting in some degree that I must now sometime or other have all that disagreeable Work to do over again" (*Writings* 1354). The substitute father leads Franklin to a substitute death, and Franklin memorializes both with unusually frantic punctuation that repeatedly brings his story to the abrupt divide of a colon or of his signature dash. The end of Denham's life is the end of Franklin's merchant career, a professional expiration for Franklin at the same time that it is a personal loss. Instead of regretting death, Franklin comically regrets life: the need to face death a second time coinciding with the need to find a new trade. This is the humorous inverse of the fantasy of the relived life—Franklin suffers from the disagreeable need to relive the "Work" of death. By using the word "Work" to describe the process of dying, Franklin creates a further connection between his employment dilemma and his experience of illness. In both cases, the change of roles can be understood as an unofficial death, and Franklin's conception of the self-mortifications entailed in worldly performances is reinforced. The underlying sense of grief at the loss of his protector Denham also suggests that the near-death experience can be read as a kind of mourning for the lost parent figure.

Franklin sheds these ghostly selves, these alternative would-be lives, to begin his life as a printer in earnest. He returns to Keimer, eventually sets up shop as a printer on his own, and marries Deborah Read. The circumstances of his marriage, which closes the first part of the *Memoir*, are of characteristic complexity. After Read was alienated from her first husband, Franklin reopened his friendship with her and found their "mutual Affection was revived" (*Writings* 1371). However, there were now "great Objections" to a union because of her first marriage. Indeed, it is the rumored death of Read's husband that both makes remarriage possible, and also makes it difficult and risky. "Tho' there was a Report of his [the first husband's] Death, it was not certain. Then, tho' it should be true, he had left many Debts which his Successor might be call'd upon to pay" (*Writings* 1371). Another unofficial death, this one allows Franklin to correct his "great *Erratum*" (*Writings* 1371) without officially dying himself. For, as Franklin reports, "We ventured however, over all these Difficulties, and I took her to Wife Sept. 1, 1730" (*Writings* 1371). Successor, again, to a dead man, Franklin fares better here than when he set out to replace the deceased Aquila Rose: "None of the Inconveniences happened that we had apprehended, she prov'd a good & faithful Helpmate, assisted me much by attending the Shop, we throve together, and have ever mutually endeavour'd to make each other happy" (*Writings* 1371). The only ghosts in their marriage, then, are the ghosts of Franklin's earlier selves.

If Franklin's narrative haunts American literature, Franklin himself is also haunted by his own life, by his past lives. The reproducible Franklin, the Franklin who serves as a template for so many reproductions, in fact reproduces *himself* many times before he allows himself to be reproduced by others. When Cathy Davidson wrote in 1986 that "The early national era antedated the Romantic period's notions of the author as the prime creator" and that "During the postrevolutionary period, a residual Puritan emphasis on relating 'truth' or 'history' still underscored the older notion that the writer merely formulated what everybody knew,"[25] she set the tone for the rest of the Franklin scholarship of the last century. The undervaluing of early American literature and the increasing interest in print culture as opposed to literary culture have gone a long way to reinforce Davidson's characterization of the period. But while her characterization of the general reading public of the early republic is amply supported, Franklin's oeuvre cannot be assimilated to this model. He is a prime creator for whom the role of simple truth teller or historian was long dead. Indeed, the guise of commonsense author was just one of Franklin's repertoire of literary ghosts. Even from the grave, Franklin always has the last laugh.

Notes

1. I have chosen Leo Lemay's edition of Franklin's *Writings* for use throughout this essay as the official *Franklin Papers* edition of the memoir is not yet available (1150).

2. A popular retelling can be found in the opening of Richard Morris's *Seven Who Shaped Our Destiny: The Founding Fathers as Revolutionaries*, which highlights the rivalry between Adams and Franklin.

3. See Lemay and Zall xxiii.

4. If Franklin's friends and fellow signers of the Declaration of Independence, Adams, Thomas Jefferson, and Benjamin Rush, all indulged in visions of death with decidedly Romantic overtones in their memoirs, Franklin's afterlives were, by comparison, decidedly Augustan. Franklin's *Memoirs* are presented, indeed, in a way that resembles the presentation of his other satiric first-person fictions and is continuous with Defoe and Swift.

5. Sacvan Bercovitch puts it well when he explains, "Through all his provisional

personae, Franklin, as even his first readers saw, assumes an identity representative of the rising nation. The link between the Franklins of the particular moments in his career and the 'essential Franklin' is the *exemplum* of corporate selfhood, ascending from dependence to dominance" (234 n12). See also Mitchell Breitwieser, *Cotton Mather and Benjamin Franklin: The Price of Representative Personality*.

6. The best discussion of Franklin's relationship to print culture is in Ziff 83-106.

7. See Michael Warner's excellent reading 73-75.

8. See Jefferson's memoir 100-101.

9. The memoir was written in four parts—the first being the most famous. Part 2 is largely an exposition of Franklin's unwritten book *The Art of Virtue*, and part 3 is a somewhat dry account of the years 1731-1757. Part 4 consists of a few pages added on to part 3. It is the first part that I will be considering here.

10. Quoted in Van Doren 631. Van Doren notes that Franklin was actually 74 at the time of his letter, so Franklin seems to be on the third repetition of his life.

11. As she was dying, Catherine Drinker Bowen made notes for the end of a biography of Franklin that she never finished. The penultimate quotation from Franklin she recorded is about cheating death, and it suggests another way Franklin imagined endless life: "'Live as if you are to live forever'" (251).

12. Douglas Anderson has an excellent reading of "Poor Richard," in *The Radical Enlightenment of Benjamin Franklin* 90-119. He points out that "Death is a recurrent and traditional subject for almanacs, whose ephemeral nature as texts corresponds perfectly to the ephemeral nature of human life" and shows how "Over the first decade of *Poor Richard's* existence, birth and death played roles in Franklin's life that inevitably sharpened his sense of the almanac's mortal analogy" (110-11). He also provides interesting new data on the question of how the death of Franklin's son, Francis Folger Franklin, is memorialized in *Poor Richard* (111).

13. Warner sees Franklin as using death here to dramatize "the problem of the subject who writes," and claims that "This extraordinary fantasy of ghostwriting dramatizes a discrepancy between persons and texts. As in the epitaph of twelve years earlier, the writing subject is necessarily cut off from the body. There is considerable emphasis on the separation of the two, since the writing subject is an incorporeal agent acting not only separate from the body but also to violate it. In the epitaph the body is decomposed; in the preface it is entered through the nose and handled like a puppet" (77).

14. Franklin also experiments with imagined temporalities when he invents the idea of daylight savings time. See Wright 357.

15. For a concise review of the various critical evaluations of Franklin's notion of self, as well as a critique of the standard view, see Kuklick 105-11.

16. For an interesting comment on Franklin's bifocals, see Jay Fliegelman, *Declaring Independence: Jefferson, Natural Language, and the Culture of Performance*.

17. I have given the modern English translation for ease of comparison.

18. Malini Schueller sees Franklin's focus on the supposed "usefulness" of his project as crucial here, and points out that "Perhaps the most recurrent word in Franklin's *Autobiography* is 'useful.'" She notes that "This should hardly be surprising in a work intended as a guidebook for posterity," but sees it as a manifestation of Franklin's "moral utilitarian ethics" (95, 96).

19. Cox puts it beautifully when he writes, "Thus, having organized a philosophical society, a university, a hospital, a lending library, an efficient postal system, and having invented the stove, the smokeless street lamp, bifocals, electrical conduction, the harmonica, and a host of other items too numerous to mention, Franklin at the age of sixty-five embarked upon what one wants to call his great invention—the invention of himself, not as a fiction, but as a fact both of and in history" (259).

20. In a wild and free-ranging article on colonial mapping (understood in the broadest sense) William Boelhower touches on the strange characteristics of memory in *The Autobiography* in his discussion of Philadelphia: "In Franklin's foundation story, Philadelphia is presented as an unpretentious functional space, a city without origin or the mechanism of memory built into it" (406). Philadelphia as Franklin helped to build it refuses to remember—Boston, London—even as it fails to forget them, much as Franklin remembers and forgets the *Spectator.*

21. For a detailed description of how the *Spectator*'s style did, indeed, come to resemble Franklin's own, see Furtwangler 15-35.

22. For a discussion of the importance of theatricality and role playing in Franklin's autobiography, and its relation to questions of authority, see Patterson 13-16.

23. Ziff makes an interesting observation about the novelistic quality of the memoirs in *Writing in the New Nation*: "Franklin, with his belief that to write is, in effect, to publish, offered the represented self as a representative history. As a result, his *Autobiography* more closely resembles a novel than do the recollections of his contemporaries. It centers on the formation of character, on, that is, his construction of a character, rather than on public events; it lets us hear a range of voices and dialects; it dramatizes incidents. In general it conveys the feeling that the writer's delight in literary construction plays as important a part in determining what he elects to represent as does his governing sense of the typical and the useful" (118-19).

24. Ada Van Gastel has argued, in "Franklin and Freud: Love in the *Autobiography*," that Franklin slights Read in his memoir. Gastel's argument is that Franklin is the model of Freud's notion of sublimation, and that as such he is a model of American civilization. She cites his use of the technical word "errata" to describe his mistake with Read as evidence of this claim: "By using the term 'erratum' to refer to his neglect to keep in touch, Franklin gives a professional as well as a didactic twist to his relationship with Deborah Read" (175). Without reference to Franklin's infamous extratextual hedonism, it is possible to refute the claim that Franklin's language is unfeeling by reference to the sincerity and even intimacy with which he deploys the printer's metaphor throughout the memoir.

25. Davidson 30.

Works Cited

Anderson, Douglas. *The Radical Enlightenment of Benjamin Franklin*. Baltimore: Johns Hopkins, 1997.

Bercovitch, Sacvan. *The Puritan Origins of the American Self.* New Haven: Yale University Press, 1975.

Boelhower, William. "Stories of Foundation, Scenes of Origin." *American Literary History* 5.3 (Fall 1993) 391-428.
Bowen, Catherine Drinker. *The Most Dangerous Man in America: Scenes from the Life of Benjamin Franklin*. Boston: Little, Brown, 1974.
Breitwieser, Mitchell. *Cotton Mather and Benjamin Franklin: The Price of Representative Personality*. Cambridge: Cambridge Univ. Press, 1984.
Butterfield, L. H., ed. *The Adams Papers: The Diary and Autobiography of John Adams*. New York: Atheneum, 1964.
Chaucer, Geoffrey. *Canterbury Tales/Tales of Caunturbury*. New York: Bantam, 1964.
Cox, James. "Autobiography and America." *Virginia Quarterly Review* 47.2 (1971): 256.
Davidson, Cathy. *Revolution and the Word. The Rise of the Novel in America*. New York: Oxford Univ. Press, 1986.
Fliegelman, Jay. *Declaring Independence: Jefferson, Natural Language, and the Culture of Performance*. Stanford: Stanford Univ. Press, 1993.
Furtwangler, Albert. "The *Spectator*'s Apprentice," in *American Silhouettes: Rhetorical Identities of the Founders*. New Haven: Yale Univ. Press, 1987.
Kuklick, Bruce. *Benjamin Franklin, Jonathan Edwards, and the Representation of American Culture*. New York: Oxford Univ. Press, 1993
Lemay, Leo, ed. *Benjamin Franklin: Writings*. New York: Library of America, 1987.
Lemay, Leo, and P. M. Zall, eds. *The Autobiography of Benjamin Franklin: A Genetic Text*. Knoxville: Univ. of Tennessee Press, 1981.
Looby, Christopher. *Voicing America: Language, Literary Form, and the Origins of the United States*. Chicago: Univ. of Chicago Press, 1996.
Morris, Richard. *Seven Who Shaped Our Destiny: The Founding Fathers as Revolutionaries*. New York: Harper and Row, 1973.
Patterson, Mark R. *Authority, Autonomy, and Representation in American Literature, 1776-1865*. Princeton: Princeton Univ. Press, 1988.
Peterson, Merrill D., ed. *Thomas Jefferson: Writings*. New York: Library of America, 1984.
Schueller, Malini. "Authorial Discourse and Pseudo-Discourse in Franklin's *Autobiography*." *Early American Literature* 22.1 (1987): 94-107.
Van Doren, Carl. *Benjamin Franklin*. New York: Viking, 1938.
Van Gastel, Ada. "Franklin and Freud: Love in the *Autobiography*." *Early American Literature* 25.2 (1990): 168-182.
Warner, Michael. *The Letters of the Republic: Publication and the Public Sphere in Eighteenth-Century America*. Cambridge: Harvard Univ. Press, 1990.
Wright, Esmond. *Franklin of Philadelphia*. Cambridge: Harvard Univ. Press, 1986.
Ziff, Larzer. "Writing for Print." In *Writing in the New Nation: Prose, Print, and Politics in the Early United States*. New Haven: Yale Univ. Press, 1991.

Two Texts Told Twice:
Poor Richard, Pastor Yorick, and the Case of the Word's Return

Christina Lupton

Christina Lupton looks at two towering eighteenth-century figures together and gives an account of how an author's early works can be recycled in later ones and put to use in new contexts. Laurence Sterne, an eccentric Irish clergyman, is most famous for his bizarre novel *The Life and Opinions of Tristram Shandy, Gent.*, published in nine volumes from 1759 to 1767. In integrating one of his own early sermons into his novel, Sterne engaged in a kind of self-recycling.

In the same way, Franklin gathered up many of his early sayings from *Poor Richard's Almanack* and other writings in *The Way to Wealth*. The writings were, to use a favorite word of modern business writers, *repurposed* to suit a new context. Lupton's essay becomes an exploration of literary transformation: Franklin's and Sterne's texts, she argues, "make their reappearance across periods of historical and personal transformation in a way that directly affects how they are to be read." Both works raise the "question of how words are to be read by having the sermon and the aphorisms reappear in settings where their own reception is a problem." — J.L.

Laurence Sterne's first published sermon, *The Abuses of Conscience*, appeared in 1751 as a six-penny pamphlet just three weeks after Sterne had preached it at the summer assizes in York. Apart from a few pointedly political pieces published in the *York Courant* and his election pamphlet, "Query Upon Query, Being an Answer to J.S.'s Letter Printed in the *York Courant*" (1741), this sermon was also Sterne's first publication. Eight years later, in 1759, as the success of the first two volumes of *Tristram Shandy* augmented Sterne's rise to fame as an author, the sermon appeared again with only a few minor changes as a text within the novel. Here, as it is read aloud by Trim in the secular forum of the Shandy drawing room, the sermon is continuously interrupted by the central cohort of the novel's male characters: Toby, Walter, and Dr. Slop. The Anglican sermon, which connects religion and morality, and rebukes the idea that either can rely on reason alone, can seem difficult to take seriously in the witty, highly intellectual context of Sterne's *Tristram Shandy*. For Carol Kay, "the sermon appears as play in the novel, but assures us that there are times and places for law as well as play" (225). Sterne's contemporary readers saw its inclusion, alternately, as evidence of Sterne's contestable standing as a preacher, and as a harbor of generic familiarity and piety in an otherwise bawdy novel. Horace Walpole praised the sermon discreetly, without associating it with the novel's humor: "The characters are tolerably kept up," writes Walpole of *Tristram Shandy*, "but the humor is forever attempted and missed. The best thing in it is a sermon" (qtd. in Howes, 56).

In 1766, well into the period in which Sterne's career as writer of fiction had overtaken his career as country pastor, *The Abuses of Conscience* was published a third time under Sterne's editorship in the fourth volume of *Yorick's Sermons*. Capitalizing on *Tristram Shandy*'s success, Sterne took his literary character, Yorick, the pastor held responsible in *Tristram Shandy* for the authorship of *The Abuses of Conscience*, and made him the pretext for publishing the collection of his stock of sermons.[1] In its second incarnation as moral text, the sermon, like many such collections circulating in Europe's eighteenth-century literary circles, was popular with the same readers who had applauded *Tristram Shandy*. This volume of sermons appeared with a subscription list of 693 including Diderot and Voltaire. The acclaim for Yorick's sermons was hardly to be distinguished from the celebrity that Sterne had won for himself as a writer of literature.

During the decade in which Sterne's *Abuses of Conscience* remained a pamphlet of little significance, Benjamin Franklin's *Poor Richard's Almanack* was one of the best-selling items in the colonial literary marketplace. Providing American readers with its annual blend of proverbs, recipes, and prophecy, Franklin's almanac sold over

10,000 copies annually at a time when the population of Philadelphia was less than 15,000 (Nash 195-96). Franklin's best-selling piece, known since 1780 as *The Way to Wealth*, was written in 1757 as the preface to the twenty-sixth and final edition of the almanac. The preface format was not new: the previous editions of the almanac had all included an address by Poor Richard to his "Courteous Reader," and had used this device to develop and maintain the character of Richard Saunders, arguably Franklin's finest, and certainly best-sustained, literary creation.[2] Yet this final preface expanded the realm of the address to new proportions. While previous issues of the almanac had devoted only the first page to the introduction, in this issue the introduction extends to the second page, fills all available space on the right-hand pages devoted to covering the 12 months of the year, and warrants a final page that follows the month of December. The introduction was quickly republished in its own right, first by Franklin's nephew under the weighty but descriptive title "Father Abraham's Speech To a great Number of People at a Vendue of Merchant-Goods; Introduced to the Publick by Poor Richard, a famous Pennsylvania Conjurer, and Almanack-Maker," but then in a succession of new editions, condensed versions, and translations. In the eighteenth century alone, *The Way to Wealth* was reprinted 145 times, including 36 in the colonies and 51 in England, and continued in the nineteenth century to outsell the *Autobiography*.[3] Its content, given as the proverbial advice of Poor Richard, promotes the policy of thrift and hard work for which Franklin is still best remembered and has secured aphorisms such as "God helps them that help themselves," and "There are no Gains without Pains" their place in the American popular imagination.

Like *Tristram Shandy*, *The Way to Wealth* serves as a venue for the presentation of material that had appeared elsewhere. Taking the form of a speech given by Father Abraham, "a plain clean old Man, with white Locks" (7:340), Franklin's composition brings together a collection of aphorisms, culled, with the exception of two new ones that deal with the ideal brevity of words, from the previous 25 editions of the almanac.[4] Franklin arranged this montage of economic advice in the summer, just prior to and during his second voyage to England, which he took as ambassador to the Pennsylvania assembly in their case against the proprietor, Thomas Penn. The general editors of Franklin's collected works suggest that in *The Way to Wealth* "one can recognize the skill with which Franklin wove his maxims together into a connected discourse, and appreciate the fun he had doing it while on his long voyage to England" (7:340).

This posture puts Franklin in the position, structurally akin to Sterne's, of revisiting his own writings at a distance of more than a decade of personal and historical change and sifting through his own words at a dramatically new moment in his own political career. Having invented Poor Richard for colonists who were not yet Americans and who openly enjoyed the benefits of imperial prosperity, Franklin reprinted a select harvest of aphorisms focusing on thrift and hard work at a time when the issue of how American money was spent was becoming an increasingly political issue.[5] By 1760, when the sale of *The Way to Wealth* was at its height, the colonies were at the end of a period in which the consumption of foreign goods (in which Franklin himself partook) had radically increased and in which excessive consumption was now explosively linked with dependence on Britain.[6] Although not as affected by changing political moods as Franklin's *Autobiography*, whose later parts are divided from its first by the event of Revolution, in its intertextuality *The Way to Wealth* registers the discontinuities of history.[7] The same can be said of Sterne's anti-Catholic sermon, which had been composed in a time of Jacobite uprising in Britain and was published as the work of Yorick during a decade of relative stability for the monarchy, for the Anglican community, and for Sterne as an established literary celebrity. In 1750, Sterne preached the moderation of Anglican doctrine against the irrationality of Catholicism in his sermons, but when he inserts the *Abuses of Conscience* into his novel, its tones of serious antagonism are heard in a domestic scene where *Tristram Shandy* tackles a much more playful version of the Anglican-Catholic divide.

Franklin and Sterne's texts, then, make their reappearance across periods of historical and personal transformation in a way that directly affects how they are to be read. The political changes that both Sterne and Franklin had experienced since the 1740s and early 1750s make it significant that they elected to revisit earlier material in their mature work at the end of the decade. Underlying their shifts of tone is a more general question about the way each author conceives of language and its relationship to meaning in the first place. If it were important that these original texts be read right, why stage a reencounter with them in contexts that invite readers to revoke these first interpretations?

I want to answer this question by comparing how *The Way to Wealth* and *Tristram Shandy* present scenes of fictional characters auditing already published texts. While neither Franklin's aphorisms nor *The Abuses of Conscience* are enduring or universal in the sense we might expect of reissued and best-selling works, they reappear in contexts that tell us much about the principles underlying the eighteenth-century sense of what it means to write and, especially, to read, well. Franklin's aphorisms and Sterne's sermon depart from their original contexts and put into practice the logic of Franklin's insistence in pieces such as "On Literary Style," that good language cannot be pegged to the credentials of a speaker or the logic of a cause and that it must monitor and produce its own integrity. As Franklin and Sterne revive previously published material in the presence of their fictional publics, they make the contingency of reception an issue, activating uncertainty in words that have been, as Franklin would have it, "bound down in print" (1:328). *The Way to Wealth* and the sermon reading insist materially on the multiple meanings that even an established text is capable of generating, and on the active kinds of reception its perpetuity requires. As the form of the sermon and the aphorism intersect with their supporting narratives, they introduce dynamic and conversational models of discourse into their framing texts—and suggest the logic of reception to which their framing narratives are also vulnerable. The endurance of these best-selling works offers evidence of the political and generic dexterity Sterne and Franklin saw built into language while encouraging an eighteenth-century reader whose literary experience could absorb and refract multiple interpretations of a single text.

Tristram Shandy and *The Way to Wealth* introduce this question of how words are to be read by having the sermon and the aphorisms reappear in settings where their own reception is a problem. As words that have become distended, distorted, or opaque to their original meaning, these published texts reappear in contexts where their reception seems to pit the possibility of reading for pleasure against the original mood of the advice given in the almanac or the sermon. Walter Shandy, the most insistent member of the audience at Trim's sermon reading, experiences an impatience and curiosity about the sermon that would have been untoward in a congregation member seated in his pew. "But prithee Trim," he urges toward the end of the reading, before himself stepping in to read these last pages when Trim retires, overcome by tears, "make an end,—for I see thou hast but a leaf or two left" (1:161/ii.xvii). Walter's mistake, James Swearingen argues, is that when "he listens to Trim read Yorick's sermon, which should speak to him directly on the power of self-deception, his remarks show that his concern is with literary surfaces rather than with the meaning that informs them" (174). His willingness to be entertained by a text originally intended for moral instruction is borne out in his final verdict on the sermon: "'tis dramatic,—and there is something in that way of writing, when skillfully managed, which catches the attention" (1:165/ii.xvii). This mode of being entertained appears, at least momentarily, to override the possibility of reading the sermon didactically. In *The Way to Wealth*, a similar drift toward pleasure takes place as Poor Richard, the author of the almanac, encounters his own aphorisms being quoted as part of a speech given by Father Abraham at the market square, heard by an audience who takes them less as advice than as entertainment and relates them only promiscuously to the moral they ostensibly deliver. While Poor Richard wants to hear his own words as advice, Father Abraham's auditors are at least partly interested in them as rhetoric.

Critical commentary on *The Way to Wealth* and the sermon reading in *Tristram Shandy* shares the argument that Franklin and Sterne foresee the misuse of their own words as entertainment.[8] If the possibility of not taking moral advice seriously is raised by Franklin, then it is, Grantland Rice has argued, because Franklin wants to point out the dangers of sedition and misreading accruing to published authors. Suggesting that *The Way to Wealth* reveals Franklin's anxiety about having his own words circulating in print, Rice claims that "the Father Abraham story reveals how an intractable traditional culture could continue to threaten Franklin's idea of a purely 'rational' print realm by merely appropriating and embodying such objectified discourse" (47). This picture of Franklin threatened by the contingencies of print can be compared to the argument, made first by Arthur Cash, that *Tristram Shandy* wants, despite appearances to the contrary, to uphold the doctrinal position expressed in *The Abuses of Conscience*. With few exceptions, modern scholarship has tended to look for ways in which *Tristram Shandy* explicates and upholds the sermon's original import.[9] Wolfgang Iser has pointed to the way in which the sermon reading "caricatures assumed readers," and therefore reminds the real reader of the dangerous "denaturing of occurrences" that renders our knowledge fallible (66). In both Rice and Iser's accounts of these scenes, staging the pleasurable reception of potentially serious advice appears as an accusation to aberrant readers, and as proof of Sterne's, or Franklin's, desire to check the vagrancy of the intended meaning.

Reading either the sermon or *The Way to Wealth* in this way suggests that Sterne and Franklin, while conscious that their own words risk the status of sheer entertainment, see pleasure in "literary surfaces" having a tense or even antithetical relation to what real appreciation of their text would be: sermons turn up a second time as literature in order to reinforce their own status as sermons. Yet, while we know that Franklin, to take the less obvious example, actively worried about the uncoupling of literary quality from educational or moral improvement, his own version of an educative literary practice relied more on wit and double-meaning than on the straightforward delivery of advice. In accepting the charted, generic distinction between literary reading and more instrumental forms of writing, critics like Rice and Cash accept the terms of a binary that Franklin himself rejected. It is not that Franklin and Sterne have nothing at stake in revisiting these earlier pieces. I agree with Rice and Cash that these scenes of return are lessons in and about reading. But my argument differs from theirs in contending that these lessons undermine, rather than support, the literal interpretation of the original liturgical and economic advice presented. I believe that Franklin and Sterne recast the idea of good reading as a dynamic act, bringing into their own texts what Derek Attridge has described as the literary work's constitution, "not by an inviolable core but by the singular putting into play—while also testing and transforming—the set of shared codes and conventions that make up the institution of literature and the wider cultural formation of which it is a part" (246). In revisiting their own works, Sterne and Franklin play, I propose, with modes of literal understanding and entertainment, not to reprimand those who would read the "literary surfaces" of these serious texts, but to promote a model of reading that accommodates the contingency of language without reducing the reader to a state of disbelief.

* * *

Franklin described *Poor Richard's Almanack*'s realm of advice-giving as one in which words should be "both entertaining and useful."[10] In the *Autobiography* he describes Poor Richard practicing a particular art of "inculcation" that made use of, but also underscored, the almanac's popularity:

> [O]bserving that it was generally read, scarce any Neighborhood in the Province being without it, I condsider'd it as a proper Vehicle for conveying Instruction among the common People, who bought scarce any other Books. I therefore filled all the little Spaces that ocurr'd between the Re-

> markable Days in the Calendar, with Proverbial Sentences, chiefly such as inculcated Industry and Frugality, as the Means of procuring Wealth and thereby securing Virtue, it being more difficult for a Man in Want to act always honestly as (to use here one of those Proverbs) it is hard for an empty sack to Stand upright. (397)

The Way to Wealth represents the readers who, Franklin observes here, routinely buy his almanac. A group of "common People" appears in the narrative and solicits from Father Abraham the words of instruction they had long been purchasing from Poor Richard. In contrast to the time-killing, pipe-smoking occupants of the Shandy parlor, who agree to hear the sermon on the premise that it has no partisan or political import, these are listeners whose predilection for entertainment does not prevent them from seriously seeking out advice on their private economy. Father Abraham speaks "in answer to the flowing questions. Pray, Father Abraham, what think you of the times? Won't these heavy Taxes quite ruin the Country? How shall we ever be able to pay them? What would you advise us to do?" (7:331). He replies, promising to give his advice "in short," and drawing extemporarily on his mental stock of Poor Richard's advice. While much of the advice Franklin had given in the almanac over the years was openly witty or anecdotal, Father Abraham's selection focuses on the aphorisms, advising thrift and frugality:

> So what signifies *wishing* and *hoping* for better Times. We may make these Times better if we bestir ourselves. *Industry need not wish*, as Poor Richard says, and *He that lives upon hope will die fasting. There are no Gains, without Pains*; then *Help Hands, for I have no Lands*, or if I have, they are smartly taxed. And, as Poor Richard likewise observes, *He that hath a Calling hath an Office of Profit and Honour*; but then the *Trade* must be worked at, and the *Calling* well followed, or neither the *Estate* nor the *Office*, will enable us to pay out Taxes. If we are industrious we shall never starve; for, as Poor Richard says, *At the working Man's House Hunger looks in, but dares not enter.* (7:342)

The sober tone of address—in this passage, Father Abraham has even changed the more mischievous "farting" of the original almanac passage to "fasting"—seems not to deter Father Abraham's auditors. They "join'd in desiring him to speak his Mind," and "gather[ed] round him" (7:340), listeners who, as Franklin's assessment of Poor Richard's readers reminds us, were well adjusted to the habit of finding words "both entertaining and useful."

The main indication that entertainment has a role to play in the dynamic of the speech comes at the end of the piece. Here, the market finally opens and claims the attention of the crowd. It now appears that Poor Richard's auditors have, all along, only been waiting to shop:

> [T]he old man ended his Harangue. The People heard it, and approved the Doctrine, and immediately practiced the contrary, just as if it had been a common Sermon; for the Vendue opened, and they began to buy extravagantly, notwithstanding all his Cautions and their own Fear of Taxes. (7:350)

This material agenda signifies a break in attention, and the call of the marketplace inverts much of the earnestness Franklin has initially attributed to the members of Father Abraham's audience. Their spirit of reckless consumption suggests the economic prosperity and thriving market economy in which most Philadelphians participated at the end of the 1750s. By the mid-eighteenth century, shopping constituted an important part of American identity, and the new world of consumer choice and the prosperity in Philadelphia during the period registers in Franklin's scene. But as it becomes clear that these listeners were held in the spirit of consumption rather than of frugality, a new explanation also emerges for the way in which they have listened so long to this "Harangue." The impression that they have been entertained by Father Abraham's performance, rather than by a direct interest in his advice, is underscored by the revaluation of the time in which they have sought his words as a waiting time, excessive to the temporal economy of the day's activities.

In describing a speech given by a member of the clergy and advising against expenditure at the threshold of the market, Franklin juxtaposes economic theory and consumer practice. The simplest irony here lies in Franklin's awareness that *Poor Richard's Almanack* belonged inside the marketplace it ostensibly scorns. He boasts in the *Autobiography* of it being "in such Demand that I reap'd considerable Profit from it, vending annually near ten Thousand" (397). As a best-selling item warning its auditors away from expenditure, *Poor Richard's Almanack* suggests the capacity for reading against the grain that Franklin is anticipating in those reading, and buying, *The Way to Wealth*: advising his readers not to consume too much, he counts on them not to take this advice literally when it comes to buying the almanac. When Franklin celebrates the success he has in selling the *Poor Richard's Almanack*—an item that he printed, advertised, and distributed himself—he makes it clear that he expected at least some degree of entertainment value to accrue to his words and to support their profitable circulation. The crowd that enthusiastically hears Father Abraham's advice in favor of thrift before beginning to "buy extravagantly" responds with a will to actively, and even paradoxically, translate what they hear into a practice commensurate with the material evidence of the almanac's popularity. But this liberal spirit of interpretation is something that Franklin had reason to endorse in Father Abraham's audience, and in the readers of *The Way to Wealth*, on at least two more elaborate fronts.

First, encoded in the questions that Father Abraham is asked is the possibility that the accumulation of capital may not involve a simple prescription of frugality so much as an assertion of the right to spend money in American, rather than imperial, venues. In 1757, the taxes that Father Abraham's audience complains of are war taxes levied by Britain during the Anglo-French wars. Despite the generally harmonious Anglo-American relations at this time, the colonists were often reluctant to furnish the troops and money required by the British, and had profited from trade with the French. In this context, Father Abraham's injunction against expenditure has symbolic value and is as much about producing American money as it is about limiting personal excess. Franklin retrospectively describes the popularity of *The Way to Wealth* in Pennsylvania as having "discouraged useless Expense in foreign Superfluities" and led some to think "it had its share of Influence in producing that growing Plenty of Money which was observable for several years after its Publication" (1398). Long before throwing tea in the Boston harbor put the issue of consumption firmly on the political agenda, the colonial consumer was linking the question of foreign expenditure, and the discourse about taxes, to larger questions of independence. Whatever the original status of the aphorisms, Father Abraham's speech is unavoidably political, and the fact that the crowd refuses to take its injunctions against spending literally does not count straightforwardly against the avid shoppers, who may nevertheless understand its political import as an encouragement to spend liberally on domestic goods.

Second, Franklin condones the idea of a congregation of people prepared to actively, if not critically, interpret advice given by a member of the clergy. The ostensibly spontaneous (though obviously memorized and derivative) nature of Father Abraham's speech, given in an open-air setting, registers the enthusiastic spirit of the Puritan congregation and the Great Awakenings. But Poor Richard's charge that Father Abraham's audience responds to his speech "just as if it had been a common Sermon" checks this impression of piety with a reminder that the crowd and the preacher are capable of experiencing such involvement without serious commitment. This demonstrates Franklin's resistance to Puritan enthusiasm. His staged and secular version of sermonizing appeals to the critical spirit in which he advised his own readers to attend church and to receive advice, and would also have resonated with the real critical distance prosperous colonial communities were establishing to the Puritan clergy. The Great Awakenings took place against the background of declining Puritan faith, and the increasing popularity of published Enlightenment sermons, particularly Tillotson's, over those given by Congregational ministers.[11] Despite its claim to be incited by the audience, and despite its invocation of the sermon form, Father Abraham's speech is not necessarily ensured of a positive reception, nor does Franklin assume this to be the case. The fact that words have to win authority in a dynamic and critical public forum is much more suggestive of the context of political and religious advice-giving Franklin observed and, more importantly, idealized.

In sum, while *The Way to Wealth* does not straightforwardly parody the advice it gives, it draws on political and religious models of argument that Franklin saw rewarding and encouraging critical public response. The setting in which Franklin stages the circulation of Poor Richard's advice is a critical one, where part of the pleasure of finding oneself a member of the public comes from registering the complexity of language that is witty, symbolic, and contentious, and of entering the marketplace once one has heard it. Through the figure of Father Abraham, Franklin identifies the skill of the itinerant minister in repeating sermons from memory but, as Jay Fliegelman suggests, he also implies that such "repetition turned speeches into scripts" (92). On this count, Poor Richard loses out on the experience of being part of the public that can recognize and enjoy repeated language as script. Hearing his own advice being given, he "resolve [s] to be the better for the Echo of it": "though I had at first determined to buy Stuff for a new Coat, I went away resolved to wear my old One a little longer" (7:350). Poor Richard's literal obedience to his own advice singles him out as oddly simple amongst his fellow members of the crowd and separates him from the other members of the audience.

* * *

Carol Kay is one of the few critics to read the appearance of the sermon in *Tristram Shandy* as evidence of Sterne's critical relation to its argument. For Kay, the originality of *Tristram Shandy* is that it allows Sterne "to approach the notion of the literary as a practice or realm that is autonomous, free from social intent or social influence" (205). She sees Sterne securing a space still uneasy before the mid-century—a space in which the airing of differences takes place, not in the realm of the didactic or political but in the "golden haze of English Liberalism" that she attributes to the Shandy parlor. It is into "this scene of time-killing leisure" that Kay imagines the sermon "drifting" (202) and taking up its place in a historically new, though closely defined, space of play:

> As originally delivered by Sterne, this sermon figured in the anti-Catholic propaganda intended to consolidate the nation against the Jacobites, but in the context of *Tristram Shandy* this function is attenuated. In the novel the sermon merely suggests that the scene of play is limited. Some matters are crucial and subject to religious law interpreted by public regulation, rather than personal whimsy; but at the same time the contrast of the novel to the seriousness of the sermon defines a large space for play. (11)

Kay's argument is an important counterweight to Cash's argument that Sterne wants to uphold the sermon's moral integrity. It suggests that the play of interpretation, which Sterne engages in by juxtaposing an old text and a new context, constructively balances what can be taken seriously against what can—and should—be rendered witty and subject to playful interpretation.

The appearance of *The Abuses of Conscience* in *Tristram Shandy* dramatizes an unoccupied audience's encounter with words as entertainment, distinct in this aspect from the way they would have appeared as religious advice. While, with *The Way to Wealth*, this defamiliarization involves a time bracketed out from the labor of everyday life, *Tristram Shandy* adds to the device of temporal disjuncture by imagining a spatial disjuncture connected with the reading of texts in a domestic setting. The Shandy brothers, Walter and Toby, sit in a parlor for most of the first and second volumes of the novel awaiting the arrival of Tristram, the narrator who is in the process of being born in the room overhead. In the course of this prolonged period of waiting, a series of conversations, disputes, naps, and visits take place, of which the sermon reading is only one example, which show missives from a more public and historically dynamic space (for instance, a sermon that has been preached elsewhere) transposed into the unprogressive and notoriously distorting time/space of the parlor. The fact that the reading itself more than triples the length of the original sermon by way of interjections, emotional outbreaks, and distraction represents *Tristram Shandy* as a novel in which actual events are forced into the eddies of a domestic dialogue and its many byways of interpretation.

The series of coincidences that takes the sermon into *Tristram Shandy* reinforces a climate of preoccupation and contingency in which words, for Sterne, often stray from meaning one thing to meaning something quite different. Toby has sent Corporal Trim to fetch his copy of *Stevinus*, hoping to find a picture in the book of Stevinus's sailing chariot. *Stevinus* arrives, however, too late to settle the case:

> —You may take the book home again, Trim, said my uncle *Toby*, nodding to him.
>
> But pri'thee, corporal, quoth my father, drolling,—look first into it, and see if thou can'st spy aught of a sailing chariot in it. (1:137/ii.xv)

Responding with the capacity for taking words literally that characterizes Sterne's fascination with language, Trim shakes the book in search of the sailing chariot. What falls out, however, are the words of the sermon:

> There is something fallen out, however, said *Trim*, an' please your Honour; but it is not a chariot, or any thing like one:—Prithee Corporal, said my father, smiling, what is it then?—I think, answered *Trim*, stooping to take it up,—'tis more like a sermon. (1:137/ii.xv)[12]

The ensuing reading of the sermon is prompted by disinterested curiosity. Although Trim has identified the genre of the text, its author and denomination remain unknown. A "smiling" and "drolling" Walter Shandy wants to hear it because he has "a strong propensity . . . to look into things which cross [his] way" (1:137/ii.xv). Dr. Slop consents to this reading because he has no indication that the sermon will offend him as a Catholic; Toby, because he is amicable to almost any form of social intercourse.

The sermon's reception makes conspicuous Franklin's hint that words can be actively sought by an audience reluctant to take them too seriously. The difference is only that, rather than seeking Father Abraham's advice in a leisured time or space where idiosyncratic and imaginative diversion leads it astray, Franklin's auditors misread his thrifty advice in a time and space palpably subversive of its missive. Father Abraham's speech is not propounded in the parlor of domestic privilege and self-interest (although it is well worth imagining exactly what Toby and Walter might have done with such a text if it had drifted their way), but at the gates to a market about to open. The relationship between Father Abraham's advice and the way it is interpreted is, therefore, directly ironic in a way that the misreading of the sermon is not. The auditors to Trim's reading are able to engage with his performance because the piece of paper that has fallen out of *Stevinus* makes no ideological demands on them: it is not that its original content is subverted by the text's excursion in this direction, but that the whole idea of its having such a content at all becomes questionable. In Kay's words, "[T]he sermon functions not to prove the superior didactic force of the novel that surrounds it, but to work a peculiarly modern magic: to convert moral writing into literature" (211). This "conversion" involves as much a change to the reader as to the text. Sterne constructs for his reissued sermon a reader who is distinct in his or her disinterest and open hostility to being educated by a text from Franklin's reader, whose mood of interpretation arises more from a willingness to ride a text through various reversals of interest and layers of meaning than to see literature directly as a term of disinterest. The setting of the Shandy parlor allows us to imagine a private and relaxed space, where aesthetic disinterest becomes the alternative to the public demands of the anti-Catholic sermon, while Franklin imagines a critical public sphere, where an excess of time allows discourse to reverberate outside the strict temporal constraints of the household economy within which Poor Richard's aphorisms are normally read.

* * *

Sterne's and Franklin's listeners embody the spirit in which a sermon, or economic advice, might be pleasurably distended. These auditors are not, however, the only audiences Franklin and Sterne invoke in imagining the reception of their texts. *The Way to Wealth* and *Tristram Shandy* both introduce the ostensible author of the text being read or cited as a listener whose presence is inscribed in the work being written. *The Way to Wealth* begins with Poor Richard narrating the experience of hearing his own advice being passed on. The piece introduces Poor Richard's arrival at the speech as itself a coincidental encounter: "I stopt my Horse lately where a great Number of People were collected at a Vendue of Merchant Goods" (7:340). Poor Richard, for all that he remains the eighteenth-century paragon of frugality and the collector of useful advice, is at this Vendue, but is not one of the crowd who asks after advice or one of "the Company" who are "Conversing on the Badness of the Times" (7:340). Reining in his horse apparently at the outskirts of this crowd, Poor Richard is drawn and held by the pleasure of vicarious involvement, which comes from hearing his own words rehearsed while he remains invisible as their author.

The crowd's sense of interested pleasure differs from the attitude of disinterested pleasure that Poor Richard appears initially to have toward his own words. It is with "Pleasure" that he introduces his 1757 almanac: "I have heard that nothing gives an Author so great Pleasure, as to find his Works respectfully quoted by other learned Authors"

(7:340). Though he has "seldom enjoyed" this pleasure in the past—as a character Richard Saunders normally assumes, rather, the posture of a reluctant author—he finds himself in its full sway as he listens to Father Abraham, and he relates hearing the speech as an experience of gratification: "Judge then," writes Poor Richard before handing over the stage to Father Abraham, "how much I must have been gratified by an Incident I am going to relate to you" (7:340). As if to confirm how gratifying it is to hear oneself quoted, Franklin added yet another level of audience to *The Way to Wealth* when he reported on his own response to its popularity in the third part of the *Autobiography*. Of Poor Richard's proverbs Franklin writes:

> I assembled and form'd [them] into a connected Discourse prefix'd to the Almanack of 1757, as the Harangue of a wise old Man to the People attending an Auction. The bringing all these scatter'd Counsels thus into a Focus, enabled them to make a greater Impression. The piece being universally approved was copied in all Newspapers of the Continent, reprinted in Britain on a Broadside to be stuck up in Houses, two Translations were made of it in French, and a great Number bought by the Clergy and Gentry to distribute gratis among their poor Parishioners and Tenants. (397)

Franklin echoes Poor Richard's posture of mild surprise at the success of his own texts, reserving for himself a space from which he, like Poor Richard, ostensibly testifies to the experience of watching his words make their way in the world without connecting this pleasure to their moral import.

Sterne, too, was fascinated with the possibility of an author encountering his own work in public. As a narrator, Tristram continually ascribes responsibility to his pen, his heart, or his imagination for his words, making credible the idea that even an author might bump into something he has written as a novelty: "Ask my pen,—it governs me—I govern not it," he claims in protest at being asked to account for why something has been mentioned (2:500/vi.vi). The premise that his text is thoroughly out of his hands plays descant to his claim that he "is resolved never to read any book but my own, as long as I live" (2:661/viii.v). So thoroughly has he assured us of *Tristram Shandy*'s autonomy, that he can assert his relation to it as reader. This celebration of literary estrangement lends credibility to Sterne's packaging his own sermons as the work of the fictional Pastor Yorick. In the novel, Tristram becomes editor and caretaker of the dead Yorick's work, discovering the moral value of these religious texts as they cross his path in their most accidental and spontaneous guise. While a suspension of disbelief is still required in order to imagine Sterne discovering his own compositions, his emphasis on creative inspiration as a force alien to the author helps render this posture genuine and positive.

As authors who wrote from within—or at least, just off to the side of—the respective traditions of Puritanism and Anglicanism, Franklin and Sterne each found support for this model of authorship in the religious view of words as a divine creation. In fact, responsibility for the texts they each wrote could be traced to traditional and secular sources, but the credo of inspiration was still largely religious. As an author of Anglican sermons, Sterne had to contend with the genuinely derivative nature of his compositions. Almost all of Sterne's sermons drew on arguments standardized by Swift or Butler, and *The Abuses of Conscience* is itself modeled on Swift's sermon *On the Testimony of Conscience*. In terms of his performance as a preacher, this was not necessarily a problem for Sterne—a certain lack of originality produced legitimacy for the tradition of Anglican sermons, where "textual forms ordained by the church hierarchy or produced by individual ministers promised a stable social order protected from the volatility of more immediate spiritual experience" (Gustafson 15). Some aspect of authorial estrangement came along with the idea that the individual author's role was to relay words of authority.

Rejecting the mediation of the scriptural canon, Puritan sermons drew more directly on the idea of divine inspiration. Yet they were also routinely composed according to strict guidelines laid down by convention, or found in the Puritan ministers' handbook, William Perkins's *The Art of Prophecying* (1592). Father Abraham's method of citation, in which he draws together already published material into an ostensibly spontaneous oral performance, testifies to the way in which Franklin observed sermons as blends of plagiarized and original ideas, which circulate between print and performance.[13] Although Puritan sermons were usually memorized or delivered from notes, these sermons were often no more original than Father Abraham's speech. In general, then, Father Abraham's role as conduit for words that are not his own and Poor Richard's experience of these words as foreign are examples contiguous with the composition of the Puritan sermon.[14] Franklin's choice of the aphorism as a unit of speech taps into what remained for most eighteenth-century readers a common and primarily religious idea: that knowledge could be, as Poor Richard claims his is, "the *Gleanings* . . . of the Sense of all Ages and Nations" (7:350) rather than the creation of an individual author.[15]

Involving members of the clergy, Pastor Yorick and Father Abraham, in the delivery of their texts, Franklin and Sterne link up with Anglican and Protestant explanations for why a text might exceed the responsibility of its author. In the secular contexts of *Tristram Shandy* and *The Way to Wealth*, this link allows Franklin and Sterne to shore up the secular and creative version of authorial estrangement claimed by Tristram and Poor Richard. The religious model of inspiration, memorization, and oral performance becomes a way of presenting the distance that Sterne and Franklin claim from their own texts as a result of creative inspiration, and the process of publication. These are cases which exemplify McKeon's argument, that the objectification of discourse which takes place as modern words become print, and as print becomes an object available for sale and circulation, cannot be cleanly distinguished from the disavowals of authorship associated with a religious tradition of composition and with an oral model of circulation. McKeon speaks of the "historical conjunction of two antipathetic 'systems,'" which imposed upon literary productions analogous demands that they be disowned or fetishized" (123). Arguing against the attribution to Puritanism alone of a hostility to human creation, McKeon stresses that this hostility is in fact at the heart of "empirical capitalist" thought itself, and that it is reconciled with the "modern cult of human creativity" in "the post-typographical notion that an idea does not really belong to you until you alienate it through publication" (121).

McKeon's willingness to conceive of the connections between a version of alienation that occurs with print, a creative version of authorship that is based on this distance, and a much older disavowal of creativity based on God's being the only legitimate author, helps in imagining *The Way to Wealth* and the sermon reading as cases where these claims converge. With Poor Richard, Yorick, and Tristram, Franklin and Sterne each go to great lengths to create characters whose experience of authorship combines humility verging on religious piety, the technical alienation of print, and the pleasure of the word's return as something that was never really the author's property. This network of fictional and real authors produces a structure through which words are relayed, responsibility disavowed, and authorship experienced in the moment of pleasurable recognition. Sterne and Franklin make an author's alienation from his work a sign both of the modern conditions of print authorship and of religious experience, a place where alienation and ownership conspire.[16]

Pastor Yorick most explicitly embodies the claim that it is possible to find pleasure as a reader of something one has written. Yorick is a zealous composer of sermons, and a literary scholar, but he is also the most alienated of all the characters in *Tristram Shandy* from his work of writing. Sterne presents him as a forgetful and modest character whose "carelessness of heart" and "invincible dislike and opposition . . . to gravity" (1:28/i.xi) extend to his careless relationship to the documents he produces. The way in which *The Abuses of Conscience* has got into—and out of—*Stevinus* testifies to his spirit as an author:

> It seems that Yorick, who was inquisitive after all kinds of knowledge, had borrowed *Stevinus* of my Uncle Toby, and had carelessly popp'd his sermon, as soon as he had made it, into the middle of *Stevinus*; and by an act of forgetfulness, to which he was ever subject, he had sent *Stevinus* home, and his sermon to keep him company. (1:166/ii.xvi)

Such oversights place Yorick loosely in relation to his sermon, which seems to make its own spontaneous transition into the public arena, but also to the very words that he speaks: "It was his misfortune all his life long to bear the imputation of saying and doing a thousand things of which . . . his nature was incapable" (1:385/iv.xxvii). In this position, Yorick resembles Poor Richard as a somewhat unwitting gatherer and distributor—rather than author and inciter—of words. Because Yorick and Poor Richard never really own their creations, they illustrate at the level of narrative the larger turn by which Franklin and Sterne re-approach texts they have written as pleasantly unfamiliar objects.

* * *

At this point I want to stress that Rice's argument, that Franklin experiences the publication of his own words as a form of alienation, is highly problematic. According to Rice, Franklin's anxiety in *The Way to Wealth* stems from his perception that once language enters print it becomes objectified and subject to the control of the market, much in the terms of the Marxian commodity: "[B]ecause this objective 'print' reality both obscured and mystified the human activity which created it, authors were left passive with the sense that they were outside such an objective realm" (66). For Rice, Franklin's role as metanarrator of Father Abraham's speech is to clamp down on the misreading his text suffers in the minds of the marketgoers. His aphorisms' flight is portrayed only as a way to call them home to the protection of a stronger authorial presence, which is required if printed texts, in their potential for anonymity, are to be managed.

The process of objectification Rice describes is certainly applicable in one way to both the textual histories shown here. It is, for instance, significant that Sterne chose his only published sermon as the document that should drift into his novel: the agency he attributes to it as a text relates to his experience of its having had such a life as a pamphlet. But it should by now be clear that neither Poor Richard nor Pastor Yorick can easily be described as simply alienated from their earlier creations. What keeps Poor Richard enthralled throughout the speech is his position as invisible author and active recipient of the language he hears. Once he has finished reporting Father Abraham's speech, Poor Richard concludes:

> The frequent Mention he made of me must have tired any one else, but my Vanity was wonderfully delighted with it, though I was conscious that not a tenth Part of the Wisdom was my own which he ascribed to me, but rather the *Gleanings* I had made of the Sense of all Ages and Nations. (7:350)

Like Franklin himself, who, as an elderly man, observes with ostensible surprise and modesty the fact that *The Way to Wealth* was "universally approved," "copied in all Newspapers of the Continent," and "reprinted in Britain on a Broadside to be stuck up in Houses," Poor Richard is comfortable with playing off his encounter with his own text between the confession of vanity and the denial of authorship. The latter—which Rice imagines as the distance of "alienation"—becomes the precondition of bringing him into legitimate and pleasurable contact with his own creation. In McKeon's terms, the conditions of empirical capitalism produce the conditions of creativity under which the alienability of print makes Poor Richard's (or Franklin's) words recognizable as his own. Poor Richard's assuming a back-seat position in relation to his own composition does not hinder him in this drama of representation. Here, Rice's understanding of alienation, which makes no distinction between what Marx conceives of as the more neutral, even constructive, process of objectification, and the process of alienation as it refers to the alienation of the worker from himself, becomes too general. For, in Franklin's case, the objectification of his own words (an objectification that can be explained as much in Protestant as in capitalist terms) becomes the precondition for his characteristically deferential brand of self-recognition as an author of print; what seems to alienate him as a worker is exactly what enables him to partake, at a time when consumption is emerging as a strong axis of colonial choice, as a consumer of his own advice.

If there is a negative form of objectification enacted in Poor Richard's encounter with his own texts, it is a problem registered in the fiction of temporal distance, which leaves him unable to experience his pleasure and his fidelity to the speech at the same time. *The Way to Wealth* and the sermon reading share the ideal of being able to read seriously and pleasurably at the same time, but in their own chronologies they explore this ideal through the comparatively less desirable separation of these modes by having words be first disowned and then rediscovered. In Sterne's case, *The Abuses of Conscience* reappears in Tristram's narrative 10 years after it was first published, a temporal lag that *Tristram Shandy* registers as the period in which Yorick's manuscript lay inside *Stevinus*. The effect of even an unpublished text's distance in time (for instance, the effect of discovering a diary or letter one had written long ago) helps license the author's involvement as disinterested reader, and both Sterne and Franklin use this historical trajectory to distinguish between the moral gravity of a text's first incarnation and the later moment of reading it in a state of disinterest and pleasure. Neither proposes, however, that such a chronological separation of these moods is necessary. In fact, Poor Richard's lapse into all-too-credulous reading at the end of *The Way to Wealth* suggests that he would have been better off to hold onto his sense of pleasure in hearing Father Abraham's advice.

Yorick is the best positive example of what it might look like to treat a text as rhetorically pleasurable while remaining true to its content. Yorick's legacy in *Tristram Shandy* is quite literally a textual one. As a writer of sermons, he has left behind at his death a sizable collection that is now in the keeping of the Shandy family. Tristram, being the only surviving member of this family, therefore owns these sermons, and is able to acquaint us with this collection and to draw *The Abuses of Conscience* out from it for the purposes of recreating the scene in which it is read aloud. He is also able to describe another sermon composed by Yorick for the funeral of Le Fever, the hero of *Tristram Shandy*'s sentimental set-piece in which a young soldier is attended by Toby and Trim on his deathbed. This sermon, Tristram explains, is preserved in a state that testifies to Yorick's complex relationship to his own work:

> The funeral sermon upon poor Le Fever, wrote out very fairly, as if from a hasty copy.—I take notice of it the more, because it seems to have been his favorite composition—It is upon morality; and is tied up length-ways and cross-ways with a yarn thrum, and then rolled up and twisted round with half a sheet of dirty blue paper which seems to have been once the cast cover of a general review, which to this day smells horribly of horse-drugs.—Whether these marks of humiliation were designed,—I something doubt;—because at the very end of the sermon, (and not at the beginning of it)—very different from his way of treating the rest, he had wrote—
>
> Bravo! (2:515-16/vi.xi)

Yorick has clearly returned to his own work lovingly, not only to copy it out a second time but also to annotate it with signs of his enthusiasm. Sterne makes much of this "Bravo," excusing it as "more like a *ritratto* of the shadow of vanity than of VANITY herself" (2:516/vi.xi), and using it to illustrate the way in which Yorick's sermons become palimpsest to the various tenors of emotional engagement and rhetorical response that can come to bear on a single body of words. Yorick has read through his sermon on morality and in the process of reading been moved to comment on his words as if he were audience to their operatic feat of emotion. Yorick applies the musical terms *lentamente*, *grave*, *adagio*, *moderato*, and *Con l'arco* to his own work, and wraps his sermons in copies of the *General Review*, explicitly using the secular language of critical appreciation to appraise language written for the pulpit. Rather than debasing him as cleric, Yorick's "Bravo" reminds us that his integrity relies on the virtue of self-reflection. "It is as if," Tristram conjectures, Yorick "has snatched the occasion of unlacing himself with a few more frolicksome strokes at vice, than the straitness of the pulpit allowed" (2:517/vi.xi). These wayward strokes of his pen, though "they skirmish lightly and all out of order, are still auxiliaries on the side of virtue" (2:517/vi.xi).

Situating Yorick as a literary critic in this way, Sterne suggests a rebellious propriety that Yorick brings to his own productions as their first reader. If they slip, as Downey suggests Sterne's sermons come very close to doing, into the realm of entertainment, then it is Yorick who determinedly sends them on their way, reappearing barely a change of clothes away in his guise as opera-lover to meet them at the other side.[17] In revisiting his sermons with the second wind of self-criticism, Yorick does not always produce the spontaneity of his self-congratulatory "Bravo." He is often deeply critical of his own tone:

> [I]t was Yorick's custom . . . on the first leaf of every sermon which he composed, to chronicle down the time place, and the occasion of it being preached: to this, he was ever want to add some short comment or stricture upon the sermon itself, seldom, indeed, much to its credit: For instance, *This sermon upon the jewish dispensation—I don't like it at all; though I own there is a world of WATER-LANDISH knowledge in it, but 'tis all tritical, and most tritically put together.—This is but a flimsy kind of a composition; what was in my head when I made it?* (2:515-16/vi.xi)

Whether Yorick reads his own sermons as successful or as "flimsy compositions," "tritically put together," he pursues a vein of literary appreciation which has little or nothing to say about their moral content.[18] He can be compared in his approach to many of the readers and auditors populating *Tristram Shandy* and *The Way to Wealth*—for instance, to Walter with his concern for "literary surfaces rather than the meaning that informs them" or to Father Abraham's audience, who turns out to be more interested in shopping than obeying his advice about saving. As the author of the sermons, though, Yorick is in the special position of demonstrating that literary response can be suitable to serious composition. Given that his piety as a member of the clergy is not in question, his willingness to apply secular terms of criticism and praise to serious sermons becomes part of his sincerity. It is not bracketed out as a contradictory or temporally distinct mood of sedition from which he must return to sober contemplation of his advice. Yorick turns out, moreover, to be a good literary critic. The scheme by which he classifies his sermons as "*so-so*'s" or "*moderato*'s," for all its appearance of arbitrary and self-punitive judgment, has a consistency Tristram attests to: "the *moderato*'s are five times better than the *so-so*'s;—shew ten times more knowledge of the human heart;—have seventy times more wit and spirit in them" (2:514-15/vi.xi).

Poor Richard, who shares Yorick's pleasure in hearing his own words, never critically comprehends his own work in this way. He moves, rather, between disjointed modes of understanding. Initially, he hears the speech with amusement, confessing to the "vanity" and "pleasure" commonly associated by eighteenth-century authors with the indulgence of publication. And then, as we have seen, he takes what he has heard more literally than any of Father Abraham's common auditors and leaves the market without buying the new material he had come for. Although, as author of the advice being given, he lends some credit to each way of receiving it, ultimately Poor Richard's move from being a casual passer-by who finds pleasure in the words spoken, to being the only one of the crowd with a singular reading of the advice given, fails to reconcile these extreme positions. This division gives rise to the idea that *The Way to Wealth* sets up rhetorical and serious reading as alternatives, allowing Franklin to approach the first as an aberration of the second. But in fact Poor Richard's two approaches to the speech are a bit like the equally unsatisfactory ways of reading Sterne ascribes to Walter and Trim as recipients of the sermon. Walter's argument that the sermon has no relation to fact and must be performed and judged as an exercise in oratory misses the point of its content: "Why, Trim, said my father, this is not a history,—'tis a sermon thou art reading;—pri'thee begin the sentence again." Yet Trim's state of emotional identification with the victims of the Catholic church, which overwhelms him as he reads the strongly anti-Catholic sermon, is too literal a response: "Behold this helpless victim delivered up to his tormentors,—his body so wasted with sorrow and confinement—(Oh! 'tis my brother, cried poor Trim in a most passionate exclamation, dropping the sermon upon the ground and clapping his hands together)" (1:162/ii.xvii).

If Franklin were concerned only with the liability of overrhetorical reading, Poor Richard's transformation, from rhetorical reader and alienated author, to serious recipient of advice, would be a positive development. His distance to his own words would decrease as he came closer to their literal meaning. This is not, however, what happens in *The Way to Wealth*, which remains as much a parody of Poor Richard's credulous approach to his own advice as it does of his vanity and pleasure in his reputation. Despite his authorship of the words, Poor Richard remains, of all the readers represented by Franklin, the least qualified to understand Father Abraham's speech, whose complexity eludes him at both of the irreconcilable moments of his own response to it. In contrast, Yorick, who uses the distancing apparatus of literary criticism, applying pages of the *General Review* literally to his sermons, stands out as an empowered owner of his own work. Embracing the estrangement that accrues to the author of the divinely or creatively inspired text, Yorick reclaims his words as the object of pleasure and critique across this aesthetic distance without compromising his fidelity to their original spirit.

Franklin is loath to attribute to Poor Richard—or, indeed, to any of his character narrators—the sophistication or propriety as authors that he reserved for himself. Unlike Sterne, who identified almost seamlessly with Yorick, Franklin does not attempt to reproduce the complexity of his own position at the level of Poor Richard's character. The ideal of author-reader that Yorick embodies is, however, more generally represented in *The Way to Wealth*. Franklin's public, his "common People," are, I have suggested, good rather than seditious readers of Father Abraham's speech. Their critical distance to the words, evidenced in their willingness to shop after hearing them, exonerates them from the kinds of uncritical enthusiasm practiced by Poor Richard himself and makes them constitutive members of the critical, literary public sphere that Franklin imagined for colonial America. Although this public does not author the words they read in the sense that Yorick authors his sermons, the marketgoers come close to being the public self that Franklin projected for himself as author: they are wholly defined by the situation at hand, but never entirely commensurate with it. The fact that the words the public hears and responds to are aphorisms rooted in common wisdom, suggests, too, that the words "gleaned" by Poor Richard are actually generated here in the space of the marketgoers. Franklin's public is clearly no more real than the fictional character, Yorick. The marketgoers invoke the real consumers and readers of *Poor Richard's Almanack*, but ultimately they project a kind of critical consciousness and capacity for sophisticated literary pleasure that Franklin actively cultivated in his readers. Both Yorick and this public involve fantasies of what it would mean to have work responsibly owned and critically read by the same author. *The Way to Wealth* and the sermon reading show that this fantasy is enabled, and not undermined, by print culture, by ideas of creative and divine inspiration, and by a text offering its reader—and its author—multiple interpretative possibilities.

From *Early American Literature* 40, no. 3 (2005): 471-498.

Notes

I am grateful to Myra Jehlen, Michael Warner, and Michael McKeon for their invaluable readings of this essay in earlier drafts.

1. The importance of Sterne's sermons remains hotly debated and it is unclear whether they would have been publishable at all, were it not for the success of *Tristram Shandy*. Downey argues for their importance in bringing the genre of the sermon into the realm of literature and finds evidence for this in the texts themselves. For Melvyn New, their editor, they remain typical Anglican sermons—typical in both their borrowings and their thematic standardization. It is clear, however, that the market for sermons in the eighteenth century was growing and that Sterne was keen to make use of this opportunity. For more information on how sermons were read in the eighteenth century, see Downey.

2. Sappenfield writes, "[T]he fact that Poor Richard, Philomath, was recognizable from year to year is Franklin's greatest achievement in characterization."

3. The bibliographic figures and details here are taken from the extensive introduction given by the editors of Franklin's Papers to *The Way to Wealth* (7:328).

4. The new aphorisms are "a Word to the Wise is enough" and "Many Words won't fill a Bushel" (7:340). Franklin has also made minor changes to many of the other aphorisms he uses. Details are given by the Yale editors (7:326-50).

5. Many of the aphorisms that Franklin does not recycle in his 1757 almanac refer explicitly to pleasure and gratification, for instance, "He that can take Rest is greater than he that can take Cities" or "An egg today is better than a Hen tomorrow." For this argument, see Larrabee.

6. Timothy Breen dates this shift of enthusiasm from 1750, when taxes caused them to "turn back the clock" on their spending of the past decade: "They claimed that they wanted to reverse the consumer tide, and in a series of increasingly successful boycotts against British manufacturers, they redefined the symbolic meaning of imported goods. In public discourse these items became politicized, badges of dependence" (499).

7. For an account of the way in which the *Autobiography* registers the event of the Revolution, which occurred between Franklin's writing of its first and second parts, see Christopher Looby's chapter on Franklin.

8. A notable exception, in the case of Franklin, is Harold Larrabee's 1957 essay that argues against the seriousness with which *The Way to Wealth* has been read in America: "[T]he unnumbered throngs who were influenced by *The Way to Wealth* and its reinforcing illustration, the *Autobiography*, were unaware that Franklin never intended in these books to write a philosophy of life for everyone. Father Abraham was talking about way to wealth for those at the bottom of the ladder, and not about the worth of wealth itself, or what ought to be done with it, much less about the perils of its pursuit. His approach was hypothetical. He was saying in substance, *if* what you want is to be 'healthy, wealthy, and wise' (as apparently you do), *then* my advice to you is 'early to bed, and early to rise'" (65).

9. In support of this observation, but also suggesting his own exception to it, New comments: "Modern scholarship, taking the sermon seriously (not to say gravely), has

passed over the possibility that a nervous first novelist was simply padding out the material of his second volume" (100).

10. Franklin here restates the Horatian dictum, which says that the aim of the poet is either to benefit, to please, or to make his words do both. This principle shows up many times in Franklin's work, for instance, in his suggestion, when *The New England Courant* was temporarily reissued under his name, that the education of a community could take place through diversion: "The main Design of this Weekly Paper will be to entertain the Town with the most comical and diverting Incidents of Humane Life, which in so large a Place as Boston, will not fail of a universal Exemplification" (1:49).

11. See Fiering, for instance, who describes Whitefield's attempt to rid New England of the works of Tillotson.

12. For a different reading of this event, see Homer Obed Brown, who reads the performance of the sermon as connecting the novel's themes of loss and problems with repetition. Speaking of the life of the sermon as a text lost and reread at several levels, Brown writes: "This stress on repetitions of an outside text which is itself an event inside the text again sets in motion a certain play of opposition between outside and inside, between event and representation. Since an 'event' is precisely what cannot be repeated, this event is lost among its repetitions and representations. In the heterogeneity of its various situations and occasions, the primary definitiveness of any single 'context' is challenged" (732). Although I like Brown's reading, it lacks, I think, an emphasis on the way Sterne implicates his readers in this dynamic of loss and recovery.

13. As Sandra Gustafson has shown, the importance of the oral tradition for Puritan society extended far into the period when print discourse seems, according to many accounts of modernization, to have overtaken the spoken word in importance.

14. One of the characteristics of religious practice in colonial America, and certainly the one that lent it its greatest appeal during the Great Awakening of the 1740s, was its basis in long, seemingly spontaneous and inspired performances which combined oral performance with a print-mediated public consciousness. Itinerant ministers such as George Whitefield (about whom Franklin wrote in appreciative terms) drew enormous crowds in the early 1740s, delivering seemingly unrehearsed sermons in which events, such as a passing thunderstorm and the immediate setting, were deftly incorporated into written texts. See Stout.

15. On the question of how ownership of intellectual property emerges for authors in the eighteenth century, see Martha Woodmansee, who asserts that "at the outset of the eighteenth century it was not generally thought that the author of a poem or any other piece of writing possessed rights with regard to these products of his intellectual labor. Writing was considered a mere vehicle of received ideas that were already in the public domain, and, as such a vehicle, it too, by extension or analogy, was considered part of the public domain" (42).

16. McKeon's argument also offers an explanation for why Tristram's claim that the practice of "writing the first sentence—and trusting to Almighty God for the second," which ostensibly makes him "the most religious of compositors" (2:656/viii.ii), does confound the instances where Tristram outlandishly advertises his own—or Yorick's—work for sale, at one point incorporating into the fourth volume of *Tristram Shandy* mention that the next volume of Yorick's sermons is shortly to be published in London.

17. For the argument that Sterne's sermons are more literary than those of his contemporaries, see Downey's chapter on Sterne.

18. Sterne himself practiced this habit of annotating his sermons in a space of private entertainment and self-irony. A manuscript of Sterne's sermon *Our Conversation in Heaven* was lightheartedly written on by the author: "Made for All Saints and preach'd on the Day 1750 for the Dean.—Present: one Bellows Blower, three Singing Men, one Vicar and one Residentiary.—Memorandum: Dined with Duke Humphrey" (3:410). To dine with Duke Humphrey means to go without dinner—a phrase common in Elizabethan literature, said to be from the practice of the poor gentry, who beguiled the dinner hour by a promenade near the tomb of Humphrey, Duke of Gloucester, in Old Saint Paul's.

Works Cited

Attridge, Derek. "Literary Form and the Demands of Politics: Otherness in J. M. Coetzee's Age of Iron." *Aesthetics and Ideology*. Ed. George Levine. New Brunswick, N.J.: Rutgers Univ. Press, 1994. 246-59.

Breen, Timothy. "An Empire of Goods: The Anglicization of Colonial America, 1690-1776." *Journal of British Studies* 25 (1986): 467-500.

____________. "'Baubles of Britain': The American and Consumer Revolutions of the Eighteenth Century." *Past and Present* 119 (1988): 73-104.

Brown, Homer Obed. "Tristram to the Hebrews: Some Notes on the Institution of a Canonic Text." *Modern Language Notes* 99 (1984): 727-47.

Cash, Arthur. "The Sermon in *Tristram Shandy*." *ELH* 31 (1964): 395-417.

Downey, James. *The Eighteenth-Century Pulpit. A Study of the Sermons of Butler, Berkeley, Secker, Sterne, Whitefield, and Wesley*. Oxford: Clarendon Press, 1969.

Fiering, Norman. "The First American Enlightenment: Tillotson, Leverett, and Philosophical Anglicanism." *The New England Quarterly* 54 (1981): 307-44.

Fliegelman, Jay. *Declaring Independence: Jefferson, Natural Language, and the Culture of Performance*. Palo Alto, Calif: Stanford Univ. Press, 1993.

Franklin, Benjamin. *The Autobiography of Benjamin Franklin*. Ed. Leonard W. Labaree et al. New Haven: Yale Univ. Press, 1964.

____________. *The Papers of Benjamin Franklin*. Ed. Leonard W. Labaree et al. New Haven: Yale Univ. Press, 1959- .

Gustafson, Sandra. *Eloquence Is Power: Oratory and Performance in Early America*. Chapel Hill: Univ. of North Carolina Press, 2000.

Howes, Alan B., ed. *Sterne: The Critical Heritage*. London: Routledge and K. Paul, 1974.

Iser, Wolfgang. *Laurence Sterne: Tristram Shandy*. Trans. David Henry Wilson. Cambridge: Cambridge Univ. Press, 1988.

Kay, Carol. *Political Constructions: Defoe, Richardson, and Sterne in Relation to Hobbes, Hume, and Burke*. Ithaca: Cornell Univ. Press, 1988.

Larrabee, Harold. "Franklin's Way to Wealth." *Harper's*, July 1957: 62-65.

Looby, Christopher. *Voicing America*. Chicago: Univ. of Chicago Press, 1996.

McKeon, Michael. *The Origins of the English Novel, 1600-1740*. Baltimore: Johns Hopkins Univ. Press, 1987.

Nash, Gary B. *Urban Crucible: Social Change, Political Consciousness, and the Origins of the American Revolution*. Cambridge, Mass.: Harvard Univ. Press, 1979.

Sterne, Laurence. *The Life and Opinions of Tristram Shandy, Gentleman*. Ed. Melvyn New and Joan New. Gainesville: Univ. Presses of Florida, 1978-1984. 3 vols.

____________. *The Sermons of Laurence Sterne*. Ed. Melvyn New. Gainesville: Univ. Press of Florida, 1996.

Rice, Grantland. *The Transformation of Authorship in America*. Chicago: Univ. of Chicago Press, 1997.

Sappenfield, James A. *A Sweet Instruction: Franklin's Journalism as a Literary Apprenticeship*. Carbondale: Southern Illinois Univ. Press, 1973.

Stout, Henry. *New England Soul: Preaching and Religious Culture in Colonial New England*. New York: Oxford Univ. Press, 1986.

Swearingen, James. *Reflexivity in Tristram Shandy: An Essay in Phenomenological Criticism*. New Haven: Yale Univ. Press, 1977.

Woodmansee, Martha. *The Author, Art, and the Market: Rereading the History of Aesthetics*. New York: Columbia Univ. Press, 1994.

The Moral Reform of a Scurrilous Press

Ralph Frasca

Ralph Frasca shows how Franklin translated his thoughts on freedom of the press from theory into practice in his support of two young newspapermen, first Francis Childs, editor of the *New-York Daily Advertiser,* and then his own grandson, Benjamin Franklin Bache, who edited the Philadelphia newspaper the *Aurora.* He lectured them on a journalist's duty to the public—Franklin himself, when he edited the *Pennsylvania Gazette,* "carefully excluded all Libelling and Personal Abuse"—and hoped to inculcate in both of them a similar devotion to the greater good. He was disappointed by both his charges, however; both ended up continuing the kind of scurrilous journalism that he found so dispiriting. — J.L.

"He that best understands the World, least likes it," a cynical Benjamin Franklin wrote in 1753 under the guise of "Poor Richard."[1] Franklin had grown pessimistic during the middle decades of the eighteenth century due in part to stories about crime, greed, and immorality that he read, wrote, and published in the colonial press. His misanthropy was augmented by failed printing partnerships, particularly in the West Indies and the Pennsylvania German community.

However, he was most resentful of public attacks on his character. During Franklin's 1764 bid for re-election to the Pennsylvania Assembly, his opponents appeared "sworn to load him with all the Filth, and Virulence that the basest Heads and basest Hearts can suggest," a Franklin supporter commented. After his defeat and subsequent appointment as colonial agent to Parliament, critics denounced him as unacceptable. He is "very unfavorably thought of by several of his Majesty's Ministers," and his character "is so extremely disagreeable to a very great Number of the most serious and reputable Inhabitants of this Province of all Denominations and Societies," according to a newspaper editorial signed by many prominent Pennsylvanians.[2]

Franklin was keenly aware of the animosities awakened by his political prominence and ability to influence public opinion. "I have many enemies (all indeed on the Public Account, for I cannot recollect that I have in a private Capacity given just cause of offence to any one whatever) yet they are Enemies and very bitter ones," he informed his daughter a month after the 1764 election. The longer he was in public life, the more the press assailed him. Exhibiting bitterness after two decades of vilification, Franklin warned a new political officeholder, "the Publick is often niggardly even of its Thanks, while you are sure of being censured by malevolent Criticks and Bug Writers, who will abuse you while you are serving them, and wound your Character in nameless Pamphlets, thereby resembling those little dirty stinking Insects, that attack us only in the dark, disturb our Repose, molesting & wounding us while our Sweat & Blood is contributing to their Subsistence."[3]

However, the conclusion of the American Revolution rejuvenated Franklin and restored a flicker of his faith in humanity. "Thank God, the world is growing wiser and wiser; and as by degrees men are convinced of the folly of wars for religion, for dominion, or for commerce, they will be happier and happier," he wrote in 1788.[4] The attacks on his reputation by adversaries in Pennsylvania politics, the Stamp Act crisis, and the quest for independence were burnished with the creation of a new country—and a new national identity—for Americans. As his fears of an American mobocracy subsided in the 1780s, Franklin hoped his new countrymen could be coaxed to lead more virtuous lives as citizens of an infant nation than they had as British colonists. Writing to British scientist Joseph Priestley during the war, he lauded scientific advances but lamented, "O that moral Science were in as fair a Way of Improvement, that Men would cease to be Wolves to one another, and that human Beings would at length learn what they now improperly call Humanity!" Conveying his desire to see "the Discovery of a Plan" for improving moral philosophy, an exasperated Franklin wrote to another friend the same week, "When will human Reason be sufficiently improv'd to see the Advantage of this!"[5]

Once the Treaty of Paris furnished diplomatic assurance of the new nation's viability, the aged Franklin saw for himself an enormous opportunity to implement just such a plan. Although still skeptical about human rectitude, Franklin was willing to resume his efforts to trumpet virtue. He had been frustrated in his efforts to lead American *colonists* to uprightness, but *United States citizens*, developing their own identity after nearly two decades of rebellion, might prove more malleable. He optimistically informed Europeans that the infant United States was a land of "Industry, Frugality, Ability, Prudence and Virtue," and he wrote that the American lifestyle and economic system "are great preservatives of the Morals and Virtue of a nation." However, Franklin privately viewed Americans as rougher, simpler, more incitable, and less refined than their trans-Atlantic counterparts. They needed an instructor in morality to guide them to the virtuous conduct necessary for a successful republic.[6]

Although well past seventy years old, his fame and fortune secure, Franklin embraced the resumption of his lifelong ambition to disseminate a moral ideology. As a result, while serving as a wartime American ambassador in France, he wrote and published numerous essays extolling virtue. In a "Dialogue Between Franklin and the Gout," Franklin inserted himself into a moralistic essay to show that illness is the result of indolence and gluttony.[7] The game of chess is a microcosm of life, Franklin explained to readers of his bagatelle "The Morals of Chess," because success in both requires foresight, circumspection, and perseverance. "The game is so full of events," Franklin wrote, "that one is encouraged to continue the contest to the last, in hopes of victory by our own skill, or, at least, of giving a *stale mate*, by the negligence of our adversary." In a pamphlet designed to laud virtue and persuade Europeans of the integrity of United States citizens, Franklin advised prospective immigrants seeking "to live upon the Public, by some Office or Salary" due to prominent lineage against journeying to the new nation, for they "will be despis'd and disregarded." Noble birth "is a Commodity that cannot be carried to a worse Market than that of America," he noted, adding that the United States would welcome people with vocational skills who are laborious, frugal, and well-behaved.[8]

Franklin's *Autobiography* was the capstone of his didactic writings. Begun in 1771, its first part contained what he called "several little family Anecdotes of no Importance to others."[9] He discontinued it that summer. However, after friends urged him to "think of bettering the whole race of men" by leading "the Youth to equal the Industry & Temperance of thy early Youth," Franklin resumed in 1784, his tales now "accordingly intended for the Publick."[10] Galvanized by his admirers, Franklin embraced the project as a means of providing moral instruction to the masses. His own assessment of the memoirs was that it "will be of more general use to young readers, exemplifying strongly the effects of *prudent* and *imprudent conduct* in the commencement of a life of business," he informed a French duke.[11]

Franklin had long regarded it essential to teach morality to the young. He wrote to American theologian and educator Samuel Johnson, "I think with you, that nothing is of more importance for the public weal, than to form and train up youth in wisdom and virtue." Teaching morals to the young was vital, Franklin noted, for "virtue is more probably to be expected and obtained from the *education* of youth, than from the *exhortation* of adult persons; bad habits and vices of the mind, being, like diseases of the body, more easily prevented than cured."[12]

While Franklin was trying to prevent moral cankers from infecting youthful souls, he also endeavored to cure them in adults—especially printers. Franklin perceived that most of his printing brethren, especially younger members who had entered the vocation during the Revolution, had no scruples about publishing defamation. While in France, Franklin sometimes refused to lend American newspapers because "the Pieces of Personal Abuse, so scandalously common in our newspapers . . . would disgrace us."[13] Besides their tendency to embarrass, Franklin believed that scurrilous newspapers jeopardized press freedom. He wrote in a newspaper editorial, "nothing is more likely to endanger the liberty of the press, than the abuse of that liberty, by employing it in personal accusation, detraction, and calumny." He found this particularly true in Philadelphia, where "the Spirit of Rancour, Malice, and *Hatred* that breathes in its NewsPapers" fueled the fires of party factionalism. Reading the city's newspapers would lead outsiders "to conclude, that Pennsylvania is peopled by a Set of the most unprincipled, wicked, rascally, and quarrelsome Scoundrels upon the Face of the Globe," he complained.[14]

To Franklin, the character and credit of the new nation was on trial in the court of international public opinion, and a fractious domestic press injured its case. "The Conductor of a Newspaper should, methinks, consider himself as in some degree the Guardian of his Country's Reputation, and refuse to insert such Writings as may hurt it," Franklin exhorted in 1782.[15] American journalism's penchant for obloquy made his job as ambassador to France more difficult and presented a stark contrast to Franklin's emerging European identity as the quintessential American—simple, honest, peaceful, and virtuous. "The British Newswriters are very assiduous in their endeavours to blacken America," Franklin warned a printer. He cautioned the proprietors of his old newspaper, the *Pennsylvania Gazette*, that European newspapers delighted in reprinting calumnies from the United States press to portray America as divisive and chaotic.[16]

Early in his journalism career Franklin adopted a posture of placid neutrality and suggested that printers were mere laborers who were obliged to publish virulent essays provided they were accompanied by money. He informed readers that "Printers naturally acquire a vast Unconcernedness as to the right or wrong Opinions contain'd in what they print" and thus "print things full of Spleen and Animosity, with the utmost Calmness and Indifference." Vituperative writings are continually submitted to printers, he claimed, "because the People are so viciously and corruptly educated that good things are not encouraged."[17]

However, as he matured and realized printing's unique ability to influence public beliefs and conduct, his editorial policy became more selective. Franklin adopted the editorial posture that his newspaper was not like a stagecoach, providing space to everyone who paid. He excoriated people who communicated malicious gossip, comparing them to flies for whom "a *sore Place* is a Feast."[18]

Franklin's solution to the problem of scurrilous submissions was to print them privately, rather than include them in his *Pennsylvania Gazette*. Pamphlets were attractive not only because essays of greater length could be presented in a unified form, but also because they allowed printers to distance themselves from defamatory or polemical writings. However, their newspapers were more closely linked to their identity in the community and more integral to their ideology of public service. "If People will print their Abuses of one another, let them do it in little Pamphlets, and distribute them where they think proper. It is absurd to trouble all the World with them; and unjust to Subscribers in distant Places, to stuff their Paper with Matters so unprofitable and so disagreeable."[19]

Franklin viewed his newspaper as a means to instruct the masses about the blessings of virtuous conduct, but he feared its noble purpose would be nullified by the hypocrisy of printing calumny. "In the Conduct of my Newspaper I carefully excluded all Libelling and Personal Abuse, which is of late Years become so disgraceful to our Country," Franklin wrote in his *Autobiography* in 1788:

> Whenever I was solicited to insert any thing of that kind, and the Writers pleaded as they generally did, the Liberty of the Press, and that a Newspaper was like a Stage Coach in which any one who would pay had a Right to a Place, my Answer was, that I would print the Piece separately if desired, and the Author might have as many Copies as he pleased to distribute himself, but that I would not take upon me to spread his Detraction, and that having contracted with my Subscribers to furnish them with what might be either useful or entertaining, I could not fill their Papers with private Altercation in which they had no Concern without doing them manifest Injustice.[20]

However, most printers in the new nation seemed to be under no such moral stricture, as scurrility and virulent writings filled the pages of the nation's newspapers in the 1780s. This type of press freedom was merely an absence of restraint, rather than a service to society, Franklin lamented. Editor Benjamin Russell concurred, asserting that "the liberty of the press" in the early republic had become "very little short of the liberty of burning our houses." Published defamation only detracted from the press's role of conveying republican enlightenment, useful education, and moral teachings. Franklin believed printers had an obligation to refuse space to rancorous writings. "Now many of our Printers make no scruple of gratifying the Malice of individuals by false Accusations of the fairest Characters among ourselves, augmenting Animosity even to the producing of Duels, and are moreover so indiscreet as to print scurrilous Reflections on the government of neighbouring States, and even on the Conduct of our best national Allies, which may be attended with the most pernicious Consequences," Franklin warned in his *Autobiography*. "These Things I mention as a Caution to young Printers."[21]

Franklin's challenge in the new country was formidable—impart moral instruction to a mass audience and overcome the deleterious effects of scurrilous journalism, which eroded the edifice of public virtue Franklin had spent a lifetime trying to erect.

To enlist assistance in this mission, Franklin decided to rejuvenate his moribund printing network. Franklin had only minimal direct involvement with his printing associates after his formal link to journalism, the Hall partnership, expired in 1766. Although its termination meant "a great Source of our Income is cut off," Franklin wrote to his wife, it freed him to be a full-time diplomat. It also relieved him from the burden of managing the disputes that were tearing apart the network, as Peter Timothy contended with radicals and his former apprentice Charles Crouch in Charles Town, Hall was at odds with Proprietary pacifists in Philadelphia, and James Parker was waging financial and editorial battles against all his former partners. Franklin's desire to distance himself from the worries of publishing prompted him to decline a printing partnership in 1767 "because I did not care to be again concerned in Business," he wrote.[22]

As time passed, Franklin's connections to members of his printing network faded. Franklin outlived most of his old partners, including Parker, Hall, and Timothy, all of whom died during the Revolution. After succumbing to a fever while traveling on postal business, Parker died July 2, 1770.[23] Hall died two years later, on Christmas eve at age fifty-eight, after a long illness.[24] Timothy died in a shipwreck off the Delaware capes in 1782, shortly after being released by the British following a year's captivity as a political prisoner.[25]

Their sons had succeeded the three stalwart partners, with William Hall and David Hall Jr. printing in Philadelphia, Samuel Franklin Parker in New York, and Benjamin Franklin Timothy (along with his mother Ann Timothy) in Charles Town. Franklin enjoyed seeing the next generation thrive. Upon learning of the elder David Hall's death, Franklin wrote, "I lament the death of my good old Friend Mr. Hall, but am glad to understand he has left a Son fit to carry on the Business, which [I] wish he may do with as good a Character and as good Success as his Father." However, there was no contractual relationship between Franklin and the sons. They respected him, but their businesses required neither his formal partnership nor his moral guidance.[26]

Franklin's family connections to the printing trade had likewise dissipated. His nephew James Franklin Jr. and sister-in-law Ann Franklin died in 1762 and 1763, respectively, and their *Newport Mercury* passed to Ann Franklin's son-in-law Samuel Hall.[27] In 1776, nephew Benjamin Mecom wandered away from the New Jersey insane asylum where he was confined and vanished.[28] Franklin's cousin by marriage, William Dunlap, left the business in 1766 to become an Episcopal clergyman.[29]

Of those few network members remaining, their bodies had been weakened by age and their finances depleted by business setbacks. Anton Armbruster, once Franklin's partner in publishing German-language newspapers, wrote him pathetic letters pleading for alms after his press and printing materials had been confiscated in partial satisfaction of his long-standing debt to Franklin. "And as there are Bonds between us I think it Reasonable, in Your Honor's own candid Consideration, they are to be given up, as I lost all," Armbruster wrote in 1785 to Franklin, who had just been chosen president of the Supreme Executive Council of Pennsylvania. The following year Armbruster suggested "some Assistance could perhaps, set me in a way, to make out a living." However, by 1788 Armbruster, writing in a tremulous hand, was more desperate. "I humbly obediently intreat your Excellencys kind and generous Heart" for "a little Assistance and Alms," he implored, as "I am almost incapable of working" due to being "ailing and old."[30] Franklin appears never to have responded, probably because Armbruster still owed him money and because Franklin's son-in-law Richard Bache gave Franklin an unflattering report of Armbruster's character. Armbruster "is an idle, drunken good for nothing Fellow," Bache wrote.[31]

With the veteran network members gone and no extant partnerships, Franklin decided to resuscitate his printing network. His objectives were to convey moral virtue to the new nation and plant worthy young printers into influential positions within the firmament of American journalism. Franklin's intention was that these new partners not only educate their readers, but also set an example for contemporary printers, as Franklin had done during his publishing career.

Relying upon familiar and comfortable methods, Franklin re-established his network with two young printers whose character, conduct, and skill impressed him. Benjamin Franklin Bache and Francis Childs both enjoyed success as printers in the early years of the new nation. Childs became the official printer for New York State and commenced the second daily newspaper there. Bache became the standard-bearer for the Jeffersonian Republicans in the 1790s and the foremost journalistic foe of presidents Washington and Adams.

The two printers attained their prosperity by very different paths.

Bache was Franklin's grandson. He came from a prosperous family, grew up in Europe amid wealth and the highest social circles, and received an elite education in France and Switzerland. Childs, by contrast, was a stranger to Franklin. He was raised in a large and impoverished family, warranting Franklin's attention only because he had been recommended by one of Franklin's trusted political allies. They were a study in contrasts in other ways, as well. Bache learned printing from his grandfather and typefounding from the most prominent typographer in France; Childs served a humble apprenticeship to a Philadelphia printer. Bache was a prolific and vituperative writer; Childs wrote little. Bache was aggressive and prominent; Childs was sedate and inconspicuous. Despite their dissimilar backgrounds and characters, Franklin saw in both men the qualities he sought in partners from years past. This impelled him to set up both in partnerships. The results were not what Franklin expected.[32]

When Franklin was dispatched to France in 1776 to serve as the United States ambassador, he brought his two grandsons with him. William Temple Franklin, age sixteen, served as his personal secretary, and seven-year-old Bache entered a French boarding school. The younger boy having impressed Franklin as "a good honest lad" who will become "a valuable man," Franklin sought to train him in the arts of printing and typefounding. He established a typefoundry in Passy and had a printing press operating by 1779.[33]

The notion of establishing a letter-casting business had intrigued Franklin for decades. "I am much oblig'd to you for your Care and Pains in procuring me the Founding-Tools; tho' I think, with you, that the Workmen have not been at all bashful in making their Bills," Franklin wrote to his English colleague and supplier William Strahan in 1744. There is no other evidence Franklin succeeded in forming a type foundry, but the quality of printing type was still a concern to him thirty-five years later. "I thank you for the Boston Newspapers," he wrote from France to a family member in Boston, "tho' I see nothing so clearly in them as that your Printers do indeed want new Letters. They perfectly blind me in endeavouring to read them. If you should ever have any Secrets that you wish to be well kept, get them printed in those Papers."[34]

Franklin recognized a need for proficient typography in the United States. While creating and defining a national character, Americans were developing a credo of self-sufficiency; it became a source of national pride to fill nearly all their needs with domestic products. This sentiment extended to the printing trade. Printers had been obligated to import their presses and types from England until 1769, when Connecticut craftsmen cast the first type and constructed the first printing press made in America. Silversmith Abel Buell produced the type, and New Haven clockmaker Isaac Doolittle erected the press for William Goddard. A Boston newspaper reported that Doolittle "has lately compleated a Mahogany Printing-Press on the most approved Construction, which, by some good Judges in the Printing Way, is allowed to be . . . equal, if not superior, to any imported from Great-Britain."[35] Papermaking was a related industry that commenced during the Revolution and flourished afterward. As one entrepreneur wrote in 1785, "the art of Manufactureing of Paper" is "of Great Public Utility."[36]

These domestic industries grew following the completion of the Revolutionary War, as printing became a vital means of unifying the new republic. Believing that typefounding was essential to a strong and self-sufficient domestic press, Franklin arranged for his grandson to study under the tutelage of French expert François-Ambroise Didot. Franklin acknowledged Didot "has a Passion for the Art" of printing, and his "Zeal & indefatigable Application, bids fair to carry the Art to a high Pitch of Perfection." His grandson agreed. "I am now learning to print at Mr. Didot's, the best Printer that now exists & maybe that has ever existed," Bache informed his parents, adding that he was also receiving lessons in engraving type.[37]

Franklin vowed to provide Bache with "a Trade that he may have something to depend on, and not be oblig'd to ask Favours or Offices of anybody." As Bache grew to manhood, though, Franklin became increasingly convinced that printing was the appropriate profession for him. By 1788, he was able to inform a French friend that Bache "is preparing to enter into Business as a Printer, the original Occupation of his Grandfather."[38] Franklin still desired that Bache ply the typefounding trade in America, prompting the patriarch to purchase the requisite supplies from Didot, but Franklin's plans for the boy's future had changed.

Franklin esteemed his grandson's character so highly that he believed Bache could better serve the nation by propagating information, education, and opinion among a large audience, rather than working as a craftsman in a foundry. "He is docile and of gentle Manners, ready to receive and follow good Advice, and will set no bad Example," Franklin wrote. "He gains every day upon my Affections." Bache's formidable intellect, philosophical demeanor, and virtuous character prompted Franklin to see Bache as his ideological successor, imparting ethical instruction and serving as a moral bellwether amid the turmoil of a scurrilous press. "I am too old to follow printing again myself, but loving the business, I have brought up my grandson Benjamin to it, and have built and furnished a printing-house for him, which he now manages under my eye," Franklin wrote with pride in 1789, His dedication to the art—and the mission he sought to accomplish by its means—was rekindled by the hope that Bache represented.[39]

Francis Childs was another symbol of Franklin's hope for the future of American journalism. He was born in Philadelphia in 1763 and raised in what John Jay described as "a large and helpless family" in New York.[40] Childs was apprenticed to Philadelphia printer John Dunlap through the patronage of Jay, who would later author some of the Federalist Papers, negotiate the infamous Jay Treaty with Great Britain, and become the first Chief Justice of the United States.[41] Jay paid for Childs's education and encouraged his interest in printing, counseling him that "Professional Knowledge, added to Diligence and Prudence, must sooner or later be successful; especially in a Country like ours."[42]

On January 1, 1783, Childs informed Jay that he aspired to re-establish a New York print shop that had been evacuated by British troops as the Revolutionary War drew to a close. Then in Paris serving as secretary of foreign affairs, Jay encouraged Childs's enterprise. "You do well to look forward to the means of exercising your profession to advantage," he wrote, adding, "You shall continue to have my aid and protection in such measure and season as circumstances may render proper and expedient." This was an important promise, as many early American printers relied on powerful backers for economic support, often in the form of government publishing contracts. This method of official subsidy could be used to encourage certain printers at the expense of others.[43]

Having learned about Franklin's printing network from Dunlap, whose uncle William had been a member, Childs asked Jay to solicit Franklin's advice on printing prospects. Jay told Childs of a press belonging to Franklin that the British army had commandeered, but which would soon be retrieved. Jay added that Franklin told him, "when the enemy left Philadelphia they carried from thence to New York a printing-press of his, and that it is now in the possession of one Robinson, a printer, at New York. As by the provisional treaty the British forces are not to carry away any effects of the inhabitants, this press may perhaps be recovered."[44]

To help his nineteen-year-old charge, Jay recruited Franklin's benefaction. Franklin wrote to Childs, acquainting him with the names of other members of the printing network. Franklin expressed "a willingness to assist you in setting up your business, on the same terms as I had formerly done with other young printers of good character, viz., Whitemarsh and Timothy in Carolina, Smith and afterwards Mecon in Antigua, Parker at New York, Franklin at Rhode Island, Holland [and] Miller at Lancaster, and afterwards Dunlap, and Hall at Philadelphia." Franklin was persuaded to assist Childs because of "The good character given of you by Mr. Jay," which, he noted, "is my inducement to serve you if I can."[45]

The importance of Franklin's phrase "good character," which he used twice in the same letter, cannot be underestimated. Since young adulthood, when he had been deceived and disappointed by callous and self-indulgent people, Franklin had been a vigorous exponent of virtue. "He is ill-cloth'd, who is bare of Virtue," he counseled in his inaugural *Poor Richard's Almanack.* He returned to the theme many times in the almanac. "You may be more happy than princes, if you will be more virtuous," he instructed readers in 1738, adding, "Sell not virtue to purchase wealth, nor Liberty to purchase power."[46] He saw—and encouraged readers to see—a clear connection between virtue and eternal rewards. "Learning to the Studious; Riches to the Careful; Power to the Bold; Heaven to the Virtuous," he noted in 1754. He believed that maintaining such virtues as industry, frugality, logic, and self-discipline represented the best service to God and man and was essential to prudent government and social tranquility. These beliefs remained intact throughout his life.[47]

Three other factors aided Childs in securing Franklin's patronage. That Childs successfully served an apprenticeship under the tutelage of Dunlap, publisher of the *Pennsylvania Packet* and a relative of Franklin's wife, enhanced Franklin's estimation of Childs's character. The second factor was Franklin's lifelong affinity for assisting neophyte tradesmen. Motivated by gratitude for kindnesses extended to him when he was a struggling young printer in the 1720s, but recalling some of his failed partnerships, Franklin wrote in his memoirs that he was "often more ready than perhaps I should otherwise have been to assist young Beginners." The third—and perhaps most important—reason Franklin sponsored Childs was his dedication to countervailing the abundance of journalistic invective in the early republic. From his vantage point in France, he had observed that American newspapers influenced European opinions about the United States. "The excesses some of our papers have been guilty of in this particular, have set this State in a bad light abroad," Franklin asserted.[48]

To help his young protégé get started, Franklin informed Childs he would carry "a very large quantity of types" on his return trip to America in the summer of 1785, "when we may carry this proposal into execution, if it shall suit you." In the interim, Franklin encouraged Childs to seek other opportunities, "for I am old and infirm, and accidents may prevent us," and suggested he visit Parker's widow in New Jersey to see a sample Franklin partnership contract. He noted, "she can show you the agreement between her husband and me, and you may consider the terms of it before my arrival."[49]

Once he became Franklin's partner, Childs took possession of the printing press and opened his shop in New York, then the nation's capital and a thriving city of thirty thousand. Childs described the municipality as the "peaceful seat of the happiest empire in the universe." Situated at "17 Duke-Street, the first Door from the Corner of the Old-Slip and Smith-Street," Childs unveiled the *New-York Daily Advertiser* on March 1, 1785. It was the first newspaper in American history to commence as a daily, and only the fourth daily ever on the continent.[50]

The twenty-one-year-old Childs had set up shop in a city governed by commercial interests, and he fashioned his newspaper accordingly. Finally free of the British occupation forces and the Revolution's hardships, New York warmly embraced economic development. "The history of the City of New York," early republic diarist Elihu Hubbard Smith complained, "is the history of the eager cultivation & rapid increase of the arts of gain." This history was unflaggingly recorded by newspapers such as the *Daily Advertiser*, which, by their focus on "the history of public contests & private intrigues," contribute to "the fatal progress of the demon of Speculation," Smith wrote.[51]

Childs endeavored to fashion the *Daily Advertiser* as New York's chief source of business information. He chose the title to reflect his newspaper's primary function, proclaiming in its nameplate, "ADVERTISEMENTS INSERTED ON THE LOWEST TERMS." True to its name, the *Daily Advertiser* relied heavily on commercial interests for revenue, usually filling about two-and-a-half of its four pages with advertisements, including the entire front page. The use of illustrations and aggressive persuasion techniques in advertising was rare in early America, with little more attention-grabbing than a "headline" in slightly larger type than the standard text. Other commercial information Childs published for the benefit of his readers included ship and stagecoach travel schedules and commodities prices. In a regular feature called "Price Current," Childs listed London prices for such goods as turpentine, mahogany, flax, beeswax, "Pot ashes," and "Rackoon."[52]

Childs's idea to establish a newspaper with an economic focus, designed for a major port city during an era of rapid domestic growth, proved to be an excellent one. Childs enjoyed immediate success, enabling him to proudly inform Franklin, "I am convinced you will with pleasure receive the information that my Paper is one of the best established in N. Yk." Franklin replied that he was glad to hear Childs's newspaper "is well established, and likely to be profitable."[53]

Within one year, Childs's advertising revenue had increased to justify creation of a second publication. He opted to divert much of the financial news and some of the advertisements to a new venture, the *American Price-Current*. Launched May 1, 1786, it was one of the first business publications in American journalism. In it, Childs told readers they could find the market prices of every commodity, as well as stock prices, insurance premiums, auction sales, and "a variety of other useful information." Childs later yielded daily management of this publication to Aeneas Lamont (who was likely one of his journeymen), preferring to devote all his time to the *Daily Advertiser.* In August 1786, the *American Price-Current* was restructured into a new publication, the *New-York Price-Current*, which functioned as a supplement, "given free (gratis) every Monday, to the Subscribers for this Paper," according to a *Daily Advertiser* notice.[54]

Business fare was the *Daily Advertiser*'s chief content, but it also contained social and political news, most of which had been reprinted from Philadelphia, Boston, and London newspapers. Childs seldom wrote for his own newspaper, preferring to solicit reader contributions, especially those promoting moral improvement. To underscore the point, Child included the phrase "The Noblest Motive is the Public Good" on the nameplate.

Following his partner Franklin's advice, Childs often printed essays championing public virtue. One of these, by "Bartholemew Plaintruth," offered "to cultivate the minds, [and] regulate the manners" of his fellow New Yorkers to the extent that it "will be honourable to themselves and promotive of the happiness of society."[55] In another, "Monitor" warned what steps the fledgling United States must take to retain its freedom, writing, "it behoves every citizen of our infant empire, to contribute his mite towards the public weal; to check in their progress the vices of the age [and] to encourage virtue." Otherwise, "liberty will degenerate into licentiousness, commerce deviate from national interest to selfish mercenary views, freedom become a curse."[56]

Others were even more strikingly Franklinesque. "An Admirer of the Fine Arts" observed that "Those efforts of genius are the most laudable which, while they please the fancy . . . communicate to the mind the most useful instruction. Virtue is taught most successfully by being recommended under the appearance of amusement; and those lessons make the deepest and most lasting impression, which, at the same time, convince and interest." Betraying some of Franklin's pessimism, "A Curious Fellow" wrote of how regrettably rare it was "to see merchants oeconomical, mechanicks industrious, politicians sensible and unbiased, magistrates conforming strictly to the laws, and honest men receive encouragement."[57]

Secure in its niche, the *Daily Advertiser* endeavored to broaden its appeal. Childs added the subtitle "Political, Commercial, and Historical" to the nameplate and added poetry and history to its content. To capitalize on the fame of his partner, Childs published some of Franklin's writings, laudatory accounts of Franklin's diplomatic accomplishments, and news about celebrations and testimonials given in Franklin's honor upon his return from France.[58]

Although press freedom was not yet formally guaranteed in the First Amendment, Childs relied on early American journalism's tradition of freedom as he steered his newspaper's editorial course. He opened the *Daily Advertiser*'s pages to harsh criticism of the New York legislature, which "A Litchfield-County Farmer" suggested "is made up principally by a set of selfish knaves and ninnyhammers." Underscoring the emerging conflict between state and federal authority, an unnamed correspondent wrote, "that we have a wise CONGRESS, is not doubted, but they cannot guide the helm for want of a necessary power, which is withheld by a certain *small number of designing men*, who are pursuing *selfish plans*, to the ruin of national prosperity." The writer laid the blame on the state legislature, asserting, "New York is the political curse of the nation."[59] Childs also published criticism of other governments. When the Massachusetts legislature instituted a stamp tax on newspaper advertisements, just two decades after the British Stamp Act had inspired overwhelming resentment and helped incite the American Revolution, "Your Friend and Humble Servant" labeled it "a tax, of extraction truly British, of name ever odious, and of operation mischievous in the extreme, not only to the printers, but the readers of newspapers." Childs himself decried the "ill-judged" and "infamous" levy's economic impact on printers. Echoing James Parker's complaints of three decades earlier, Childs claimed the tax "shackles the Press, by robbing it of its subsistence."[60]

Childs occasionally allowed individuals to express their grievances in print. Irishman "Paddy Whack" railed against ethnic prejudice suffered by his countrymen in the United States. Childs also published personal quarrels. Patrick Dunn accused auctioneer Robert Hunter of cheating him in the consignment sale of soap, branding him a "knave" and a "highwayman." Two days later, Hunter branded the charge "A MALICIOUS and defamatory libel" filled with "abusive epithets."[61]

Childs even published lengthy and vitriolic attacks on his benefactor Jay. He filled nine full columns, or more than half of an entire issue, with a bitter anti-Jay diatribe from Lewis Littlepage, a social climber whom Jay had once befriended but who had later fallen into the statesman's disfavor. Littlepage cursed and mocked Jay, describing him as scheming and greedy. Having printed this polemic, Childs then published Jay's response to "this Young Man's Ebullitions" in pamphlet form, and he also published Littlepage's retort.[62] Their virulent exchange prompted one New Yorker to observe that Childs's publications "have given Rise to a most violent Quarrel between them and occasioned considerable Parties in this City."[63]

Such rancorous essays were not in Childs's newspaper because they served the public interest. Rather, Childs was utilizing a longstanding tradition in the early American press, of which Franklin disapproved: publishing personal attacks in newspapers if their authors paid for them. For example, Franklin partner Peter Timothy requested that letters from political factions intended for print "be paid for proportionably as advertisements." The payment would thus signify the writings as "properly recommended." During a controversy involving fees charged by a medical clinic, Timothy claimed he would not publish opinions on the subject unless they were "properly and sufficiently recommended."[64] Network member John Holt announced his decision "to prefer those Pieces that come attended with Money." Bache also notified readers that he would "shut his paper against" additional submissions regarding a protracted quarrel "except on the footing of advertisements."[65] No surviving evidence confirms that Littlepage paid to attack Jay in print, but on January 30, 1786, Jay paid Childs fifty-six pounds sterling to print two hundred copies of his pamphlet response.[66]

To Franklin's chagrin, Childs adopted an editorial posture of placid neutrality to promote financial success. Childs was influenced by Franklin's early advocacy for journalistic detachment, which was well known in the early republic through publication and distribution of many of Franklin's writings. As a young printer in 1732, Franklin asserted that "Being thus continually employ'd in serving all Parties," printers become ideologically insouciant about the essays they publish, satisfied to "chearfully serve all contending Writers that pay them well." However, as his moral code developed, and as printers became more influential in the middle decades of the eighteenth century, Franklin recognized that such editorial apathy could cause unjust and severe damage to reputations. Franklin's financial stability also played a role in his evolving editorial philosophy: in 1732, he was deeply in debt and thus rationalized the publication of scurrility accompanied by payment. In later years, free of debt, he revised his professional values to abhor defamatory writings.[67]

Having spent his youth in poverty, the ambitious Childs was eager to adopt the remunerative posture of neutrality, just as Franklin had as a young printer. However, after a long career in journalism and government service, the older and wiser Franklin had seen the ill effects of libel, and he sternly advised young printers like Childs to avoid it. By resisting the temptation to defame for pay, printers will be more likely to gain many important friends, Franklin counseled in his *Autobiography*. Directly addressing the concern for money, he assured them, "such a Course of Conduct will not on the whole be injurious to their Interests."[68]

As Franklin wrote these words in August 1788, he may well have been thinking of Childs. Franklin surely thought Childs went too far by allowing a minor figure like Littlepage to repeatedly skewer Jay, whom Franklin respected as "so able a Minister" and whose service "gave me the Pleasure of seeing the Affairs of our Country in such good Hands." Franklin was also appalled that Childs would publish an attack on Jay, who had fostered Childs's rise from poverty to prominence, and then make Jay pay to reply.[69]

Relations between Franklin and Childs were further strained by Childs's repeated complaints about supplies that Franklin sent from France, and particularly the type that Bache had cast. Upon receiving a shipment from Franklin, Childs wrote, "I have the misfortune to find that the types are in very bad order—all the paper and Cords being rotten." After several such letters, Franklin sharply reproached his young partner, prompting Childs to respond, "There is nothing Sir, I prize more than your good opinion, and believe me that your last has given me very severe sensations. I hope Sir you will never occasion again to be disple[ased]."[70] However, Childs persisted in his complaints. "It has been a great misfortune that the Letter has been so imperfect," he wrote, adding, "I find still a considerable deficiency of some sorts." An exasperated Franklin vigorously defended his grandson's craftsmanship, replying, "You are always complaining of Imperfections in the Founts, which I suppose to proceed from your not having right Ideas of that Matter. They were all cast after the best Rules of the Founderies in England, and in the same Proportions." As a further expression of annoyance, Franklin pressed his demands for his share of the partnership's profits, with which Childs had been delinquent.[71]

Franklin acceded to Childs's request for more time to pay, but after several broken promises, the elder statesman's patience had worn thin. He sternly reminded Childs of the debt, cautioned him to "remember that Punctuality is the Life of Credit," and informed him that the expense of building five houses in Philadelphia had left him "in *real & great* Want of Money." He concluded, "I hope and entreat that as I have shown my self willing and ready to serve you, you will now in return exert yourself to me by paying off the Debt, at a time when I so much want it."[72] However, Childs never paid during Franklin's lifetime. Franklin bequeathed to his son-in-law Richard Bache the responsibility of collecting from Childs.[73]

The matters of editorial philosophy, supplies, and money had created a rift between Childs and Franklin, so Childs took journeyman John Swaine into partnership on July 2, 1789. The two men had served their apprenticeships together in Dunlap's shop, and had remained friends since. It is open to conjecture whether the pact with Swaine signaled the cessation of Franklin's partnership with Childs, or whether Swaine joined Childs in partnering with Franklin. The fact that only one letter apparently passed between Franklin and Childs after July 2, 1789—offering no indication the partnership was extant—suggests they may have ended their affiliation in 1789, with the understanding that Childs would eventually buy out Franklin's interest.[74]

Childs later formed an alliance with Philip Freneau to publish the *National Gazette*, a Republican newspaper in Philadelphia. This was another example of Childs's paradoxical proclivities in an era of growing partisan sentiment. By setting up Freneau as a junior partner, who under Thomas Jefferson's protection would spearhead the opposition to the Federalist policies of George Washington, John Adams, Alexander Hamilton, and Jay, Childs displayed the same surprising catholicity of politics as in the Jay-Littlepage dispute several years earlier. Seemingly, neither loyalty to person nor party could deter Childs from his Janus-faced journalism.[75]

Assessing Childs's political sentiments, the shrewd Hamilton dubbed him "a very cunning fellow." Hamilton wrote to New York Senator Rufus King that "In Philadelphia in the person of his proxy Freneau, he is a good Antifederalist Clintonian; in New York he is a good Federalist and Jayite—Beckley & Jefferson pay him for the first & the Federal Citizens of New York for the last."[76] New Jersey Congressman Jonathan Dayton underscored the paradoxical nature of Childs's political loyalties, informing Hamilton about Childs's involvement with Freneau's *National Gazette*, "He, you know, is one of the printers, and interested in the paper, and altho' I am well assured that he entirely disapproves the manner in which it is conducted, yet it is natural to suppose that he would not willingly be instrumental in the establishing of any fact which might operate to it's disrepute or prejudice." Dayton's assertion about Childs's true political sentiments may have been more a reflection of what the Federalist congressman wanted to believe, or what Childs wanted him to believe, than reality.[77]

Franklin's involvement with Bache was more satisfying than his partnership with Childs. Bache had been molded in his grandfather's image and imbued with his ideals and work ethic. After nine years in France, the sixteen-year-old Bache returned with Franklin to Philadelphia, receiving a gradual introduction to American printing. His grandfather established a printing house for him to do typefounding and book publishing while he learned about American society and politics.

Bache also attended the University of Pennsylvania. "Ben is at College to compleat his Studies," Franklin noted. Moral philosophy was one of his courses. After his graduation, Bache and Franklin worked in their Philadelphia typefoundry and print shop.[78]

Bache's moral education was furthered by close exposure to the precepts in his grandfather's memoirs. Franklin, saddled with three "incurable" ills, "the gout, the stone, and old age," felt his life slipping away. "I am on the whole much weaker," he reported to one correspondent in the fall of 1788. "But possibly that may be the effect of age, for I am now near eighty-three, the age of commencing decrepitude." He finally had to enlist Bache's help in 1789 as an amanuensis in copying the *Autobiography*. He admitted wishing he had enlisted Bache's help earlier; if he had, "I think I might by this time have finished my Memoirs, in which I have made no progress for these six months past," he reported to a friend late in 1789.[79]

He never finished it, though, spending his final year taking opium to ease his suffering from the kidney stones. "For my own personal Ease, I should have died two Years ago," he wrote to George Washington in the fall of 1789, adding, "those Years have been spent in excruciating Pain."[80]

After considering Franklin's thirteen-point "Project of arriving at moral Perfection" in the memoirs, Bache found himself intrigued by the question of mankind's inherent disposition to virtue. He concluded, just as his grandfather had a half-century earlier, that people's inclination to be virtuous is contrary to their nature. Like his grandfather, he concluded people needed to be taught virtuous conduct, as it was not inherent in them. And like his grandfather, he concluded that his desire to be useful to his new country required that he take on the role of moral educator. Finally, his method for serving the public good required a newspaper, just as it had for his grandfather.[81]

Bache issued a prospectus for a newspaper he intended to publish in Philadelphia. He invited submissions from writers who "deliver their sentiments with temper & decency, and whose motive appears to be, *the public good*," Bache announced. "The strictest impartiality will be observed in the publication of pieces offered with this view."[82]

Bache's plan to publish a newspaper concerned some of his friends, who feared he might not be able to maintain the impartiality he promised in the prospectus. After reading the prospectus, Pennsylvania Senator Robert Morris cautioned him, "it is difficult for a Press of such Reputation as you would choose yours to be, to maintain the Character of Freedom & impartiality, connected with Purity." Rather than publishing a newspaper, Morris advised, "you might be more honorably & more lucratively employed by the printing of Books."[83]

Bache was not dissuaded, and by age twenty-one announced he was ready to fill the role of moral instructor his grandfather had intended for him. He thus commenced his *General Advertiser* as a Philadelphia daily newspaper on October 1, 1790, promising "that no consideration whatever shall induce him blindly to submit to the influence of any man or set of men: His PRESS SHALL BE FREE." Its editorial focus on useful knowledge and instruction was inspired by "the advice which the Publisher had received from his late Grand Father," he informed readers.[84] Bache's interest in printing was partly inspired by the fact that "it is lucrative," as he informed the father of one of his apprentices, but also by his sincere belief that "it is first in respectability on the score of usefulness in a free state." Bache regarded the press as the protector of civic prosperity because "it leads legislators to be cautious in enacting laws, lest they infringe on the rights of man" and enables the people to discern "errors or designs of an administration which have an unfavorable aspect on the public interest and happiness."[85]

In the early years of his journalism career, Bache furnished didactic instruction as his grandfather had. Cautioning readers, "It is a sign of great prudence to be willing to receive instruction," he noted that "the felicity of life . . . arises only from virtue." A month after he began publishing his newspaper, Bache informed young readers that "The ORNAMENTS of YOUTH" consist of such virtues as modesty, cheerfulness, serenity, reverence, "a pleasing benevolence and readiness to do good to mankind."[86]

Emulating his grandfather, Bache intended his newspaper as a purveyor of moral teachings. "Many people read newspapers who read little else," he acknowledged. "To a retired man, a newspaper is always company—sometimes instruction." Bache's exhortative early issues prompted his great-aunt Jane Mecom to comment that his newspaper "Apears to me very Respectable." If he continues to steer this editorial course, she wrote to Bache's wife Margaret, "it may soon create for him an Estate in the clouds as his Venerable Grandfather used to say of His Newspaper."[87]

Franklin viewed his journalism as service to God and humanity, and hoped it would merit him a heavenly estate. However, Bache's journalism gradually strayed from this course. Despite promising that "Impartiality and independence shall still be the characteristic" of his newspaper when he changed its name to *The Aurora and General Advertiser* in 1794, Bache had by this time succeeded Philip Freneau as the most aggressive and partisan of the nation's Republican editors.[88] Inspired by Federalist affronts to his father and grandfather, Bache became a virulent critic of the Washington and Adams administrations.[89] Bache claimed that "If ever a nation was debauched by a man, the American nation has been debauched by Washington," who had held himself up as "an idol" during his Presidency, and he branded Adams an inept, war-mongering monarchist. One of his correspondents, "Codrus," warned readers, "You are on the verge of tyranny" and "Your Constitution is in danger" because of Washington's malfeasance.[90] When Washington left office, Bache delighted in his departure. "If ever there was period for rejoicing, this is the moment," he wrote, "that the name of WASHINGTON from this day ceases to give a currency to political iniquity; and to legalize corruption."[91]

Federalists reacted with alarm at Bache's lack of restraint. "Mr. Bache has thrown off every appearance of Modesty" and has been "profuse in his abuse of the President," Director of the U.S. Mint Elias

Boudinot wrote. He lamented that Bache's writers regularly vilify Washington and "will scarcely admit that he possesses even the semblance of any one Virtue." Bache took obvious pleasure in his task of excoriating the first two Federalist presidents. "The art of Printing is that which men in office dread exceedingly," Bache noted gleefully.[92]

John Adams saw Bache's scurrilous journalism as a perpetuation of his grandfather's animosity toward Adams. Franklin "had conceived an irreconcilable hatred to me" and "had propagated and would continue to propagate prejudices, if nothing worse, against me in America from one end of it to the other," Adams wrote Philadelphia physician Benjamin Rush. "Look into Bache's Aurora . . . and see whether my expectations have not been verified."[93]

In donning the mantle of Republican standard-bearer, Bache abandoned his own early advice to readers—to demonstrate a "hatred of calumny and slander"—and ignored his own recommendation that they form "a habit of speaking well of others."[94] More significantly, he abandoned the ethical teachings of his grandfather, who made dissuading printers from scurrility one of his foremost ambitions in his final years. Franklin's most satirical and pointed attack on journalistic defamation was "An Account of the Supremest Court of Judicature in Pennsylvania, viz., The Court of the Press," published seven months before his death. In it he decried that the press can "promulgate accusations of all kinds, against all persons and characters" and "condemn to infamy, not only private individuals, but public bodies" with impunity. The sole guardians and beneficiaries of this power are the "one citizen in five hundred, who, by education or practice in scribbling," can write or publish. "This five hundredth part of the citizens have the privilege of accusing and abusing the other four hundred and ninety-nine parts at their pleasure; or they may hire out their pens and press to others for that purpose," Franklin mused.[95]

Franklin claimed that the concept of press freedom is highly regarded but misunderstood by the public. To Franklin, it meant the free flow of political discourse in the public interest. "If by the *liberty of the press* were understood merely the Liberty of discussing the Propriety of Public Measures and political opinions, let us have as much of it as you please: But if it means the Liberty of affronting, calumniating, and defaming one another, I, for my part . . . shall cheerfully consent to exchange my *Liberty* of Abusing others for the *Privilege* of not being abus'd myself." To avoid infringing on the liberty of the press, Franklin sarcastically posited that people should be granted "the *liberty of the cudgel*."[96]

This alternative liberty was taken several times with Bache. His harsh writings prompted Clement Humphreys, the son of a ship architect, and Federalist editor John Ward Fenno to publicly assault Bache in separate incidents.[97] The former occurred on board a U.S. Navy ship being built in a Philadelphia harbor. "I was thus standing, alone as I thought, still looking at the bell, when I felt a violent blow on my head," Bache informed readers. He recalled that Humphreys was angered because Bache "abused the President on the day of his resignation." In the latter incident, Bache reported that Fenno "scratched the nose of his antagonist and his teeth took off the skin of the editor's knuckles; for which he got in return a sound rap or two across the head and face."[98]

Bache's rabid anti-Federalist partisanship crippled his newspaper. Fellow Philadelphia printer Mathew Carey observed, "the attacks on Gen. Washington blasted Bache's popularity, and almost ruined the paper. Subscribers withdrew in crowds—and the advertising custom sank to insignificance."[99]

The Franklin printing network finally expired with the dissolution of the Childs partnership and Bache's death in the 1798 yellow-fever epidemic. The disease killed more than 3,600 of the 15,000 people who remained in Philadelphia. Five of every six people who contracted the fever died from it.[100] The twenty-nine-year-old Bache opted to stay in the city, which had also been ravaged by the disease five years earlier, rather than escape to the countryside. Although acknowledging "The disorder still increases, & Kills more than it did in '93," he never expected it to claim his life. As the fever spread throughout Philadelphia, Bache reassured his parents that "our danger now is nothing to what it then was." Bache remained in the city to publish the *Aurora*, choosing to risk disease "rather than sacrifice my interest so materially as an abandonment of my paper at this time would," he wrote. "I cant fly and ask others to stay & mind my business; besides it would not be done to my mind." Eight days later, he was dead.[101]

Childs enjoyed a much longer life, turning the *Daily Advertiser* over to John Morton in 1796 before entering politics. In his valedictory Childs acknowledged public support for the newspaper and noted, "Duty and interest, combined to render the *Daily Advertiser* an impartial, and free depository of speculative and political opinions."[102] He later served as a United States governmental agent in France and Germany and ambassador to Great Britain. Upon returning to the United States, he settled in Vermont, where he was elected to that state's legislature. He died in 1830.[103]

Of all Franklin's network printers, Francis Childs was one of the most remarkable. In addition to producing a pioneering daily newspaper and contributing to the fledgling American business press, his was among the last and least satisfying of the partnerships Franklin established to aid the development of early American journalism. Childs used the partnership to great advantage, as other network members had, but he alienated Franklin with his willingness to peddle defamation for profit and with his repeated complaints about the printing supplies Franklin furnished. Also, in an era of intense ideological inclinations, Childs allowed monetary concerns and his conception of editorial neutrality to override his loyalty to his benefactor Jay, thus allowing him to be attacked in print by a disappointed office-seeker.

Childs was unusual for his curiously apolitical stance in an era of intense partisanship, particularly among printers. While conducting a Federalist newspaper in New York, he also helped establish the opposition Republican press in Philadelphia. In doing so, he exhibited the same impartiality and "vast Unconcernedness" about defamatory writings that

Franklin advocated early in his printing career but later repudiated.[104] Although not possessing Franklin's creative genius and apparently reluctant to contribute his own commentary to his newspapers' columns, Childs tailored Franklin's strategy of editorial neutrality to his own use, enabling him to outlast many more controversial and partisan printers.

Bache was an equally intriguing study in contrast. Resolute in his convictions, he launched one of the most effective challenges to the Federalists' creation of central government in the United States. His newspaper criticism of executive policies contributed to American political thought and provided an early test of the new nation's support for press freedom. Although he adhered to Franklin's republican principles and fostered press scrutiny of public officials during his career, Bache descended into obloquy and became the very sort of journalist about whom Franklin expressed dismay in his public writings.

Despite showing early promise, both Bache and Childs ultimately disappointed Franklin's aspiration to set up young printers who would teach moral virtue while eschewing calumny. Childs's querulous business practices and pecuniary neutrality, and Bache's character assassinations and indifference to his grandfather's concern for the nation's image diverged from Franklin's reasons for reviving the network.

Franklin's ambition to reform the United States press from within, as a legacy to his beloved profession, had been foiled. In the last months of his life, he was forced to conclude that printers, editors, and writers enjoy "tearing your private character to flitters" and thereby inviting "the odium of the public." This was an abuse of the understanding of press freedom Franklin had long supported. Since, as he told one writer, "Such personal public Attacks are never forgiven," the only remaining remedy to scurrility and defamation was an expression of private resentment. "Thus, my fellow-citizens, if an impudent writer attacks your reputation, dearer to you perhaps than your life, and puts his name to the charge, you may go to him as openly and break his head."[105]

Abbreviations

AAS = American Antiquarian Society
APS = American Philosophical Society
BF = Benjamin Franklin
HSP = Historical Society of Pennsylvania
PBF = Labaree, Leonard W., et al., eds. *The Papers of Benjamin Franklin*
PG = *Pennsylvania Gazette*
WoBF = Bigelow, John, ed. *The Works of Benjamin Franklin*
WrBF = Smyth, Albert Henry, ed. *The Writings of Benjamin Franklin*

Notes

1. *Poor Richard*, 1753, in *PBF*, 4:405.

2. *The Scribler*, 8; *Pennsylvania Journal*, October 26, 1764. For other political attacks on Franklin's character, see Ketcham, "Benjamin Franklin and William Smith"; Miles, "American Image of Benjamin Franklin."

3. BF to Sarah Franklin, November 8, 1764, in *PBF*, 11:449; BF to Robert Morris, July 26, ibid., 35:311-12.

4. BF to Louis Le Veillard, June 8, 1788, in *WrBF*, 9:657.

5. BF to Joseph Priestley, February 8, 1780, in *PBF*, 31:456; BF to Richard Price, February 6, 1780, ibid., 453.

6. See e.g. "Comparison of Great Britain and America as to Credit, in 1777," ibid., 24:508-14; "Information to Those Who Would Remove to America," 1782, in *WrBF*, 8:603-14. For the link between virtue and a republic, see Peter Berkowitz, *Never a Matter of Indifference: Sustaining Virtue in a Free Republic*.

7. "Dialogue Between Franklin and the Gout," October 22, 1780, in *WrBF*, 8:154-62. Privately, Franklin claimed "disease was intended as the Punishment of Intemperance, Sloth, and other Vices; and the Example of that Punishment was intended to promote and strengthen the opposite Virtues" (BF to John Fothergill, March 14, 1764, in *PBF*, 11:101).

8. "The Morals of Chess," in *PBF*, ca. 1779, 29:755; "Information to Those Who Would Remove to America," 1782, in *WrBF*, 8:605-6.

9. *Autobiography*, 72.

10. Benjamin Vaughan to BF, January 31, 1783, in *Autobiography*, 185-89; Abel James to BF, 1782, ibid., 184-85; *Autobiography*, 72.

11. BF to the Duc de La Rochefoucauld, October 22, 1788, in *WrBF*, 9:665. For Franklin's aims in writing his memoirs, see Paul M. Zall, *Franklin on Franklin*.

12. BF to Samuel Johnson, August 23, 1750, in *PBF*, 4:41.

13. BF to Francis Hopkinson, December 24, 1782, in *WrBF*, 8:647.

14. "To the Editors of the *Pennsylvania Gazette*," 1788, ibid., 9:639-42.

15. BF to Francis Hopkinson, December 24, 1782, in *WrBF*, 8:648.

16. "To the Printer of the *Evening Herald*," n.d., in *WrBF*, 9:627; "To the Editors of the *Pennsylvania Gazette*," 1788, ibid., 9:639-42.

17. "Apology for Printers," *PG*, June 10, 1731.

18. *Autobiography*, 95; "On Ill-Natured Speaking," *PG*, July 12, 1733.

19. BF to Francis Hopkinson, December 24, 1782, in *WrBF*, 8:648. For pamphlets' role as the primary repository of controversial writings that did not involve immediate public concerns, see Bernard Bailyn, *Pamphlets of the American Revolution, 1750-1776*.

20. *Autobiography*, 94-95.

21. [Boston] *The Columbian Centinel*, June 21, 1797; *Autobiography*, 95.

22. BF to Deborah Franklin, June 22, 1767, in *PBF*, 14:193; BF to DH, April 14, 1767, ibid., 127. For Franklin's chance to be a partner in another Philadelphia newspaper, see John J. Zimmerman, "Benjamin Franklin and the *Pennsylvania Chronicle*," 351-64.

23. Mary Parker to BF, August 12, 1770, in *PBF*, 17:204.

24. Deborah Franklin to BF, November 16, 1773, ibid., 19:373; Richard Bache to BF, January 4, 1773, ibid., 20:6.

25. Thomas, *History of Printing in America*, 569.

26. Ibid., 390, 397, 483, 495, 580-81; BF to Richard Bache, March 3, 1773, in *PBF*, 20:88.

27. "Account with the Estate of James Franklin, Junior," April 4, 1763, in *PBF*, 10:238-41; Thomas, *History of Printing in America*, 315-17, 325.

28. John Lawrence and William Smith to BF, July 19, 1776, in *PBF*, 22:517-18; Jane Mecom to BF, August 15, 1778, ibid., 27:257; Jane Mecom to BF, February 14, 1779, ibid., 28:541.

29. Dwight L. Teeter Jr., "John Dunlap: The Political Economy of a Printer's Success," 3-9, 55; Turnbull, "William Dunlap."

30. Anton Armbruster to BF, November 12, 1785; April 26, 1786; June 26, 1788, Franklin Papers, APS (the Armbruster correspondence appears to be as yet unpublished in a print volume; it is published online at http://franklinpapers.org/franklin/framedNames.jsp). Other network members sought money from Franklin. In 1768 Samuel Franklin Parker, James Parker's ne'er-do-well son, tried unsuccessfully to borrow from Franklin. See JP to BF, October 17, 24, 1768, in *PBF*, 15:232-33, 241. Ann Franklin's son-in-law and printing partner Samuel Hall succeeded, though he appears never to have repaid the debt. Seven years later, Franklin was still trying to collect. In a letter to his sister, he likened Hall to "a whimsical man in Pennsylvania, of whom it was said that it being against his Principle to pay Interest, and against his Interest to pay the Principal, he paid neither one nor t'other" (Jonathan Williams Sr. to BF, September 19, 1771, ibid., 18:219-20; BF to Jane Mecom, January 13, 1772, ibid., 19:28).

31. Richard Bache to BF, January 4, 1773, in *PBF*, 20:5. For more on Armbruster's debt to Franklin, see BF to Richard Bache, October 7, 1772, ibid., 19:315; Anton

Armbruster to BF, June 13, 1763, ibid., 10:289; Anton Armbruster Chattel Mortgage and Inventory, October 29, 1765, ibid., 12:342-45.

32. On Bache's life and journalism, see Richard N. Rosenfeld, *American Aurora: A Democratic-Republican Returns*; Jeffery A. Smith, *Franklin & Bache: Envisioning the Enlightened Republic*; James Tagg, *Benjamin Franklin Bache and the Philadelphia Aurora*.

33. BF to Richard Bache, June 2, 1779, *PBF*, 29:600. For Passy, see Luther S. Livingston, *Franklin and His Press at Passy*, 6-16, 78-80.

34. BF to William Strahan, July 4, 1744, in *PBF*, 2:410; BF to Elizabeth Partridge, October 11, 1779, in *PBF*, 30:514.

35. [Boston] *Massachusetts Gazette*, September 7, 1769; Wroth, *Colonial Printer*, 98-101.

36. David Bemis to the Massachusetts Legislature, October 1785, Book Trades Collection, AAS.

37. BF to William Strahan, December 4, 1781, in *PBF*, 36:193; Benjamin Franklin Bache to Richard and Sarah Bache, May 11, 1785, Society Collection, HSP. For American papermaking, see Dard Hunter, *Papermaking: The History and Technique of an Ancient Craft*. On Didot, see Albert J. George, *The Didot Family and the Progress of Printing*.

38. BF to Richard Bache, November 11, 1784, in *WrBF*, 9:279; BF to Madame Brillon, April 19, 1788, ibid., 644.

39. BF to Mary Hewson, September 7, 1783, in *WrBF*, 9:89; BF to Catherine Greene, March 2, 1789, ibid., 10:4.

40. [Washington] *National Intelligencer*, October 27, 1830; *Burlington Sentinel*, October 15, 1830; John Jay to Francis Childs, May 11, 1783, in Henry P. Johnston, ed., *The Correspondence and Public Papers of John Jay*, 3:45-46.

41. John Jay to John Dunlap, July 10, 1779, Jay Papers, Columbia University.

42. John Jay to Francis Childs, December 20, 1784, Franklin Papers, APS. On Jay's career, see Walter Stahr, *John Jay: Founding Father*; Phil Webster, *Can a Chief Justice Love God? The Life of John Jay*. On the treaty for which he is known, see Joseph Charles, "The Jay Treaty: The Origins of the American Party System," 581-630; Jerald A. Combs, *The Jay Treaty: Political Battleground of the Fathers*; Todd Estes, "Shaping the Politics of Public Opinion: Federalists and the Jay Treaty Debate," 393-422.

43. John Jay to Francis Childs, May 11, 1783, in Johnston, ed., *Papers of John Jay*, 3:45. On government printing contracts as subsidy, see Boorstin, *The Americans*, 324-40. For a Jacksonian printer who defied his party and was punished with the loss of government printing, bankrupting him, see Robert K. Stewart, "Jacksonians Discipline a Party Editor: Economic Leverage and Political Exile," 591-99.

44. John Jay to Francis Childs, May 11, 1783, in Johnston, ed., *Papers of John Jay*, 3:45. Jay likely erroneously referred to "Robinson" when he meant Alexander and James Robertson, Loyalist printers who published the *Royal American Gazette* in New York under British auspices until the departure of British troops in 1783. See Thomas, *History of Printing in America*, 476-77.

45. BF to Francis Childs, February 8, 1785, in *WoBF*, 11:8-9.

46. *Poor Richard*, 1733, 1738, in *PBF*, 1:315, 2:194.

47. *Poor Richard*, 1754, ibid., 5:185. For Franklin's concepts of virtue, see Norman S. Fiering, "Benjamin Franklin and the Way to Virtue," 199-223; David M. Larson, "Franklin on the Nature of Man and the Possibility of Virtue," 118.

48. Thomas, *History of Printing in America*, 386-87, 393-94; *Autobiography*, 60; "To the Editors of the *Pennsylvania Gazette*," 1788, in *WrBF*, 9:639.

49. BF to Francis Childs, February 8, 1785, in *WoBF*, 11:9.

50. [New York] *Daily Advertiser*, March 16, 1785, December 12, 1789; Frank L. Mott, *American Journalism: A History*, 115-16. The date of the *Daily Advertiser*'s inaugural issue is estimated, based on the earliest extant issue, number 14, dated March 16, 1785. Three other newspapers started as weeklies, then converted to daily publication. One of them, the first daily in New York, was the *New-York Morning Post, and Daily Advertiser*. It switched from semiweekly status to daily on February 23, 1785 just one week before Childs's newspaper.

51. James E. Cronin, ed., *The Diary of Elihu Hubbard Smith*, 77, 126-27.

52. By 1800, twenty of the twenty-four daily newspapers published in the United States denoted their commerce function by using the word "Advertiser" in their titles. The percentage declined in the early nineteenth century as newspapers became increasingly reliant on political parties for income. See Alfred M. Lee, *The Daily Newspaper in America*, 59.

53. Francis Childs to BF, April 3, 1787, Society Collection, HSP; BF to Childs, May 8, 1787, *WrBF*, 9:580.

54. *Daily Advertiser*, May 2, 9, August 10, 1786. Although its roots extend to the eighteenth century, the American business press was slow to develop. Now it represents more than half of the magazines published in the United States. See Kathleen L. Endres, "Ownership and Employment in Specialized Business Press," 996-98; Carol Smith, "Taking Stock, Placing Orders: A Historiographic Essay on the Business History of the Newspaper."

55. *Daily Advertiser*, March 16, 1785.

56. Ibid., September 23, 1785.

57. Ibid., May 11, 13, 1786. Franklin understood that "the Mob hate Instruction, and the Generality would never read beyond the first Line of my Lectures, if they were usually fill'd with nothing but wholesome Precepts and Advice." He thus sought to "humour them" by weaving moral lessons into satirical essays ("The Busy-Body, No. 4," *American Weekly Mercury*, February 25, 1729).

58. See e.g. *Daily Advertiser*, September 20-22, 1785.

59. *Daily Advertiser*, May 2, 11, 1786.

60. Ibid., May 30, September 24, 1785.

61. Ibid., September 20, 22, 1785.

62. Ibid., December 10, 16, 1785; [Francis Childs], *Letters, being the whole of the Correspondence between the Hon. John Jay, Esquire, and Mr. Lewis Littlepage*. For Littlepage's obsequious pursuit of Jay's patronage, see Lewis Littlepage to BF, February 12, 1780, in *PBF*, 31:476-77.

63. Lambert Cadwalader to John Cadwalader, January 29, 1786, Cadwalader Papers, HSP.

64. *South-Carolina Gazette*, November 21, 1754; July 8, 1755. Timothy also used

the term "well-recommended" to mean he expected payment when accepting new apprentices. See Chapter 2.

65. *New-York Journal*, March 22, 1770; [Philadelphia] *Aurora*, March 11, 1795.

66. On Jay's payment to Childs, see Frank Monaghan, *John Jay: Defender of Liberty*, 452.

67. "Apology for Printers," *PG*, June 10, 1731, in *PBF*, 1:195. Franklin explained his indebtedness in his memoirs. See *Autobiography*, 65-66, 69-70.

68. *Autobiography*, 95.

69. BF to John Jay, October 2, 1780, in *PBF*, 33:356.

70. Francis Childs to BF, March 18, 1786; February 27, 1787, Society Collection, HSP.

71. April 3, 1787, Society Collection, HSP; BF to Francis Childs, May 8, 1787, in *WrBF*, 9:580. For other letters in which Childs complained of the types, see Francis Childs to BF, April 18, 28, June 16, 1786, ibid. Nearly two years later, Childs remained dissatisfied, bemoaning "the amazing quantities of imperfections" (Francis Childs to BF, January 8, 1788, Society Collection, HSP).

72. BF to Francis Childs, October 15, 1786; April 27, 1789, Society Collection, HSP. Franklin made the same point earlier about the need for punctuality in repaying America's pecuniary debt to France. See BF to Charles Thomson, April 16, 1784, *WrBF*, 9:192; BF to Samuel Mather, May 12, 1784, ibid., 9:210.

73. "Franklin's Last Will and Testament," July 17, 1788, in *WrBF*, 10:496.

74. BF to Francis Childs, March 10, 1790, ibid., 10:86.

75. *Daily Advertiser*, July 2, 1789; Francis Childs to BF, August 24, 1786, Society Collection, HSP.

76. Alexander Hamilton to Rufus King, July 25, 1792, in Harold C. Syrett, ed., *The Papers of Alexander Hamilton*, 12:100. "Beckley" was John Beckley, clerk of the House of Representatives and a close political ally of Jefferson.

77. Jonathan Dayton to Alexander Hamilton, August 26, 1792, in Syrett, ed., *Papers of Alexander Hamilton*, 12:275.

78. BF to Mary Hewson, October 30, 1785, in *WrBF*, 9:474. Bache was to have received his college degree in July 1787, but the Constitutional Convention delayed the graduation four months. Bache finally graduated in a class of eight on November 22. See BF to Francis Childs, May 8, 1787, Society Collection, HSP; Smith, *Franklin & Bache*, 90.

79. BF to Elizabeth Partridge, November 25, 1788, *WrBF*, 9:683; BF to Jan Ingenhousz, October 24, 1788, ibid., 671; BF to Benjamin Vaughn, November 2, 1789, ibid., 10:49-50.

80. BF to Benjamin Vaughn, November 2, 1789, *WrBF*, 10:49-50; BF to George Washington, September 16, 1789, ibid., 10:41.

81. *Autobiography*, 68; Tagg, *Benjamin Franklin Bache*, 56-71.

82. Benjamin Franklin Bache, *Proposals for Publishing a News-Paper, to be Entitled The Daily Advertiser.*

83. Robert Morris to Benjamin Franklin Bache, July 28, 1790, Bache Papers, APS.

84. [Philadelphia] *General Advertiser*, October 1, 1790. Bache believed he was ready to commence newspaper publishing well before the autumn of 1790, and re-

sented that Franklin had not let him start an independent printing operation sooner. See Benjamin Franklin Bache to Margaret Markoe, June 23, 1790, in Tagg, *Benjamin Franklin Bache*, 76.

85. Benjamin Franklin Bache to Joseph Chambers, September 14, 1796, David Chambers Papers, AAS; *General Advertiser*, March 8, 1792.

86. *General Advertiser*, January 16, 1792; November 10, 1790.

87. Ibid., December 1, 1791; Jane Mecom to Margaret Bache, December 2, 1790, Gratz Collection, HSP.

88. [Philadelphia] *Aurora and General Advertiser*, November 8, 1794.

89. The affronts to which Bache objected included Federalist efforts to skewer Franklin's posthumous reputation and the Congressional dismissal of his father, Richard Bache, as postmaster without offering a reason. For the former, see [Philadelphia] *Gazette of the United States*, February 23, 1793; Cobbett, *Porcupine's Works*, 1:40, 4:32-33; Nian-Sheng Huang, *Benjamin Franklin in American Thought and Culture*, 32-36. For the latter, see Richard Bache to George Washington, April 21, 1789, in W. W. Abbot, ed., *The Papers of George Washington: Presidential Series*, 2:95-96. For the claim that boredom motivated Bache's partisanship, see Jeffrey L. Pasley, *The Tyranny of Printers: Newspaper Politics in the Early American Republic*, 83.

90. *Aurora*, November 8, 1794; March 6, 1797; March 4, 1796; [Benjamin Franklin Bache], *Remarks Occasioned by the Late Conduct of Mr. Washington as President of the United States; Letters from General Washington to Several of His Friends, In June and July, 1776*. For Bache's attack on Adams, see Arthur Scherr, "'Vox Populi' versus the Patriot President: Benjamin Franklin Bache's Philadelphia *Aurora* and John Adams (1797)," 503-21.

91. *Aurora*, March 5, 1797.

92. Elias Boudinot to John Bayard, December 7, 1795, Edward Everett Papers, Massachusetts Historical Society; *Aurora*, August 18, 1798.

93. John Adams to Benjamin Rush, April 12, 1809, Adams, ed., *Works of John Adams*, 9:619.

94. *General Advertiser*, November 10, 1790.

95. "An Account of the Supremest Court of Judicature in Pennsylvania, viz., The Court of the Press," [Philadelphia] *Federal Gazette*, September 12, 1789, in *WrBF*, 10:36-37.

96. Ibid., 38-39.

97. *Aurora*, April 6, December 9, 1797; August 9, 10, 1798; *Gazette of the United States*, August 9, 1798. For the "culture" of honor and combat prevalent in the era, see Joanne B. Freeman, *Affairs of Honor: National Politics in the New Republic*.

98. *Aurora*, April 6, 1787, August 10, 1798.

99. Mathew Carey, *Autobiography*, 39.

100. Philadelphia's population in 1798 was fifty-five thousand, but about forty thousand fled to the countryside. Thus, the fever killed nearly a fourth of those who stayed in the city. See John T. Scharff and Thompson Westcott, *History of Philadelphia, 1609-1884*, 2:1629-31. For an eyewitness narrative of the 1798 epidemic, see Thaddeus Brown, *An Address in Christian Love, to the Inhabitants of Philadelphia; on the Awful Dispensation of the Yellow Fever, in 1798*; Philadelphia College of Physi-

cians, *Facts and Observations Relative to the Nature and Origin of the Pestilential Fever* . . . .

101. Benjamin Franklin Bache to Richard and Sarah Bache, September 2, 1798, Society Collection, HSP. For the effects of the comparable 1793 Philadelphia epidemic, see J. H. Powell, *Bring Out Your Dead: The Great Plague of Yellow Fever in Philadelphia in 1793*. For firsthand accounts of the 1799 epidemic, see Charles Brockden Brown, *Arthur Mervyn; or, Memoirs of the Year 1793*; Mathew Carey, *A Short Account of the Malignant Fever, Lately Prevalent in Philadelphia*.

102. *Daily Advertiser*, January 25, 1796.

103. [Washington] *National Intelligencer*, October 27, 1830; *Burlington Sentinel*, October 15, 1830. Childs solicited powerful friends to obtain federal appointments, such as the post of American ambassador to Great Britain. For one such example, see Francis Childs to Rufus King, August 9, 1800, Rufus King Papers, New-York Historical Society.

104. For Franklin's early editorial philosophy, see "Apology for Printers," *PG*, June 10, 1731.

105. "An Account of the Supremest Court of Judicature," in *WrBF*, 10:38, 40; BF to ?, November 25, 1786, ibid., 9:549.

Works Cited

Abbot, W. W., ed. *The Papers of George Washington: Presidential Series*. Charlottesville: University Press of Virginia, 1987.

Adams, Charles Francis, ed. *The Works of John Adams*. Boston: Little, Brown, 1850-56.

[Bache, Benjamin Franklin.] *Letters from General Washington to Several of His Friends, In June and July, 1776*. Philadelphia: Federal Press, 1795.

Bache, Benjamin Franklin. *Proposals for Publishing a News-Paper, to be Entitled The Daily Advertiser*. Philadelphia: Benjamin Franklin Bache, 1790.

[Bache, Benjamin Franklin.] *Remarks Occasioned by the Late Conduct of Mr. Washington as President of the United States*. Philadelphia: Benjamin Franklin Bache, 1790.

Bailyn, Bernard. *Pamphlets of the American Revolution, 1750-1776*. Cambridge: Harvard University Press, 1965.

Berkowitz, Peter. *Never a Matter of Indifference: Sustaining Virtue in a Free Republic*. Palo Alto: Stanford University Press, 2003.

Bigelow, John, ed. *The Works of Benjamin Franklin*. 12 vols. New York: Knickerbocker, 1904.

Boorstin, Daniel. *The Americans: The Colonial Experience*. New York: Random House, 1958.

Brown, Charles Brockden. *Arthur Mervyn; or, Memoirs of the Year 1793*. Philadelphia: David McKay, n.d.

Brown, Thaddeus. *An Address in Christian Love, to the Inhabitants of Philadel-*

phia; on the Awful Dispensation of the Yellow Fever, in 1798. Philadelphia: Robert Aitken, 1798.

Carey, Mathew. *A Short Account of the Malignant Fever, Lately Prevalent in Philadelphia*. Philadelphia: Mathew Carey, 1794.

Charles, Joseph. "The Jay Treaty: The Origins of the American Party System." *William and Mary Quarterly* 12 (October 1955): 581-630.

[Childs, Francis.] *Letters, being the whole of the Correspondence between the Hon. John Jay, Esquire, and Mr. Lewis Littlepage*. New York: Francis Childs, 1786.

Cobbett, William. *Porcupine's Works*. 12 vols. London: William Cobbett, 1801.

Combs, Jerald A. *The Jay Treaty: Political Battleground of the Fathers*. Berkeley: University of California Press, 1970.

Cronin, James E., ed. *The Diary of Elihu Hubbard Smith*. Philadelphia: American Philosophical Society, 1973.

Endres, Kathleen L. "Ownership and Employment in Specialized Business Press." *Journalism Quarterly* 65 (Winter 1988): 996-98.

Estes, Todd. "Shaping the Politics of Public Opinion: Federalists and the Jay Treaty Debate." *Journal of the Early Republic* 20 (Fall 2000): 393-422.

Fiering, Norman S. "Benjamin Franklin and the Way to Virtue." *American Quarterly* 30 (Summer 1978): 199-223.

Franklin, Benjamin. *The Autobiography of Benjamin Franklin: A Genetic Text*. Edited by J. A. Leo Lemay and P. M. Zall. Knoxville: University of Tennessee Press, 1981.

Freeman, Joanne B. *Affairs of Honor: National Politics in the New Republic*. New Haven: Yale University Press, 2001.

George, Albert J. *The Didot Family and the Progress of Printing*. Syracuse, N.Y.: Syracuse University Press, 1961.

Huang, Nian-Sheng. *Benjamin Franklin in American Thought and Culture, 1790-1990*. Philadelphia: American Philosophical Society, 1994.

Hunter, Dard. *Papermaking: The History and Technique of an Ancient Craft*. 2nd ed. New York, Knopf, 1957.

Johnston, Henry P., ed. *The Correspondence and Public Papers of John Jay*. New York: G. P. Putnam's Sons, 1890-93. Reprint, New York: Burt Franklin, 1970.

Ketcham, Ralph. "Benjamin Franklin and William Smith: New Light on an Old Philadelphia Quarrel." *Pennsylvania Magazine of History and Biography* 88 (April 1940): 218-42.

Labaree, Leonard W., et al., eds. *The Papers of Benjamin Franklin*. 37 vols. to date. New Haven: Yale University Press, 1959- .

Larson, David M. "Franklin on the Nature of Man and the Possibility of Virtue." *Early American Literature* 10 (Fall 1975): 111-20.

Lee, Alfred M. *The Daily Newspaper in America*. New York: Macmillan, 1937.

Livingston, Luther S. *Franklin and His Press at Passy*. New York: Grolier Club, 1914.

Miles, Richard D. "The American Image of Benjamin Franklin." *American Quarterly* 9 (Summer 1957): 117-43.

Monaghan, Frank. *John Jay: Defender of Liberty*. New York: Bobbs-Merrill, 1935.

Mott, Frank L. *American Journalism: A History*. 3rd ed. New York: MacMillan, 1962.
Pasley, Jeffrey L. *The Tyranny of Printers: Newspaper Politics in the Early American Republic*. Charlottesville: University of Virginia Press, 2001.
Philadelphia College of Physicians. *Facts and Observations Relative to the Nature and Origin of the Pestilential Fever . . . .* Philadelphia: Printed for Thomas Dobson, 1798.
Powell, J. H. *Bring Out Your Dead: The Great Plague of Yellow Fever in Philadelphia in 1793*. Philadelphia: University of Pennsylvania Press, 1949.
Rosenfeld, Richard N. *American Aurora: A Democratic-Republican Returns*. New York: St. Martin's, 1997.
Scharff, John T., and Thompson Westcott. *History of Philadelphia, 1609-1884*. 3 vols. Philadelphia: L. H. Everts, 1884.
Scherr, Arthur. "'Vox Populi' versus the Patriot President: Benjamin Franklin Bache's Philadelphia *Aurora* and John Adams (1797)." *Pennsylvania History* 62 (Fall 1995): 503-21.
Smith, Carol. "Taking Stock, Placing Orders: A Historiographic Essay on the Business History of the Newspaper." *Journalism Monographs* 132 (April 1992).
Smith, Jeffrey A. *Franklin & Bache: Envisioning the Enlightened Republic*. New York: Oxford University Press, 1990.
Smyth, Albert Henry, ed. *The Writings of Benjamin Franklin*. 10 vols. New York: Macmillan, 1905-7. Reprint, New York: Haskell House, 1970.
Stahr, Walter. *John Jay: Founding Father*. London: Hambledon and London, 2005.
Stewart, Robert K. "Jacksonians Discipline a Party Editor: Economic Leverage and Political Exile." *Journalism Quarterly* 66 (Autumn 1989): 591-99.
Syrett, Harold C., ed. *The Papers of Alexander Hamilton*. 27 vols. New York: Columbia University Press, 1961-87.
Tagg, James. *Benjamin Franklin Bache and the Philadelphia Aurora*. Philadelphia: University of Pennsylvania Press, 1991.
Teeter, Dwight L., Jr. "John Dunlap: The Political Economy of a Printer's Success." *Journalism Quarterly* 52 (Spring 1975): 3-8, 55.
Thomas, Isaiah. *The History of Printing in America*. Edited by Marcus A. McCorison. New York: Weathervane, 1970.
Turnbull, Mary D. "William Dunlap, Colonial Printer, Journalist, and Minister." *Pennsylvania Magazine of History and Biography* 103 (April 1979): 143-65.
Webster, Phil. *Can a Chief Justice Love God? The Life of John Jay*. Bloomington, Ind.: Authorhouse, 2002.
Wroth, Lawrence. *The Colonial Printer*. New York: Grolier, 1931. Rev. ed. Charlottesville: University of Virginia Press, 1964.
Zall, Paul M. *Franklin on Franklin*. Lexington: University Press of Kentucky, 2000.
Zimmerman, John J. "Benjamin Franklin and the *Pennsylvania Chronicle*." *Pennsylvania Magazine of History and Biography* 81 (October 1957): 351-64.

RESOURCES

Chronology of Benjamin Franklin's Life

1706	Benjamin Franklin is born on January 17 in Boston to Josiah and Abiah (Folger) Franklin.
1714-1715	Franklin is enrolled in the South Grammar School in Boston.
1715-1716	Franklin attends George Brownell's English school.
1718	Franklin is apprenticed to his brother James as a printer.
1722	Franklin publishes the letters of "Mrs. Silence Dogood" in the *New England Courant* (the newspaper started by James).
1723	Franklin breaks his apprenticeship to James and leaves for New York; he eventually arrives in Philadelphia.
1724	Franklin moves to London to buy printing equipment.
1725	Franklin works in the printing shops of Samuel Palmer and John Watts.
1726	Franklin returns to Philadelphia.
1727	Franklin suffers his first attack of pleurisy. Later in the year he founds the Junto, which later becomes the American Philosophical Society.
1728	With Hugh Meredith, Franklin starts his own print shop.
1729	Franklin becomes the owner and publisher of the *Pennsylvania Gazette*. His first son, William, is born.
1730	Franklin's print shop is elected to be the official government printer, and Franklin buys Meredith's half of the business. He marries Deborah Read Rogers.
1731	Franklin joins the Freemasons, publishes "Apology for Printers," and founds the first circulating library, the Library Company of Philadelphia.

1732	Franklin's son Francis Folger Franklin is born; Franklin begins publishing *Poor Richard's Almanack.*
1735	Franklin's brother James dies.
1736	Franklin is appointed clerk of the Pennsylvania Assembly, and he founds the Union Fire Company in Philadelphia. His son Francis dies.
1737	Franklin is appointed postmaster of Philadelphia.
1743	Franklin publishes "A Proposal for Promoting Useful Knowledge Among the British Plantations in America." His daughter Sarah is born.
1745	Franklin's father, Josiah, dies.
1747	Franklin begins experimenting with electricity. He publishes *Plain Truth* and organizes a volunteer militia.
1748	Franklin retires from publishing and printing.
1749	*Proposals Relating to the Education of Youth in Pennsylvania* is published. Franklin organizes the Academy of Philadelphia, which later becomes the University of Pennsylvania.
1751	Franklin helps secure funding for the first hospital in Pennsylvania. The first volume of his *Papers, Experiments and Observations on Electricity* is published. Franklin is elected a member of the Pennsylvania Assembly. He proposes a plan for the first fire insurance company.
1752	Franklin's mother, Abiah, dies. Franklin experiments with kite and key in a thunderstorm and later explains his kite experiment in the *Pennsylvania Gazette.*
1753	Franklin is appointed joint deputy postmaster general of North America.
1754	Franklin proposes a unionization of the colonies as protection against the French.

1756	Franklin is elected to Britain's Royal Society; he meets George Washington.
1757	Franklin travels to London as the representative of the Pennsylvania Assembly. *Poor Richard Improved*, also known as *The Way to Wealth*, is published.
1759	The University of St. Andrew awards Franklin an honorary doctor of laws degree.
1762	Franklin returns to Philadelphia.
1764	Franklin travels to London after being defeated in his bid for reelection to the Pennsylvania Assembly.
1767	Franklin travels to France.
1769	The American Philosophical Society elects Franklin as the organization's president.
1771	Franklin begins writing his autobiography.
1772	Franklin is inducted into the French Academy of Science.
1773	*Rules by Which a Great Empire May Be Reduced to a Small One* and *An Edict of the King of Prussia* are published.
1774	Franklin's wife dies. He is accused of stealing the letters of Massachusetts governor Thomas Hutchinson.
1775	Franklin returns to Philadelphia and is elected as a delegate to the Second Continental Congress; he submits the Articles of Confederation. King George III declares the colonies to be in rebellion.
1776	Franklin is appointed to draft the Declaration of Independence; he is later one of the signers of the final document. He travels to France as American commissioner.
1778	Franklin negotiates and signs the Treaty of Alliance with France; France declares war on Great Britain.

1779	Franklin is appointed minister to France.
1783	With John Adams and John Jay, Franklin signs the Treaty of Paris.
1784	Franklin negotiates treaties with Prussia and other European countries. "An Economical Project for Diminishing the Cost of Light," in which Franklin proposes a form of daylight saving time, is published.
1785	Franklin describes his invention of bifocal eyeglasses. He returns to Philadelphia.
1787	The Pennsylvania Society for Promoting the Abolition of Slavery elects Franklin as the organization's president. He serves as delegate to the Constitutional Convention and signs the U.S. Constitution.
1790	Franklin dies of pleurisy on April 17 in Philadelphia.
1791	*Memoirs de la vie privée ecrits par lui-même* is published in Paris.
1793	*The Private Life of the Late Benjamin Franklin* (later known as *The Autobiography of Benjamin Franklin* or simply *Autobiography*) is published in London.

Works by Benjamin Franklin

"Silence Dogood Essays," 1722
"The Bagatelles," 1722-1784 (miscellaneous tales and sketches)
Dissertation on Liberty and Necessity, Pleasure and Pain, 1725
"The Busy-Body Essays," 1729
The Nature and Necessity of a Paper Currency, 1729
Poor Richard's Almanack, 1732-1757
"On Protection of Towns from Fire," 1735
"Self-Denial Not the Essence of Virtue," 1735
"A Proposal for Promoting Useful Knowledge Among the British Plantations in America," 1743
An Account of the New Invented Pennsylvania Fireplaces, 1744
"Old Mistresses' Apologue," 1745 (also known as "Advice to a Young Man on the Choice of a Mistress")
Plain Truth, 1747
"The Speech of Polly Baker," 1747
Proposals Relating to the Education of Youth in Pennsylvania, 1749
Idea of the English School, 1751
Observations on the Increase of Mankind, People of Countries, &c., 1751
"Physical and Meteorological Observations," 1751
Papers, Experiments and Observations on Electricity, 1751-1754 (3 volumes)
"The Kite Experiment," 1752
Post Office Instructions and Directions, 1753
Albany Plan of Union, 1754
Some Account of the Pennsylvania Hospital, 1754
Treaty of Carlisle, 1754
Poor Richard Improved, 1757 (also known as *The Way to Wealth*)
The Interest of Great Britain Considered, 1760
Cool Thoughts on the Present Situation of Our Public Affairs, 1764
Memorandum on the American Postal Service, 1764
Narrative of the Late Massacres, 1764
Examination of Dr. Franklin by the House of Commons Concerning the Stamp Act, 1766
An Edict of the King of Prussia, 1773
Rules by Which a Great Empire May Be Reduced to a Small One, 1773
The Ephemera, 1778
Treaty of Amity and Commerce Between the United States and France, 1778
Political, Miscellaneous, and Philosophical Pieces, 1779
The Whistle, 1779

Dialogue Between Franklin and the Gout, 1780
The Handsome and the Deformed Leg, 1780
Treaty of Peace Between the United States and Great Britain, 1783
"An Economical Project for Diminishing the Cost of Light," 1784
Remarks Concerning the Savages of North America, 1784
"On Smoky Chimneys," 1785
The Art of Procuring Pleasant Dreams, 1786
"Observations Relative to the Academy in Philadelphia," 1789
On the Slave Trade, 1790
Memoirs de la vie privée ecrits par lui-même, 1791 (*The Private Life of the Late Benjamin Franklin*, 1793; *Memoirs of the Life*, 1818; best known as *Autobiography*)

Bibliography

Abbott, John S. C. *Benjamin Franklin*. New York: Dodd, Mead, 1903.

Aldridge, A. Owen. *Benjamin Franklin, Philosopher and Man*. Philadelphia: J. B. Lippincott, 1965.

____________. *Franklin and His French Contemporaries*. 1957. Westport, CT: Greenwood Press, 1976.

American Philosophical Society. *Studies on Benjamin Franklin, The Two Hundred and Fiftieth Anniversary of His Birth, January 17, 1956*. Philadelphia: Author, 1955.

Augur, Helen. *The Secret War of Independence*. New York: Duell, Sloan, and Pearce, 1955.

Barretta, Gene. *Now and Ben: The Modern Inventions of Benjamin Franklin*. New York: Henry Holt, 2006.

Block, Seymour Stanton. *Benjamin Franklin, Genius of Kites, Flights, and Voting Rights*. Jefferson, NC: McFarland, 2004.

Bodzin, Eugene Saul. "The American Popular Image of Benjamin Franklin, 1790-1868." Ph.D. dissertation, University of Madison-Wisconsin, 1969.

Bowen, Catherine Drinker. *The Most Dangerous Man in America: Scenes from the Life of Benjamin Franklin*. Boston: Little, Brown, 1974.

Brands, H. W. *The First American: The Life and Times of Benjamin Franklin*. New York: Doubleday, 2000.

Breitwieser, Mitchell Robert. *Cotton Mather and Benjamin Franklin: The Price of Representative Personality*. New York: Cambridge University Press, 1984.

Brooks, Elbridge Streeter. *The True Story of Benjamin Franklin, the American Statesman*. Illus. Victor A. Searles. Boston: Lothrop, 1898.

Bruce, William Cabell. *Benjamin Franklin, Self-Revealed: A Biographical and Critical Study Based Mainly on His Own Writings*. 2 vols. New York: G. P. Putnam's Sons, 1917.

Burlingame, Roger. *Benjamin Franklin, Envoy Extraordinary*. New York: Coward-McCann, 1967.

____________. *Benjamin Franklin: The First Mr. American*. New York: New American Library, 1955.

Buxbaum, Melvin H., ed. *Critical Essays on Benjamin Franklin*. Boston: G. K. Hall, 1987.

Campbell, James. *Recovering Benjamin Franklin: An Exploration of a Life of Science and Service*. Chicago: Open Court, 1999.

Carey, Lewis J. *Franklin's Economic Views*. Garden City, NY: Doubleday, Doran, 1928.

Carr, William George. *The Oldest Delegate: Franklin in the Constitutional Convention*. Newark: University of Delaware Press, 1990.

Chaplin, Joyce E. *Benjamin Franklin's Political Arithmetic: A Materialist View of Humanity*. Washington, DC: Smithsonian Institution Libraries, 2008.

___________. *The First Scientific American: Benjamin Franklin and the Pursuit of Genius*. New York: Basic Books, 2006.

Clark, Ronald W. *Benjamin Franklin: A Biography*. 1983. London: Phoenix, 2001.

Clark, William Bell. *Ben Franklin's Privateers: A Naval Epic of the American Revolution*. 1956. Westport, CT: Greenwood Press, 1969.

Cohen, I. Bernard. *Benjamin Franklin: His Contribution to the American Tradition*. Indianapolis: Bobbs-Merrill, 1953.

___________. *Benjamin Franklin: Scientist and Statesman*. New York: Charles Scribner's Sons, 1975.

___________. *Science and the Founding Fathers: Science in the Political Thought of Jefferson, Franklin, Adams, and Madison*. New York: W. W. Norton, 1995.

Conner, Paul Willard. "Benjamin Franklin's Quest for Political Order." Ph.D. dissertation, Princeton University, 1963.

___________. *Poor Richard's Politicks: Benjamin Franklin and His New American Order*. New York: Oxford University Press, 1965.

Crane, Verner. *Benjamin Franklin and a Rising People*. Boston: Little, Brown, 1954.

___________. *Benjamin Franklin, Englishman and American*. Baltimore: Williams & Wilkins, 1936.

Currey, Cecil B. *Road to Revolution: Benjamin Franklin in England, 1765-1775*. Garden City, NY: Anchor Books, 1968.

Draper, John William. *Life of Franklin*. Ed. Ronald S. Wilkinson. Washington, DC: Library of Congress, 1977.

Dray, Philip. *Stealing God's Thunder: Benjamin Franklin's Lightning Rod and the Invention of America*. New York: Random House, 2005.

Dudley, E. Lawrence. *Benjamin Franklin*. New York: Macmillan, 1915.

Dull, Jonathan R. *Franklin the Diplomat: The French Mission*. Philadelphia: American Philosophical Society, 1982.

Eiselen, Malcolm R. *Franklin's Political Theories*. Garden City, NY: Doubleday, Doran, 1928.

Essig, Mark Regan. *Inventing America: The Life of Benjamin Franklin*. Nashville, TN: Rutledge Hill Press, 2006.

Finger, Stanley. *Doctor Franklin's Medicine*. Philadelphia: University of Pennsylvania Press, 2006.

Fisher, Sydney George. *The True Benjamin Franklin*. Philadelphia: J. B. Lippincott, 1899.

Ford, Paul Leicester. *Franklin Bibliography: A List of Books Written By, or Relating to Benjamin Franklin*. 1899. Boston: Longwood Press, 1977.

Franklin, Benjamin. *The Autobiography and Other Writings*. 1961. Ed. L. Jesse Hemisch. New York: Signet Classic, 2001.

___________. *Autobiography of Benjamin Franklin*. 1868. Ed. John Bigelow. Franklin Center, PA: Franklin Library, 1984.
___________. *The Autobiography of Benjamin Franklin*. 1896. Mineola, NY: Dover, 1996.
___________. *The Autobiography of Benjamin Franklin: A Genetic Text*. Ed. J. A. Leo Lemay and P. M. Zall. Knoxville: University of Tennessee Press, 1981.
___________. *Autobiography, Poor Richard, and Later Writings*. Ed. J. A. Leo Lemay. New York: Library of America, 1987.
___________. *Benjamin Franklin: A Biography in His Own Words*. Ed. Thomas Fleming. 2 vols. New York: Newsweek, 1972.
___________. *Benjamin Franklin: His Life as He Wrote It*. Ed. Esmond Wright. Cambridge, MA: Harvard University Press, 1990.
___________. *A Benjamin Franklin Reader*. Ed. Walter Isaacson. New York: Simon & Schuster, 2003.
___________. *The Compleated Autobiography*. Ed. Mark Skousen. Washington, DC: Regnery, 2006.
___________. *The Complete Works in Philosophy, Politics, and Morals, of the Late Dr. Benjamin Franklin, Now First Collected and Arranged: With Memories of His Early Life*. 3 vols. London: J. Johnson and Longman, Hurst, Rees, and Orme, 1806.
___________. *The Complete Works of Benjamin Franklin*. 10 vols. Ed. John Bigelow. New York: G. P. Putnam's Sons, 1887-88.
___________. *Franklin on Franklin*. Ed. Paul M. Zall. Lexington: University Press of Kentucky, 2000.
___________. *Memoirs of Benjamin Franklin; Written by Himself, and Continued By His Grandson and Others; With His Social Epistolary Correspondence, Philosophical, Political, and Moral Letters and Essays, and His Diplomatic Transactions as Agent at Longon and Minister Plenipotentiary at Versailles; Augemented By Much Matter Not Contained in Any Former Edition; With a Potliminouse Preface*. 2 vols. Ed. William Deane. Philadelphia: McCarty & Davis, 1834.
___________. *The Papers of Benjamin Franklin*. 39 vols. Ed. Leonard W. Labaree et al. New Haven, CT: Yale University Press, 1959-2009.
___________. *Writings*. New York: Literary Classics of the United States, 1987.
Gaustad, Edwin S. *Benjamin Franklin*. New York: Oxford University Press, 2006.
Granger, Bruce Ingham. *Benjamin Franklin: An American Man of Letters*. 1964. Westport, CT: Greenwood Press, 1988.
Green, James N., and Peter Stallybrass. *Benjamin Franklin: Writer and Printer*. New Castle, DE: Oak Knoll Press, 2006.
Hartsock, Pamela Ann. "Tracing the Pattern Among the Tangled Threads: The Composition and Publication History of *The Autobiography of Benjamin Franklin*." Ph.D. dissertation, University of Missouri-Columbia, 2000.
Hawke, David Freeman. *Franklin*. New York: Harper & Row, 1976.

Huang, Nian-Sheng. *Benjamin Franklin in American Thought and Culture, 1790-1990*. Philadelphia: American Philosophical Society, 1994.

Humes, James C. *The Wit and Wisdom of Benjamin Franklin*. Warsaw, Poland: Gramercy Books, 2001.

Isaacson, Walter. *Benjamin Franklin: An American Life*. New York: Simon & Schuster, 2003.

Jennings, Francis. *Benjamin Franklin, Politician*. New York: W. W. Norton, 1996.

Kennedy, Jennifer T. "Signing History: The Memoirs of Benjamin Franklin, Benjamin Rush, John Adams, and Thomas Jefferson." Ph.D. dissertation, Yale University, 1999.

Kushen, Betty Sandra. "Benjamin Franklin and His Biographers: A Critical Study." Ph.D. dissertation, New York University, 1969.

Laska, Vera. *Benjamin Franklin, the Diplomat*. New York: Eilert Print, 1982.

Lemay, J. A. Leo. *The Canon of Benjamin Franklin, 1722-1776: New Attributions and Reconsiderations*. Newark: University of Delaware Press, 1986.

___________. *The Life of Benjamin Franklin*. 2 vols. Philadelphia: University of Pennsylvania Press, 2006.

___________, ed. *Oldest Revolutionary: Essays on Benjamin Franklin*. Philadelphia: University of Pennsylvania Press, 1976.

___________, ed. *Reappraising Benjamin Franklin: A Bicentennial Perspective*. Newark: University of Delaware Press, 1993.

Lokken, Roy N., ed. *Meet Dr. Franklin*. Philadelphia: Franklin Institute Press, 1981.

McMaster, John Bach. *Benjamin Franklin*. New York: Chelsea House, 1980.

Middlekauff, Robert. *Benjamin Franklin and His Enemies*. Berkeley: University of California Press, 1996.

Miles, Richard Donald. "The American Image of Benjamin Franklin." *American Quarterly* 9.2, pt. 1 (Summer 1957): 117-43.

___________. "The Political Philosophy of Benjamin Franklin: The Beginning of the Pragmatic Tradition in American Political Thought." Ph.D. dissertation, University of Michigan, 1949.

Morgan, Edmund. *Benjamin Franklin*. New Haven, CT: Yale University Press, 2002.

Newcomb, Benjamin Havelock. *Franklin and Galloway: A Political Partnership*. New Haven, CT: Yale University Press, 1972.

Pangle, Lorraine Smith. *The Political Philosophy of Benjamin Franklin*. Baltimore: Johns Hopkins University Press, 2007.

Parton, James. *The Life and Times of Benjamin Franklin*. 2 vols. 1864. New York: Da Capo Press, 1971.

Pasles, Paul C. *Benjamin Franklin's Numbers: An Unsung Mathematical Odyssey*. Princeton, NJ: Princeton University Press, 2008.

Robitaille, Patricia Bohen. "The Paradoxes of the Diplomacy of Benjamin Franklin During the American Revolution." M.A. thesis, California State University, Long Beach, 2005.

Schiffer, Michael B. *Draw the Lightning Down: Benjamin Franklin and Electrical Technology in the Age of Enlightenment*. Berkeley: University of California Press, 2003.

Srodes, James. *Franklin: The Essential Founding Father*. Washington, DC: Regnery, 2002.

Stourzh, Gerald. *Benjamin Franklin and American Foreign Policy*. 2d ed. Chicago: University of Chicago Press, 1969.

Tierney, Mary Nulty. "A Useful Citizen: Benjamin Franklin as Defender of the 'Glorious Publick Virtue.'" D.A. thesis, State University of New York at Albany, 1998.

Van Doren, Carl. *Benjamin Franklin*. 1938. Birmingham, AL: Palladium Press, 2001.

Waldstreicher, David. *Runaway America: Benjamin Franklin, Slavery, and the American Revolution*. New York: Hill & Wang, 2004.

Weaver, Jeanne Moore. "Benjamin Franklin and Thomas Jefferson: Two American Philosophes Compared (Volumes I and II)." Ph.D. dissertation, Auburn University, 1988.

Wood, Gordon S. *The Americanization of Benjamin Franklin*. New York: Penguin Press, 2004.

Wright, Esmond. *Franklin of Philadelphia*. Cambridge, MA: Belknap Press of Harvard University Press, 1986.

Zall, Paul M. *Benjamin Franklin's Humor*. Lexington: University Press of Kentucky, 2005.

Zimmerman, John Joseph. "Benjamin Franklin: A Study of Pennsylvania Politics and the Colonial Agency, 1755-1775." Ph.D. dissertation, University of Michigan, 1956.

CRITICAL INSIGHTS

About the Editor

Jack Lynch is Associate Professor of English at Rutgers University in Newark, New Jersey. He has published both scholarly and popular books and essays, mostly on British and American culture in the long eighteenth century. He is the author of *The Age of Elizabeth in the Age of Johnson* (2003), *Becoming Shakespeare: The Unlikely Afterlife That Turned a Provincial Playwright into the Bard* (2007), and *Deception and Detection in Eighteenth-Century Britain* (2008). He is also the editor of *The Age of Johnson: A Scholarly Annual* and coeditor of *Anniversary Essays on Johnson's Dictionary* (2005). His essays and reviews have appeared in scholarly forums such as *Eighteenth-Century Life*, *The Review of English Studies*, and *Studies in Philology*, as well as in *The American Scholar*, *The New York Times*, and the *Los Angeles Times*.

About *The Paris Review*

The Paris Review is America's preeminent literary quarterly, dedicated to discovering and publishing the best new voices in fiction, nonfiction, and poetry. The magazine was founded in Paris in 1953 by the young American writers Peter Matthiessen and Doc Humes, and edited there and in New York for its first fifty years by George Plimpton. Over the decades, the *Review* has introduced readers to the earliest writings of Jack Kerouac, Philip Roth, T. C. Boyle, V. S. Naipaul, Ha Jin, Jay McInerney, and Mona Simpson, and published numerous now classic works, including Roth's *Goodbye, Columbus*, Donald Barthelme's *Alice*, Jim Carroll's *Basketball Diaries*, and selections from Samuel Beckett's *Molloy* (his first publication in English). The first chapter of Jeffrey Eugenides's *The Virgin Suicides* appeared in the *Review*'s pages, as well as stories by Edward P. Jones, Rick Moody, David Foster Wallace, Denis Johnson, Jim Shepard, Jim Crace, Lorrie Moore, Jeanette Winterson, and Ann Patchett.

The Paris Review's renowned Writers at Work series of interviews, whose early installments include legendary conversations with E. M. Forster, William Faulkner, and Ernest Hemingway, is one of the landmarks of world literature. The interviews received a George Polk Award and were nominated for a Pulitzer Prize. Among the more than three hundred interviewees are Robert Frost, Marianne Moore, W. H. Auden, Elizabeth Bishop, Susan Sontag, and Toni Morrison. Recent issues feature conversations with Salman Rushdie, Joan Didion, Stephen King, Norman Mailer, Kazuo Ishiguro, and Umberto Eco. (A complete list of the interviews is available at www.theparisreview.org.) In November 2008, Picador will publish the third of a four-volume series of anthologies of *Paris Review* interviews. The first two volumes have received acclaim. *The New York Times* called the Writers at Work series "the most remarkable and extensive interviewing project we possess."

The Paris Review is edited by Philip Gourevitch, who was named to the post in 2005, following the death of George Plimpton two years earlier. Under Gourevitch's leadership, the magazine's international distribution has expanded, paid subscriptions have risen 150 percent, and newsstand distribution has doubled. A new editorial team has published fiction by Andre Aciman, Damon Galgut, Mohsin Hamid, Gish Jen, Richard Price, Said Sayrafiezadeh, and Alistair Morgan. Poetry editors Charles Simic, Meghan O'Rourke, and Dan Chiasson have selected works by Billy Collins, Jesse Ball, Mary Jo Bang, Sharon Olds, and Mary Karr. Writing published in the magazine has been anthologized in *Best American Short Stories* (2006, 2007, and 2008), *Best American Poetry*, *Best Creative Non-Fiction*, the Pushcart Prize anthology, and *O. Henry Prize Stories*.

The magazine presents two annual awards. The Hadada Award for lifelong contribution to literature has recently been given to William Styron, Joan Didion, Norman Mailer, and Peter Matthiessen in 2008. The Plimpton Prize for Fiction, given to a new voice in fiction brought to national attention in the pages of *The Paris Review*, was presented in 2007 to Benjamin Percy and to Jesse Ball in 2008.

The Paris Review won the 2007 National Magazine Award in photojournalism, and the *Los Angeles Times* recently called *The Paris Review* "an American treasure with true international reach."

Since 1999 *The Paris Review* has been published by The Paris Review Foundation, Inc., a not-for-profit 501(c)(3) organization.

The Paris Review is available in digital form to libraries worldwide in selected academic databases exclusively from EBSCO Publishing. Libraries can contact EBSCO at 1-800-653-2726 for details. For more information on *The Paris Review* or to subscribe, please visit: www.theparisreview.org.

Contributors

Jack Lynch is Associate Professor of English at Rutgers University in Newark, New Jersey. He is the author of *The Age of Elizabeth in the Age of Johnson* (2003), *Becoming Shakespeare: The Unlikely Afterlife That Turned a Provincial Playwright into the Bard* (2007), and *Deception and Detection in Eighteenth-Century Britain* (2008). He is also the editor of *The Age of Johnson: A Scholarly Annual.*

Clark Davis is Professor of English at the University of Denver. He is the author of *After the Whale: Melville in the Wake of Moby-Dick* and *Hawthorne's Shyness: Ethics, Politics, and the Question of Engagement.*

Bradley Bazzle is an associate instructor in creative writing and composition at Indiana University. His award-winning play *The Franklin Thesis* appears from time to time in New York City.

Neil Heims is a writer and teacher living in Paris. His books include *Reading the Diary of Anne Frank* (2005), *Allen Ginsberg* (2005), and *J. R. R. Tolkien* (2004). He has also contributed numerous articles for literary publications, including essays on William Blake, John Milton, William Shakespeare, and Arthur Miller.

Gurdip Panesar earned his M.A. and Ph.D. degrees in English literature from the University of Glasgow, Scotland. He has contributed various entries to recent literary reference works and is at present teaching in the Department of Adult Education at the University of Glasgow.

Maura Grace Harrington teaches at Seton Hall University. She has published articles in *Yeats-Eliot Review*, *Edgar Allan Poe Review*, *Discoveries in Renaissance Culture*, *South Carolina Review*, *Early Modern Literary Studies*, and *Explicator.*

Matthew J. Bolton is an English teacher and the academic dean of Loyola School in New York City. He earned his Ph.D. in English literature in 2005 from the Graduate Center of the City University of New York, where he wrote his dissertation on Robert Browning and T. S. Eliot. He received the T. S. Eliot Society's Fathman Young Scholar Award for work related to his dissertation. In addition to his doctorate, Bolton holds master's degrees in teaching and in educational administration from Fordham University. His research and writing center on connections between Victorian and modernist literature.

Sherry Ann Beaudreau is Clinical Assistant Professor at Stanford School of Medicine.

Stanley Finger is Professor of Psychology at Washington University in St. Louis. His books include *The Origins of Neuroscience: A History of Explorations into Brain Function* (1994), *Minds Behind the Brain: A History of the Pioneers and Their Discoveries* (2000), *Trepanation: History, Discovery, Theory* (with R. Arnott and C. U. M. Smith, 2003), *Doctor Franklin's Medicine* (2006), *Brain, Mind and Medicine: Essays in Eighteenth-Century Neuroscience* (with H. Whitaker and C. U. M. Smith, 2007), and *History of Neurology: Handbook of Clinical Neurology* (with F. Boller and K. Tyler, 2009).

Betsy Erkkila is the Henry Sanborn Noyes Professor of Literature at Northwestern University. Her essays have appeared in such journals as *ELH*, *Tulsa Studies in Women's Literature*, *American Literary History*, and *American Quarterly*. Her books include *Walt Whitman Among the French: Poet and Myth* (1980), *Whitman the Political Poet* (1989), *The Wicked Sisters: Women Poets, Literary History, and Discord* (1992), *Breaking Bounds: Whitman and American Cultural Studies* (with Jay Grossman, 1996), and *Mixed Bloods and Other American Crosses: Rethinking American Literature from the Revolution to the Culture Wars* (2005).

A. Owen Aldridge was Professor of Comparative Literature at the University of Illinois. A renowned literary scholar, he published numerous books, including *Shaftesbury and the Deist Manifesto* (1951), *Franklin and His French Contemporaries* (1957), *Man of Reason: The Life of Thomas Paine* (1957), *Jonathan Edwards* (1964), *Benjamin Franklin: Philosopher and Man* (1965), *Benjamin Franklin and Nature's God* (1967), *Voltaire and the Century of Light* (1975), *Early American Literature: A Comparatist Approach* (1982), *Benjamin Franklin: Anecdotes and Eulogies* (1983), *Thomas Paine's American Ideology* (1984), *Reemergence of World Literature: A Study of Asia and the West* (1986), and *The Dragon and the Eagle: The Presence of China in the American Enlightenment* (1993).

Jennifer Jordan Baker is Assistant Professor of English at New York University. Her book *Securing the Commonwealth: Debt, Speculation, and Writing in the Making of Early America* was published in 2005, and she has published essays in *Arizona Quarterly*, *Early American Literature*, and *Prospects*.

Jennifer T. Kennedy taught at Yale University. She published articles in *American Literature*, *Early American Literature*, and *PMLA*.

Christina Lupton is Assistant Professor in the Department of English at the University of British Columbia. With Alexander Dick, she edited the volume *Theory and Practice in Eighteenth-Century Philosophy: Writing Between Philosophy and Literature* (2008). She has contributed articles to *Criticism*, *NOVEL*, *Eighteenth-Century Studies*, *Early American Literature*, *ELH*, and *Philosophy and Literature*.

Ralph Frasca has taught at Marymount University and Belmont Abbey College. He is the author of *The Rise and Fall of the "Saturday Globe"* (1992), *American War Reporting: The Mexican-American War* (2005), and *Benjamin Franklin's Printing Network: Disseminating Virtue in Early America* (2006).

Acknowledgments

"Benjamin Franklin" by Clark Davis. From *Cyclopedia of World Authors, Fourth Revised Edition*. Copyright © 2004 by Salem Press, Inc. Reprinted with permission of Salem Press.

"The *Paris Review* Perspective" by Bradley Bazzle. Copyright © 2010 by Bradley Bazzle. Special appreciation goes to Christopher Cox and Nathaniel Rich, editors for *The Paris Review.*

"Medical Electricity and Madness in the Eighteenth Century: The Legacies of Benjamin Franklin and Jan Ingenhousz" by Sherry Ann Beaudreau and Stanley Finger. From *Perspectives in Biology and Medicine* 49, no. 3 (Summer 2006): 330-345. Copyright © 2006 by The Johns Hopkins University Press. Reprinted by permission.

"Franklin and the Revolutionary Body" by Betsy Erkkila. From *ELH* 67, no. 3 (2000): 717-741. Copyright © 2000 by The Johns Hopkins University Press. Reprinted by permission.

"Feeling or Fooling in Benjamin Franklin's 'The Elysian Fields'" by A. Owen Aldridge. From *Early American Literature* 39, no. 1 (2004): 121-128. Copyright © 2004 by The University of North Carolina Press. Reprinted by permission.

"Benjamin Franklin's *Autobiography* and the Credibility of Personality" by Jennifer Jordan Baker. From *Early American Literature* 35, no. 3 (2000): 274-293. Copyright © 2000 by The University of North Carolina Press. Reprinted by permission.

"Death Effects: Revisiting the Conceit of Franklin's *Memoir*" by Jennifer T. Kennedy. From *Early American Literature* 36, no. 2 (2001): 201-234. Copyright © 2001 by The University of North Carolina Press. Reprinted by permission.

"Two Texts Told Twice: Poor Richard, Pastor Yorick, and the Case of the Word's Return" by Christina Lupton. From *Early American Literature* 40, no. 3 (2005): 471-498. Copyright © 2005 by The University of North Carolina Press. Reprinted by permission.

"The Moral Reform of a Scurrilous Press" by Ralph Frasca. From *Benjamin Franklin's Printing Network: Disseminating Virtue in Early America*, 168-191. Copyright © 2006 by The Curators of the University of Missouri. Reprinted by permission.

Index